Beryl Halley

BERYL HALLEY

*The Life and Follies
of a Ziegfeld Beauty, 1897–1988*

Jacob L. Bapst *and*
Ivan M. Tribe

McFarland & Company, Inc., Publishers
Jefferson, North Carolina

All images unless otherwise noted are from the Jean Lloyd Cooper Archives at the University of Rio Grande

ISBN (print) 978-1-4766-7643-2
ISBN (ebook) 978-1-4766-3677-1

LIBRARY OF CONGRESS AND BRITISH LIBRARY
CATALOGUING DATA ARE AVAILABLE

© 2019 Jacob L. Bapst and Ivan M. Tribe. All rights reserved

No part of this book may be reproduced or transmitted in any form or by any means, electronic or mechanical, including photocopying or recording, or by any information storage and retrieval system, without permission in writing from the publisher.

Front cover: Beryl Halley is the center of attention on stage (photograph by Richard Tucker)

Printed in the United States of America

McFarland & Company, Inc., Publishers
  Box 611, Jefferson, North Carolina 28640
  www.mcfarlandpub.com

To Chester O. Falkenhainer, Jr.
His mother will no longer be
a forgotten Ziegfeld Girl.

Table of Contents

Preface and Acknowledgments — 1
Introduction: A Representative Ziegfeld Girl — 5

1. Bladen to Rio Grande, 1897–1913 — 9
2. Rio Grande to Norfolk, Virginia, 1913–1920 — 18
3. Norfolk to Broadway, 1920–1924 — 28
4. Ziegfeld Girl, 1924–1925 — 46
5. *Palm Beach Nights*, *The Bunk* … and More, 1926–1927 — 55
6. The Bladen Beauty's "Big Apple," or Beryl Halley's New York City — 72
7. The World She Left Behind, or Gallia County in Prosperity and Depression — 86
8. Life After the *Follies*, 1927–1929 — 102
9. Surviving the Depression, 1929–1933 — 116
10. Marriage and the Ziegfeld Girls Club, 1933–1941 — 123
11. New York to Texas, 1941–1953 — 133
12. Texas, 1953–1988 — 142

Appendix: Beryl's Buddies — 153
Chapter Notes — 179
Bibliography — 197
Index — 205

Table of Contents

Preface and Acknowledgments

Beryl Halley became a familiar name in New York theatrical circles nearly a century ago. For a decade her name appeared regularly in newspapers in the "Big Apple" and, to a lesser degree, throughout the nation. Although her achievements may seem modest compared to a Marilyn Miller, Ann Pennington, Eddie Cantor, or Will Rogers, she certainly came in for her share of attention in the period between 1921 and 1929. A talented chorus girl and dancer, Beryl gained most of her fame during the "Roaring Twenties" in the employ of the legendary producer Florenz Ziegfeld and that of his rival Earl Carroll.

Much of Halley's appeal was undoubtedly based on her pleasing looks and charismatic stage personality. Yet—with one exception—she managed to avoid the scandals that destroyed the careers of one-time Ziegfeld favorite and mistress Lillian Lorraine and the short-term sensation Imogene "Bubbles" Wilson. While some Broadway beauties, to quote a song lyric, "went from man to man," her only New York romance prior to her marriage in 1933—at least, the only one that attracted press attention—was with bandleader Vincent Lopez. She seems to have concentrated on her career and her close friendships with other showgirls, including Clair Luce. After her stage career ended, she settled into a second career as a legal secretary and focused on rearing her son, Chester.

Writing a biography of Beryl Halley presented challenges. For a start, neither of us possessed a background in theatrical history. Prior study and research interests varied, but included such topics as the Civil War,

Preface and Acknowledgments

coal-mining towns, George Custer, Appalachian culture, traditional country and bluegrass music, and the small educational institution where we had spent nearly all of our academic careers. And then, a chance discovery in the archives of a photograph labeled "Beryl Halley, Ziegfeld Girl" piqued our curiosity. There were a few other scattered items in those archives, and the recollections of an octogenarian couple who hailed from the same community where Beryl spent her childhood, but beyond that, no one had any had ever heard of her. Internet research, however, yielded data far surpassing expectation. Making a connection with Beryl's son, Chester O. Falkenhainer, Jr., who lived in Austin, Texas, also proved highly rewarding. Not only did he share memories of his mother, he also donated many of her personal items, photos, and clippings she had saved from her Broadway days, and later activities with the Ziegfeld Girls Club.

Virtually all of the research and writing in this project took place in the University of Rio Grande Archives, the Davis Library on the Rio Grande campus, the Samuel L. Bossard Library of Gallia County, Ohio, and our respective homes in Gallipolis and McArthur. Record keepers Tammy Sheets and Sherri Jarrell helped locate Beryl's college transcript; Gallia County Court House employees County Recorder Roger Walker, Chief Deputy Probate Court Clerk Mary Beth Coleman, Deputy Probate Clerk Barb Swain, and Deputy Probate Clerk Patti Myers located legal documents pertaining to the Halley Family. The Gallia County Genealogical Society, under the direction of Ann Brown, provided previously missing documents. Richard and Mary James shared their knowledge of the Bladen and Eureka communities and the Halley and Porter families. Some direction, encouragement, and advice came from Rio Grande colleagues Mike Thompson, Stephanie Alexander, Scott Beekman, and

Beryl Halley in her most memorable photograph, taken by Edward Thayer Monroe.

Preface and Acknowledgments

William Plants. Our respective wives, Joann Bapst and Deanna Tribe, also helped in various ways. Among numerous online newspaper files, those of the *New York Daily News* proved to be most essential. All of the pictures used in this work are from The Jean Lloyd Cooper Archives at the University of Rio Grande, where co-author Bapst serves as the volunteer archivist.

Aside from the aforementioned scattered archival materials and that furnished by Chet Falkenhainer and a few others, the vast majority of the data contained in this study resulted from information online. The amount accumulated relating to a once well-known, but now virtually forgotten, figure thirty years after her death and another thirty years out of the limelight proved voluminous.

The authors are well aware that much of the printed source material regarding the Broadway theatre scene resulted directly, or indirectly, from the work of public relations people, and may not be 100 percent accurate. Yet, in the absence of other data and evidence, one has little choice but to accept it at face value—albeit with the proverbial "grain of salt." For instance, the most sensational moment in Beryl Halley's show business life is what might be termed the "fig-leaf" encounter in *The Bunk of 1926*. While one goes with the public reports, one nonetheless may harbor suspicions that the whole incident may have been a well-crafted publicity stunt. Such are the challenges facing those who research entertainment history.

Taking this caveat in mind, known errors in fact and interpretations are our own. It is our belief that Beryl Halley, a girl from a rural background in the foothills of Appalachia—some might even call it backwoods—has a story worth telling.

Introduction: A Representative Ziegfeld Girl

During the "Roaring Twenties," Beryl Halley became a household name, particularly among those who followed the New York theatrical scene. Her hometown newspaper, *The Gallipolis Daily Tribune*, termed her "a favorite of favorites."[1] The more cosmopolitan *New York Daily Mirror* claimed that her beauty was "responsible for a good part of the Broadway traffic congestion."[2]

However, time has dimmed the memory of the "Ziegfeld dancer" with "the incomparable beauty and histrionic talent."[3] Unlike Barbara Stanwyck and Paulette Goddard, Beryl did not go on to become a screen legend, nor did her notoriety match that of a Lina Basquette or a Louise Brooks. Nonetheless, she probably ranked as one of the most typical of Broadway showgirls of her era.

During her heyday, highlighted by three seasons as a Ziegfeld Girl, Beryl not only ranked as a major figure in her own right, but frequently interacted and associated with members of the rich and famous. Those included such major sports figures as former and current heavyweight boxing champions "Gentleman" Jim Corbett, "Manassa Mauler" Jack Dempsey. Bandleader Vincent Lopez fell in love with Beryl. Frank Crumit, W. C. Fields, Will Rogers, and Eddie Cantor shared the stage with her. Lillian Roth, of *I'll Cry Tomorrow* fame, considered her a mentor. Ziegfeld Girls who were her close friends included Clare Luce, Paulette Goddard, Lina Basquette, Fanny Brice, Ann Pennington, Dorothy Knapp, and Estelle Taylor. Even William Moulton Marston (a.k.a. Charles Moulton), inventor of the lie detector—and later creator of "Wonder Woman"—tested his

Introduction

newest device on her. Other celebrities with whom Beryl crossed paths during her show business days were the champion swimmer Annette Kellerman; former Floradora dancer (and one-third of the most notorious love triangle of the early 20th century) Evelyn Nesbitt, and perhaps even a few of the noted underworld figures who frequented and sometimes had some control over the Broadway theatres and nightclubs associated with the celebrity culture of the "Roaring Twenties."

Our own Beryl Halley awareness is not of long standing. Only in July 2016, while searching for new material for an illustrated history of the University of Rio Grande, did she come to our attention. Among a pile of old photos was a glossy 8 × 10 of an attractive 1920s-style woman. The caption on the reverse side read "Beryl Halley, Ziegfeld Girl." An online search revealed a great deal of scattered data on a person who undoubtedly ranked as Rio Grande's most notable former student in the first half of the 20th century. Her celebrity status, however, had become overshadowed by basketball legend Clarence "Bevo" Francis.

A year passed and more data was accumulated through deeper and more intense internet searches, additional material from the Rio Grande Archives, and contact with Beryl's only child, Chester "Chet" Falkenhainer, Jr. Among other things, the latter found a box in the attic containing material from his mother's show business days. We began to believe that a biography might be warranted.

A book held promise that examined the life and times of a twenty-nine-year-old girl from the Appalachian foothills of the Ohio Valley, with a year of college under her belt. Joining the navy during World War I, achieving fame on Broadway, her later career as a top-flight secretary in a major law firm, and living to the ripe old age of ninety became the stuff of Beryl Halley's life. Popular culture and songs of the early 20th century were crammed to the full about country girls who left home for the city and came to a sad end, as in Charles K. Harris's popular songs; "There'll Come a Time" and "Fallen by the Wayside"; Gussie L. Davis, "If I Only Could Blot Out the Past"; Paul Dresser (a.k.a. Dreiser); "Just Tell Them That You Saw Me"; William B. Gray; "She's More to be Pitied than Censured"; and "Pictures from Life's Other Side" by Charles E. Baer. Even more penetrating fears were expressed in a 1913 composition by Thomas Allen and Joseph Daly, titled, "In the Heart of the City That Has No Heart," which was recorded by popular balladeer Henry Burr:

Introduction

> She wanted to roam, so she left the old home,
> The old people's hearts were sore,
> She longed for the lights, and the bright city nights,
> Where others had gone before.
> She went to the heart of the city, and mingled with strangers there,
> But nobody said you're being misled,
> For what did the strangers care.
>
> In the heart of the city, that has no heart,
> That's where they meet and that's where they part,
> The current of vice has proved too strong,
> So poor little girly just drifted along.
> Nobody cared if she laughed or cried,
> Nobody cared if she lived or died,
> She's just a lost sister and nobody'll miss her
> In the city that has no heart.
>
> A year has passed by, there's a tear in her eye,
> And sorrow is on her brow,
> O what would she do if the old people knew,
> She couldn't go back home now.
> Her dear mother said when she parted,
> Remember your good old name
> And her daddy said, rather we'd see you dead,
> Than bring us disgrace and shame.[4]

Unlike the tragic figures in sentimental ballads of the time, Beryl Halley came out a winner. After her show business career wound down, she married an insurance executive and became the proud mother of a son. Although that marriage, and another, did not endure, her superior stenography skills, probably learned before or during her brief career as a navy "yeomanette," provided her with a comfortable life, spent after 1950 in the Houston, Texas, area where her second husband lived. As son Chet recalls, "At the age of eighty she could flawlessly type up to ninety words per minute" and "could make an electric typewriter sound like a machine gun." While most girls who enrolled at Rio Grande College in the early decades of the new century who followed a career outside home and hearth became public school teachers—including her only sister Cecile—Beryl followed a different path. She looked beyond the horizon and found more than a modicum of fame and success, which led to a comfortable and fulfilling life.

Her story follows.

1
Bladen to Rio Grande, 1897–1913

Gallia County lies along the west bank of the Ohio River, slightly past the halfway point between Pittsburgh and Cincinnati. The acreage near what early French explorers termed *la belle riviere* consists of rich bottom land. The interior varies from lower to higher and more rugged terrain, being more characteristic of the Allegheny Plateau that is part of the Appalachian foothills. The 1900 census recorded the county as having 27,918 residents, which decreased to 25,745 a decade later. With the exception of about 2,000 African Americans, the county was predominantly white. Since the Civil War, voters nearly always supported Republicans in national elections, but could be more bipartisan at the county level. Eleven miles south of Gallipolis lies the hamlet of Bladen, where Nannie (later changed to Nina) Beryl Halley was born on June 20, 1897. She was the second of three children, born to Samuel T. Halley (1870–1930) and his wife, Melissa Porter (1858–1949). She had an older sister, Cecile Vivian (1894–1987), whose name was always pronounced "See-cil" by the local populace, and a younger brother, Paul Porter Halley (1900–1971).

The Halleys were a numerous-membered family in southern Gallia County. Some spelled their name "Holley." According to the best information available, the family came from English forebears, migrated to Fairfax County, Virginia, about 1735, and to Gallia County about 1816. Many males of the older generation had served in the Union Army during the Civil War, including Samuel's father, Benjamin Franklin Halley (1839–1904), who enlisted in Company C of the 60th Ohio Volunteer Infantry for a

Beryl Halley

year beginning March 7, 1862. Ben's army career was only eight months long as he was discharged in Chicago on November 10, 1862. He did, however, participate in four battles—Strasburg, Harrisburg, Cross Keys, and Harper's Ferry, none of which were major. It appears that shortly after Harper's Ferry, the entire regiment was captured at Bolivar Heights, subsequently paroled, and then taken to Camp Douglas, where they were "mustered out."[1]

In keeping with a citizen soldier tradition, Samuel Halley, along with a Bladen kinsman John Halley, served for several months during the brief Spanish-American War as a member of Company C in the 7th Ohio Volunteer Infantry. The entire company organized in Gallipolis, and the regiment left Camp Bushnell at Columbus for Camp Alger, Virginia, on June 30, 1898, a few days before the Spanish capitulation at Santiago. Some weeks later they moved to Camp Meade, Pennsylvania, and then back to

In this somber picture, taken about 1900, are Beryl Halley (left), her sister, Cecile, and her mother, Melissa Porter Halley. Cecile would stay close to her mother but Beryl did not as the two were often at odds with each other. Brother Paul Porter Halley had probably not been born when this picture was taken, and father Samuel T. Halley is conspicuous by his absence.

1. Bladen to Rio Grande, 1897–1913

Columbus, where they were "mustered out" on November 6.[2] Like most of the volunteers, Sam never got close to the combat zones in Cuba or the occupancy army in Puerto Rico and the Philippines.

The Porters generally lived in the same areas of southern Gallia County. Although of limited formal education, Melissa worked as a teacher, mostly in the one-room district schools, not only in Ohio but apparently in West Virginia as well. One unverified claim is that she was the first certified teacher in the Mountain State. Melissa's brother, Daniel T. Porter (1872–1943), after presumably being well-tutored by his older sister—called "Aunt Sis" within the family—moved to Kentucky where he worked as a newspaperman and served as grand chancellor in that state's Knights of Pythias Grand Lodge. His nephew James Sherman Porter, Jr. (1908–1988) also worked in journalism, taught at Rio Grande College for a time, and, beginning in 1959, served a four-year term in the state Senate.[3]

Most of the Halleys in the area occupied small farms in the townships of Ohio, Clay, and Guyan. Bladen (sometimes

Samuel T. Halley would marry Melissa Porter, twelve years his senior, in 1893. The marriage produced three children: Cecile, Beryl, and Paul. In 1898, Samuel enlisted in the 7th Ohio Volunteer Infantry. During the summer of 1907, he went to Jamestown, Virginia, to serve as a security policeman at the Tercentenary Exposition of the first settlement in the thirteen colonies. The tempestuous marriage would end in a bitter divorce in 1915, with Samuel held at fault for "extreme cruelty." Melissa would have exclusive custody of Cecile and Beryl, and Samuel would have custody of Paul. This picture of Samuel in his security garb would be carried by Beryl for the rest of her life.

called Bladenburg, Blandenburg, or, more commonly, Bladen Landing), located along the river, was a farm community, at its largest may have contained about two hundred residents. It had a couple of general stores, several residences, and a post office, from 1890 until 1957. A half-mile away, Bethel Methodist Church—now vanished—helped serve the community's religious needs, forty-six members in 1919.[4] Many of Beryl's kinfolk, including her parents and brother, are buried in the adjacent cemetery. After Beryl had left Ohio, Bladen had an Independent Order of Odd Fellows Lodge from 1923 until 1935 and a nativist fraternal group, the Junior Order of United American Mechanics. An 1882 history mentions the recent discovery of a "valuable vein of fire clay two miles below the village of Bladensburg which is soon to be developed,"[5] but not much seems to have come of it. For a time, a coal mine operated and maps show what was termed the "Jeffers Coal Fields" there, with the "black diamonds" shipped on boats and barges down the river, hence the name Bladen Landing. According to Richard James, the leading historian of the area, there were several "coal banks," but the only effort to connect them to the larger commercial markets ended when the short line rail spur from Gallipolis went bankrupt. But Bladen was in no sense a coal-mining town, such as those once common in other Appalachian counties in Ohio and West Virginia.[6]

About a mile north of Bladen, across the township line in Clay, lay the somewhat larger community of Chambersburg, which dates back to 1852, as laid out by John Chambers (202 people in 1880, and 225 in 1950), more commonly known as Eureka (from the post office). An 1882 description noted that "there are several saw-mills and planing-mills ... but the principal business is boat-building which is carried on to quite an extent." The same minister served the Methodist churches in both Bladen and Chambersburg—which had seventy members in 1919—as well as churches at Clipper's Mill, Clay Chapel, and Swan Creek. Eureka had about the same, or a slightly larger, business community, and from 1873 until 2007, was the home of Gallia Lodge No. 469, Free and Accepted Masons, of which Samuel Halley was a faithful member. Not just active, he served as master in 1906 and 1907. The village also had lodges of Odd Fellows, an Independent Order of Foresters, and a Knights of the Golden Eagle. The latter fraternity also appealed a great deal to Sam Halley, who journeyed to Wellston in nearby Jackson County in August 1906 to join the order

1. Bladen to Rio Grande, 1897–1913

and then took the lead that December to start a K. G. E. lodge in Eureka. A few months later, the Knights of the Golden Eagle served as security police—named Powhatan Guards—at the 1907 Jamestown, Virginia, Ter-Centenary Exposition of the first settlement in the thirteen colonies, Sam Halley among them. In fact, the only surviving photo of the man, wearing a uniform, a badge, and handlebar mustache, with the word *Dad* written thereon, was part of the Halley Collection in the Rio Grande Archives.[8]

Eureka Post Office existed from 1862 until it closed in 1943, after which the Bladen Post Office relocated to Eureka, but kept the Bladen name. In their later years, Melissa and Paul Halley lived in a house nearly across the highway from the Masonic Hall, which sat on a high embankment between the road and the river. After 1938, Eureka became the site of one of the largest dams on the Ohio River, designed to keep the flow of water more even and thus maintain commercial traffic flowing year round, except in the uncommon times when the river completely froze over. Bladen and Eureka lay in different townships, and were platted separately at different times, which partly explains why they became two different communities, although they were almost one.[9]

The 1900 Federal Census Enumeration for Ohio Township showed the Halley family as residents, although there were some inaccuracies concerning ages. Samuel was listed as thirty-six, when he was actually thirty; Melissa as forty-one, when she was forty-two; Cecil [*sic*] as five, when she was six; and Beryl, correctly, at three. There is some indication of a fourth Halley child, "Daughter George Halley" in 1898, probably Georgia, who apparently died in infancy, but this cannot be confirmed. Ages are often reported inaccurately on census reports—a circumstance frequently characteristic of show business people who have a way of adjusting their age to suit their purposes. Beryl Halley would prove no exception. A 1904 theft of twelve "fair, fat young pullets" from the Halley chicken coop, located near the Ohio River, attracted press coverage in the county seat. The crime was blamed on "shantyboat" dwellers who literally lived on the river and were often regarded as being of unsavory character.[10]

Southern Gallia County in the early 20th century offered virtually no secondary education opportunity beyond the one-room district schools. The county seat, Gallipolis, could boast of Gallia Academy High School (by 1900 a public school, in spite of its exclusive-sounding name) since 1818. For a time, the city even had Lincoln High School for the sizable

African American populace, with Edward Bouchet, the first black American PhD and Phi Beta Kappa, as principal from 1908 to 1913 (racial segregation did not totally end in either city or Gallia County until just after World War II). Small academies flourished for some years in the towns of Cheshire and Ewington.[11] A better opportunity could be found via the presence of Rio Grande College.

Rio Grande College had been founded in 1876 as a Free Will Baptist institution. It existed as result of the financial endeavors of two childless, affluent, dedicated lay members, Nehemiah and Permelia Atwood of the local Calvary FWB Church, and their equally zealous, but economically less-wealthy minister Ira Z. Haning (1825–1878). The latter persuaded the Atwoods to use their funds, gained through operating a tavern on the Gallipolis-Jackson public road and income from several hundred acres of farm land, to support founding a college. Nehemiah died in 1869, but Permelia and the Reverend Haning went forward. Under their direction in 1874, surveyors laid out a college green and surrounding town lots. A rural post office, Rio Grande, had opened in 1846, at the height of the excitement generated in the neighborhood as a result of the Mexican War.[12]

Since many rural areas lacked facilities for secondary education, most colleges also had "Preparatory Departments" which filled the gap. Typically, more students were in preparatory than in the college proper. Rio Grande would be no exception, as it would be the fall of 1920 before the "collegiate" students would outnumber those in "preparatory." Both institutions would attract and prove useful to the Halley family, especially the girls. As the local press reported at the time in their "Rio Grande College" column, the parents had charge of the "boarding hall for the coming year" and could also "secure educational advantages for their children."[13]

Rio Grande College had opened in September 1876 with a student body of thirteen, all in "preparatory." It would be 1883 before any degrees were awarded, although a minimum of sixteen had completed the secondary program by that time. Two brick buildings comprised the facilities. All classes took place in Atwood Hall: college, preparatory, normal—added in 1877 for teacher training—and music added in 1889. A second structure, the "Boarding Hall," housed students, although some stayed with local families, and a few lived nearby.

Always seriously underfunded, Rio Grande College survived through the dedication of an overworked, underpaid faculty, many of them Free-

1. Bladen to Rio Grande, 1897–1913

Rio Grande College
RIO GRANDE, OHIO

Beautiful Location
Thorough Instruction
Moral and Healthful Surroundings
Moderate Expenses

Spring Term opens April 15, 1912.   Summer Term, June 24---Aug. 2, 1912
WRITE FOR BULLETIN.   SIMEON H. BING, PRESIDENT

Rio Grande College was founded in 1876 by Permelia Ridgeway Atwood Wood (1802–1885) as the culmination of a desire by her late husband, Nehemiah Atwood (1792–1869), to establish a college in southeastern Ohio. The college was "situated in a locality of much natural beauty, with no saloons in the vicinity, and would endeavor to encourage and support sound moral and religious influences without sectarianism." There were two buildings—Atwood Hall, with an impressive bell tower, and Boarding Hall. The college exists today as the University of Rio Grande, and Rio Grande Community College. Its survival as an institution of higher learning is a story as improbable as the life of one of its most famous yet forgotten alums, Beryl Halley.

Will Baptist ministers or lay persons, some of whom were women. John Merrill Davis served as president from 1887 until 1911, and an even longer period, forty-one years, on the faculty. Others among the faithful were Clarence Clark—who survived decades of jokes about his bald head—Ruth Brockett, an atypical Victorian career lady whose expertise extended from the German language to the sciences, and who established a botanical garden on a corner of the college green. There was also the ever-serious Stella May Fulton, who taught English and Latin while running the preparatory department even after Rio Grande had a public high school, still located in Atwood Hall until 1930. In 1901, Chestora McDonald Carr, a one-time educator/entertainer from the Chautauqua circuit, joined the faculty for the Spring Term only, introducing elocution, drama, and theatre to the curriculum, all of which proved not only popular but enlivening to campus and community as a whole, because local kids and adults also participated in many of her endeavors.[14]

Beryl Halley

By 1909, when the Halleys relocated to Rio Grande, the enrollment for the 1909–1910 school year with "each student counted once," the enrollment had increased to 154. The girls and young Paul enrolled in the elementary school, which was near the campus, and from 1909 to 1912, Samuel and Melissa had charge of the Boarding Hall, which, from available evidence, ranked as a thankless job at best. College trustees leased operation of the Hall to a person (or persons, in their case) for a one-time payment of one hundred dollars. The lessees then collected the room rents and boarding fees, and would hopefully make some profit thereby. The trustees did furnish funds for major improvements or replacing the nearby wooden privy which burned that year, but smaller maintenance was the responsibility of the lessees, as were losses incurred from students who might be in arrears in their payments.[15] The older Halleys enjoyed—or at least endured—Boarding Hall operation for nearly three years, but at least it provided an educational opportunity for Cecile and Beryl, an opportunity unavailable in Bladen or Eureka.

The 1910 census shows the Halleys as residents of Raccoon Township. Rio Grande would not be incorporated as a separate village until 1935, but an unofficial count gave a population of 110, and, this time, the enumerator got Sam Halley's age correct, at forty. Beryl made what was probably her first documented entertainment debut on June 10, 1910, when she appeared in Chestora Carr's "Annual Elocutionary Recital," which consisted of monologues, readings, piano duets, sketches, and a "Pantomime (In Costume)" of "Bird's Christmas Carol" by Kate Douglas Wiggin, otherwise best known as author of the classic children's novel *Rebecca of Sunnybrook Farm*. Beryl, a week way from turning thirteen, portrayed Kitty Ruggles, a character in a family of children, while ten-year old Paul played her younger brother Clem. An even younger cast member, six-year-old Donovan Allen, played a child in the Bird family, who would later become a major financial supporter of Rio Grande College as the result of a booming automobile agency in Buffalo, New York.[16] Whether Beryl's part in "Bird's Christmas Carol" provided the impetus to inspire the emerging adolescent to aspire for a career on the stage, cannot be determined, but it likely had some level of a positive impact.

The August 1911 *Rio Grande College Bulletin* indicates that both Cecile and Beryl had become well integrated at Rio Grande. The two girls are listed therein as students in the preparatory department. Both were

1. Bladen to Rio Grande, 1897–1913

also enrolled in the music program. As for elocution, Cecile was enrolled for individual lessons, while Beryl seemed to have been limited to classroom instruction. It seems likely that music and elocution would serve her well in the coming years. Taking to athletics with the same gusto, the sisters were part of Rio Grande College's first girls' "basket ball" team. Since the high school and college girls played on the same squad, both were still on the team in 1916. The girls also had two close friends as team members, Frederica (Freda) Koontz and Helen Martin.[17]

The Halleys proved popular in their Boarding Hall job, as the newspapers reported: "Mr. and Mrs. S. T. Halley cared well for the Boarding Hall last year and will have charge next year. The Hall is a good place and the Halleys are good folks." The trustees put them in charge for another year, beginning August 22, 1911. However, the third year did not prove to be a rosy one. On February 28, 1912, Mrs. Halley reported that she wished to be replaced as soon as a successor could be found. Among other reasons, trustees found that the building was in "wretched" condition, with a leaky roof and places where the wood in the floors was rotting. Before the school year ended, the Halleys departed from having charge of a building that fire would destroy five years later. Both the daughters continued as students in the preparatory department throughout the 1911–1912 school year. Cecile was listed as an honor student, having accumulated 145 hours of credit; meanwhile, Beryl had accumulated 110 hours.[18]

With the elder Halleys back in Bladen, Cecile and Beryl continued as students at Rio Grande. On October 31, 1912, the younger girl made another stage presentation at a "Rhetorical" called "The Secretary's Retort." Freda Koontz did another, this one titled "The One-Legged Goose," while Helen Martin contributed "Things Inside," among several other presentations.[19] However, it is not certain that they were enrolled for every term as their names are not always listed in the catalogues. Nor is it known whether they remained in the Boarding Hall or roomed with some of the townsfolk who rented rooms and boarded students, but the latter seems more likely given the negative image associated with "the Hall." It is, however, a certainty that Cecile graduated from the preparatory department in 1913. She later received a bachelor's degree, and Beryl later graduated from the preparatory school, by then renamed Rio Grande High School. Soon, another chapter in the Halley family saga was beginning to unfold, back in Bladen and also in the Gallia County Court House.

2

Rio Grande to Norfolk, Virginia, 1913–1920

The Halley Family, having divested themselves of responsibility of the Rio Grande College Boarding Hall, returned to Bladen. Cecile and Beryl divided their time over the next five years between continuing their education at "Old Rio" and staying with their parents in Bladen, or perhaps Eureka. As for Samuel and Melissa Halley, their marital union was coming apart.

Anyone with even secondhand recollections of Sam and Melissa describe them as a cantankerous, and perhaps quarrelsome, couple. This, in spite of generally being thought of as honorable citizens and "good people." Their nearly three years of caring for the Boarding Hall, a building badly in need of refurbishing with minimal funding for even limited upkeep for repairs, may well have strained their domestic situation. Melissa being twelve years older than her husband may also have been a factor. At any rate, their disagreements continued. In February 1914, an initial case of *Melissa P. Halley vs. Samuel Halley* was dismissed in a "court report." Lest one gets the idea that tranquility reigned, the case was back in court the next January when the court "enjoined" Sam Halley "from encumbering or disposing of 15 acres of land in Ohio Tp. and $1,000 on deposit in a Columbus bank." Apparently, Melissa thought Sam was attempting to sell and hide property from her. The property was later sold in accordance with the court order and Melissa received half of the money from the sale. However, Sam presumably retained the banked cash.[1]

Trouble continued until Melissa again filed for divorce. On June 15,

2. Rio Grande to Norfolk, Virginia, 1913–1920

1915, the Gallia County Court of Common Pleas granted her request. Samuel Halley, on grounds of "extreme cruelty," was held at fault. Paul Halley remained in his father's custody, but Melissa received the "privilege of seeing said child at any and all reasonable times." Melissa gained "the exclusive custody, care and control of ... Beryl Halley and Cecil [sic] Halley."[2] In the case of Cecile, this judgment meant little because she would reach the age of twenty-one just two months after the legal decree. In fact, in April, she had already passed the examination for a one-year teaching certificate. Paul Halley went with his father to the village of South Webster in Scioto County where Sam taught school and Paul finished high school prior to his entering the army at the end of World War I.[3]

It was common for high school and undergraduate collegians not to be in school continuously in the early decades of the twentieth century. They might be in school for a term or two, drop out for a term or even for a full year, and then re-matriculate before eventually accumulating a sufficient number of credits to graduate. For instance, another area native James Rhodes (1909–2001), who went on to serve for sixteen years as governor of Ohio, was nearly twenty-one before he completed high school in the spring of 1930.[4]

Where the Halley girls resided during their time back in Rio Grande has not been documented. However, given their parents and their own experience in the Boarding Hall, it seems unlikely that they returned to that increasingly rattletrap structure. Most likely, they resided in the Martin House. Joseph F. and Margaret Cherrington Martin not only had students who roomed and boarded in their home, they also had twin children who were students themselves. Hollis and Helen Martin, fourteen years of age in 1910,[5] became close friends of the Halley girls. Cecile, Beryl, and Helen were members of the first Rio girls basketball team, remaining close for years, although Beryl's friendship was conducted mostly by way of her older sister.

The Martins also ranked among Gallia County's best-known and respected citizenry. Joe Martin, at fourteen, along with his father Caswell, had enlisted in Company B of the 91st Ohio Valley Infantry on August 8, 1862, and both had been seasoned combat veterans in General Phil Sheridan's Shenandoah Valley campaign. They sustained heavy fire at the Battle of Winchester on September 19, 1864, where Joseph took a slight wound. But, by October, he was back in action at Cedar Creek, where he suffered a more serious wound. His father was almost fatally injured.[6]

Beryl Halley

After the war, Joe Martin engaged in a variety of business activities, including building contracting, farming, and lumbering. He also held the office of police chief in Gallipolis from 1883 until 1891, and was elected as Gallia County sheriff in 1892. While serving his first term, his wife died in 1893, leaving him with six offspring, some already adults. He remarried, in 1894, to Margaret Cherrington, a member of the county "upper-crust." Leaving office in 1897, he purchased a large farm in Perry Township, and prior to 1910, a home in Rio Grande, probably so his younger children could benefit from the same educational opportunities that had brought the Halleys to Rio. When Joe Martin died on Memorial Day 1929, he was the community's last Union veteran.[7]

What is known of the Halley sisters back in Rio Grande is based on somewhat spotty information found in the *College Bulletin* (or "Catalog"), mentions in newspapers and the Rio College yearbook *Grandion*. Both girls apparently spent the summer of 1913 in an extended visit to Porter relatives in Lexington, Kentucky, where Melissa's brother worked for a newspaper. To complicate matters, although Rio Grande College issued two or three bulletins annually, they did not always list the names of students. Cecile Vivian Halley is listed as a Summer Student in 1915 in the July 1915 *Bulletin*. The October 1915 "alumni issue" lists among the Preparatory School graduates for 1913 as Cecile Vivian Halley, Fredericka Koontz, Helen C. Martin, and her twin brother Hollis. The 1913 Senior Class Prophecy touched on all three girls. Freda Koontz attracted the most space. As an advocate for female suffrage, it described "a suffragette parade," and "this woman who so triumphantly leads them all is Freda!" It further stated that "over the entrance of a great building there is a sign which reads: 'Home for Aged Suffragettes' ... which was kept by Freda." Helen Martin must have been attracted to someone with a German connection as the prophecy read: "I understand you vas keepin' house vor a Bennsylvania Dutchman."

On the other hand Cecile Halley, must have been uninterested in men at the time since the document states "'man delights not me,' was her motto and so, after teaching school many years [true enough] she laid aside this work and now lives in her old home—alone [almost true]." In July 1916, Cecile is listed as a junior in the College while Nina (the first use of this name instead of Nannie) Beryl Halley as a Preparatory Graduate. In July 1917, Cecile is identified as a recent graduate with an Ele-

2. Rio Grande to Norfolk, Virginia, 1913–1920

mentary Education Diploma, while Beryl was a freshman for the school year just completed.[8]

Considerable additional material for what would be Beryl's senior year in the Preparatory Department (which technically had been Raccoon Township High School since the 1911–1912 school year) records that she achieved a high level of both activity and popularity among her fellow co-eds. In the fall of 1915, she "was unanimously chosen Captain" of the Girls "basket ball" team. Yearbook sports editor Esther Edwards (a team member) commented that "the girls' confidence in her was not misplaced." She had likely been on the team since 1912, but yearbook pictures do not give the names, since they all knew who they were at the time. The downside of the season saw the team on the losing end in four of their six games (all against high schools), defeating Oak Hill and Wellston, but losing by a single point to Gallipolis and Middleport, and badly twice to Catlettsburg, Kentucky, being scoreless in one game.[9]

Further Halley activities continued under the "elocution" tutelage of Chestora Carr. At the March 23, 1916, "Public Rhetoricals," Beryl presented a reading titled "The Catacombs." This was followed by a piano solo of Beethoven's "Andante" by her pal Helen Martin, who was soon to graduate from the Music Program. Six weeks later, on May 9, Beryl had a significant role as "Doris Meredith, an heiress" in the class play *The 15th of*

Beryl Halley, nicknamed "Cubby," as she appeared as a student in 1916. Captain of the girls' basketball team, she graduated from Rio Grande Preparatory School and entered Rio Grande College. She would study to be a teacher, and in 1917-1918, she would teach in a one-room school. Just as World War I was changing the world, Beryl's life would undergo major changes as well.

Beryl Halley

January, by Lindsey Barbee, described as a "college comedy in three acts." Another member of the cast was Stanley Neal, who portrayed "Billy Burton, the Varsity quarterback."[10] The latter had also played quarterback for the Rio Grande football squad, and there are vague hints that he and Beryl may have been romantically involved.

Relatively little has been unearthed concerning Stanley Crawford Neal (1896–1976). A native of Lawrence County, just south of Gallia, he had "the distinction of being in every minute of the season's play." The Rio gridiron squad was not very good, but "Scooty" Neal ranked as one of their better players, intercepting a Gallipolis forward pass and running it back for forty yards, on October 9, 1915. In the humor section of the 1916 *Grandion*, "Scooty and Beryl" are termed "Disputable" cases, and that "we know ... Beryl Halley [because of] Scootie." Neal was still around Rio on June 1, 1917, when he was registered for the World War I draft by none other than Rio Grande's President Simeon Bing. The following May, he joined the navy and served as a radio electrician at a U.S. naval base in Cardiff, Wales. Discharged on September 30, 1921, he died in Huntington, West Virginia, some fifty-five years later.[11] After their Rio days ended, it seems unlikely that he and Beryl ever saw each other again.

Another glimpse of Beryl Halley as a high school senior that may shed light on her future ambitions comes from the "preparatory senior class prophecy." The latter document, then as later, offered some insight into the personalities of seniors as seen at the time by their contemporaries, usually with a degree of humor. For Beryl Halley and a classmate named Lora Welker, the writer passed a "magnificent" theatre, the front of which had a large sign reading: "TONIGHT. The Joys of Love" with "old friends Lora and 'Cubby' playing the leading parts."[12] Whatever, happened to Lora Welker, who had also had a part in the recent school play, is not known, but for "Cubby" (a.k.a. Beryl Halley), the scenario was prescient.

Beryl Halley continued on as a freshman in the collegiate department at RGC. It appears that the 1917 edition of *The Grandion* went to press somewhat earlier than usual and, as a result, less information is available than what was usually the case. Beryl did serve the book as "Athletic [a.k.a. Sports] Editor." While pointing out that baseball served as the principal sport on campus and predicting that this was likely to be the best team ever, relying heavily on the talents of future major leaguer and really a star in the high minors Clyde Fisher, she said little else as the yearbook went to press before the season started. She was pictured as a member of the Tennis Club and was in the Ladies Glee Club, listed as one of a half-dozen "first sopranos." Her only stage appearance that spring was with the Glee Club, although she had no solo numbers.[13]

As usual, RGC did not have a very good gridiron squad, but Beryl managed to cover their lackluster performance with some degree of flair and journalistic gusto. For instance, of the first game in which Rio lost to a much stronger team from Marshall College, in which the West Virginia team won by a score of 26 to 12, the Athletic Editor wrote, "Marshall scored 19 of her points in the first quarter before our boys got over their stage fright" but "after the first quarter Rio more than outplayed Marshall." All things considered, she said, "Rio was pleased over the game." However, in a home game in which the visiting team—"Gallipolis Hi"—arrived late, she gave the excuse that "Rio was stale from waiting all afternoon" and lost by a 15–0 score in what she termed "a listless game with Rio on the short end." RGC did much better in a game with the Marshall reserve squad, in which her account states that her team "was working like a well oiled machine."[14]

"Basket Ball" had always been Beryl's favorite sport, but surprisingly little appeared in print concerning their season, except that the team looked forward to next year "on our ... indoor floor in the new gymnasium," soon to be known as Community Hall. Cecile was graduating from the Normal Department. Editor-in-Chief Charles Weed termed her a "pleasant, likeable, efficient young lady" with "keen intellect ... sufficient for solving all school problems."[15]

That same school year, the only surviving grade report for Fall 1916 thus found showed that Beryl earned a "C+" in American History. Those were the days before anything akin to 21st century grade inflation had arisen. Miss Halley, in fact, did considerably better than the only other identifiable name on the roster, that of Grayum Bing, the son of the school's president, Simeon Bing. The younger Bing only managed a "C-." A complete transcript for Winter and Spring 1917 shows a much stronger record of academic achievement. With the exception of College English and Physical Education, the remainder of her courses were related to Elementary Education. Credit was also given for participation in the Ciceronian Literary Society, in which she held an office. All her grades were either A's or B's in such classes as School Management, Public School Music, Elementary Curriculum, and History of Education. When not engaged in academic pursuits, the Halley girls and Helen Martin seemed to make the most of shopping trips to Gallipolis, especially during the holiday season. Their other close college pal Freda Koontz seems to have become something of a 1916 style social activist, identified as a "suffragette."[16]

Meanwhile, Cecile Halley began her lifelong career as a public school teacher at White Throne School in Clay Township. At any given time, there were about one hundred one-room schools in rural Gallia County in the early decades of the 20th century and many, if not most, provided jobs for Rio Grande College students who wished to teach and who passed the examinations. The number of pupils might range from as few as ten to more than thirty. The jobs sometimes had political overtones. For instance, school board members who wished to employ their eighteen- or nineteen-year-olds might do so, if their offspring could obtain the necessary certificates. The actual teaching seems not to have been political, but concentrated on the rudiments of what was often termed a "good common school education."

The average salary in 1920 was roughly $100 monthly. Eight grades were all in a single room and the concentration was usually on the basics, perhaps more so than in later decades. The oddly named White Throne was about two miles north of Eureka and perhaps a half-mile back from the river. The exact length of Cecile's tenure at the school is not known, but it was sometime between 1916 and 1918. By the fall of 1919, she had been replaced by a relative named Cecil E. Halley, who came from nearby Mercerville. Cecile moved north to the booming city of Youngstown in September 1918, then in the throes of rapid expansion (increasing in population from 79,066 to 132,358 during that decade) and higher pay for teachers. In 1920, she resided in a rooming house on Wick Avenue, owned and operated by Anna Hedges, where two other young ladies—possibly also teachers—resided.[17]

Melissa Porter Halley also returned to the classroom following her divorce. She had probably been a teacher prior to her marriage at the age of thirty-five. Her first post-marital teaching assignment was at Paw Paw School, a couple of miles south of Bladen, in 1915–1916. By 1919–1920, she had gone farther down river to Waugh Bottom. She also taught at Chambersburg for unspecified periods, and probably at other schools as well.[18]

2. Rio Grande to Norfolk, Virginia, 1913–1920

Following her freshman year at Rio Grande College, Beryl Halley also entered the teaching profession. But sometime that summer, she journeyed northward, possibly by auto but more likely by rail, to McArthur "to attend Chautauqua." In September 1917, she took a position at Story's Run School, also known as Eureka, (but nowhere near the community of Eureka) in the northern part of Gallia County's Cheshire Township. On September 7, the *Daily Tribune* reported that "Miss Beryl Halley has gone to Cheshire to take charge of her school." A 1914 photo shows about twenty students, perhaps somewhat fewer than Cecile's White Throne School.[19] Story's Run Road, in the northern part of Gallia County, extends close to the Meigs County line. The school, located in Section 10, burned in 1931, and no trace of it remains. One year in the classroom seems have been enough for Beryl to decide to seek other fields of employment and perhaps more distant options, far from the Gallia County hills.

World War I raged in Europe during the year 1918. Beryl's younger brother Paul was a volunteer in the 57th Ohio Infantry (later transferred to the 49th) Regiment. However, he did not actually go on duty until after the Armistice. On February 22, 1919, he shipped out from Hoboken, New Jersey, on the *Northern Pacific*, a troop carrier, as a private in the U.S. Transport Service. He arrived in Antwerp, Belgium, on March 1, and spent the next year probably helping to load and unload supplies and equipment. Given his residence in a community that, according to most accounts, he spent time in France, but only Antwerp shows on his military record. He returned to Hoboken on March 1, 1920, on the same ship that had taken him to Europe. Sometime before departing from the military, he survived a bout with typhoid fever; he received an honorable discharge in 1921.[20] Back in civilian life, he worked on some riverboat crews, but frequently seems not to have worked much at all, except for occasionally helping his mother in her vegetable garden.

Recent information has surfaced that another Gallia County girl may have appeared on Broadway and in motion pictures, prior to Beryl Halley. In 1916, three mentions in the *Tribune* concern a girl named Marie Hall, from the railroad crossing hamlet of Kanauga (across the Ohio River from Point Pleasant), who visited her family there, is described as an "actress." There were such printed comments as "Miss Marie Hall, recently with the Ziegfeld Follies, was here over Sunday" and "Marie Hall, a moving picture actress of New York ... passed through Pomeroy ... en route to Kanauga."

Beryl Halley

The report added "frequent mention has been made of Miss Hall in the movie magazines." The Internet Movie Database (IMDb) identifies a Marie Hall in three films in 1913: *The Winner, His Hour of Triumph,* and *The Return of Tony,* all shorts. The Internet Broadway Database (IBDb) shows Marie Hall in one drama in 1920 (although the latter may be a different person). Whether or not Beryl had an awareness of Miss Hall is indeterminate, but if so, it may have influenced her decision to go to New York. First, however, she joined the navy.[21]

On September 14, 1918, Beryl Halley enlisted in the U.S. Navy in Parkersburg, West Virginia, as a "yeomanette" (officially known as a Yeoman F, for *female* on government records). At almost the same time that Congress declared war on April 6, 1917, women were enlisted to fill a shortage of clerical workers, and by the war's end, some eleven thousand women had joined the navy. Most—including Beryl—were in clerical positions, but a few also worked as mechanics, truck drivers, cryptographers, telephone operators, and munitions makers. The *Daily Tribune* belatedly made the announcement, noting that she made a visit to another former student friend "Miss Phyllis Johnston" while "waiting her call," which came soon, as she reported for active duty in Norfolk, Virginia, on October 1. Beryl's active naval career turned out to be only about nine months long, as the armistice came exactly six weeks later.[22]

Although largely forgotten today, female navy personnel attracted a fair amount of publicity in their day. Special designs were made for their uniforms and headgear. They also attracted at least some attention from males, as is illustrated by the following lyrics:

> I've been in frigid Greenland and in Sunny Tennessee
> I've been in noisy London and in wicked gay Paree,
> I've seen the Latin Quarter with its models, wines and tights,
> I've hobnobbed oft with Broadway stars who outshone Broadway lights,
> But North or South or East or West, the girls that I have met,
> Could never hold a candle to a [Norfolk] yeomanette.[23]

The women enlisted for a period of four years, but not long after the conflict terminated, Congress began their usual efforts to reduce the defense budget. Although the last yeoman F was not discharged until March 1921, most were released from active duty in July 1919, although for Beryl Halley the date was August 5. However, many became civilian employees of the Navy Department. Beryl apparently was among these

2. Rio Grande to Norfolk, Virginia, 1913–1920

ladies as the 1920 census shows her working as a stenographer in Norfolk, Virginia, and she received an honorable discharge as yeoman first class on September 8, 1920, which meant that her actual service was nearly two years.[24] In fact, evidence suggests that once Beryl Halley departed from Gallia County to enter military service, she never returned to Bladen, Rio Grande, or Gallipolis, with the possible exception of a brief visit when her father's estate was settled.

3

Norfolk to Broadway, 1920–1924

Following Beryl Halley's honorable discharge from the U.S. Navy on September 8, 1920, she maintained a low profile for the next eleven months. She evidently remained in Norfolk for a few more months as she is listed in the city directory, but at a different address from that listed in the 1920 census. A March 1924 photograph in the *Chicago Tribune* suggests that prior to her Broadway career she was "formerly a figure model for artists and sculptors," but that may have been concurrent with her theatre work.[1] However, in August 1921, the country girl from Bladen made her modest debut in a Broadway production that, in the coming months, would make her name a household word on the "Big Apple" show business scene.

On August 9, 1921, a musical romantic comedy opened at the Casino Theatre titled *Tangerine*. The plot followed the adventures of four men, three of whom had been in "Alimony Jail," for "nonpayment." The fourth man, Dick Owens, had been having problems with his girlfriend, Shirley Dalton. Tangerine refers to a paradise island in the South Sea where the men go. The isle is ruled by a polygamy-practicing expatriate American known as King Home-Brew, who has a number of native girl spouses who make up a chorus line. As is common in such societies, the girls—virtual slaves—do all the work while the king and men "loll around, doing nothing." Eventually the estranged wives and girl friend arrive on the island and all the problems are "happily" settled except for the king who "winds [up] with not a spouse to his name."[2]

3. Norfolk to Broadway, 1920–1924

The part of Owens was played by another Ohioan, Frank Crumit (1889–1943), a native of Jackson, the next county seat up the road—northwest—from Gallia County. The son of a county clerk turned banker and prominent Mason, Frank's hometown circle included those with Rio Grande connections, including local attorney and long-time college trustee Benner Jones. (This may or may not have helped Beryl get her start in New York, but the possibility cannot be discounted.) Crumit himself had gone to Ohio University and Ohio State University, obtaining an engineering degree from the latter. His main interest, however, was music, and he had composed "fight" songs for both schools, which were in use for decades. The OSU song, "The Buckeye Battle Cry," remains their principal song at athletic events to this day and was reportedly composed at the request of the athletic director, George Trautman, who was also Crumit's brother-in law. Prior to 1920, he had made a name for himself on the vaudeville stage.[3]

Crumit made his first appearance on Broadway in 1920 in a production known as *Betty Be Good*, followed by the *Greenwich Village Follies*. He also began recording for the Columbia label and that year had his first of thirty-one hits in the decade with "Oh! By Jingo" and followed with two more from the *Greenwich Village* production. He also had a major hit in *Tangerine*, "Sweet Lady." His leading lady, Julia Sanderson (1887–1975), was much better known at the time and allegedly unhappy to be playing opposite a lesser figure. Nonetheless, the pair soon hit it off, became lovers, married in 1927, and soon turned to network radio where they became known as the "Sweethearts of the Air."[4]

Beryl's initial part in *Tangerine* was as one of King Home-Brew's "many wives" who made up the "grass-skirted chorus line." However, during the show's first run, which lasted for several months, some cast changes took place. Helen Frances, who had been "Kulikuli," shifted to become "Ahoa Oe," replacing Grace DeCarlton, who had left the show. Beryl took the role of Kulikuli through the initial run, ending on May 27, 1922, and for a short second run which terminated on August 26, 1922, a total run of 361. Ironically, one of the new cast members who moved into the chorus line-ensemble was fourteen-year-old Jeanette MacDonald, who later became famous for her MGM musicals from the mid-thirties, in which she and Nelson Eddy popularized such operetta numbers as "Indian Love Call." In addition to a possible connection with Crumit, another Gallia

Beryl Halley

native had Broadway connections that may have helped Ms. Halley make acquaintances in the New York theater world. Oscar Eagle (1861–1930) had come to the aid of some stage productions and even acted in a few, especially those associated with the Marx Brothers. While no evidence exists that they even knew each other, the possibility is less than remote. Bernice Ackerman, who later served as a bridesmaid at Beryl's 1933 nuptials, worked for Eagle at times.[5]

Persons who attained some level of Broadway celebrity could also make themselves available for other appearances. One such activity came—then as now—in style shows. In between the *Tangerine* runs, Beryl Halley made a visitation to one such venue in Hartford, Connecticut, on June 14 at "A Bather's Review" featuring Australian swimmer Annette Kellermann (1887–1975), who gained worldwide fame in 1905 when, among other achievements, she nearly became the first woman to swim the English Channel. She went on to popularize swimming among women, became a swimsuit designer, a health food advocate, and even appeared in some motion pictures. Others featured in the Hartford show were Dorothy Kitchen, "formerly of the Floridora Juvenile Sextet," who would "show children's suits," and Florence Moore (1886–1935), a stage actress then appearing in the Ziegfeld *Midnight Follies.* Later on, there appeared a picture of a swim-suited Beryl posing on a diving board at Lake Hoptacong, New Jersey, a venue where Kellerman also had connections.[6]

This magazine photograph of Beryl Halley, from about 1924, was found folded and stuck into a 1915 Rio Grande yearbook.

Not long after *Tangerine* closed for the second time, Beryl went on to start a week-

3. Norfolk to Broadway, 1920–1924

long appearance on September 5 at the Majestic in *The Demi-Virgin*. Described in the press as "Avery Hopwood's famous farce ... under the direction of A. H. Woods," and termed a "satiric farce-comedy of movie life in Hollywood," the cast also included Hazel Dawn (1890–1988), a devout Mormon who had earlier starred in a Ziegfeld production of *The Pink Lady*, which gave her that lifetime nickname, and Glenn Anders (1890–1981), who had a long career on the stage. On Broadway, the farce had a successful run of 268 performances at the Times Square Theatre, beginning on October 18, 1921, before going on the road; it was then that Miss Halley joined the company. Although controversial in many respects—mostly due to a strip-poker scene—the production was indeed popular. One later critic commented that, while *The Demi-Virgin* had no long-term literary impact, it did stimulate numerous arguments over censorship. The "famous farce," with most if not all of the original cast, then went on the road, opening at the Adelphi in Philadelphia in early October 1922. Beryl's surviving contract states that her salary was only $75 per week, suggesting that in spite of increasing fame, she remained in the lower ranks, at least by Broadway standards.[7]

Following her performances in *The Demi-Virgin*, Beryl apparently took a trip to the Far West. An undated clipping from the December 1922 *San Francisco Chronicle* states that she had been named the "most beautiful girl in the Golden West." (The *Chicago Tribune* likewise stated that she "has been awarded first prize as the most beautiful girl in California.") This seems to have been the time when Beryl was being described with such superlatives as "the Form Divine," "Venus of the 20th century," "the Most Undressed Girl," "Broadway's most beautiful showgirl," and "America's most perfect beauty." Such terms subsequently appeared in the *Washington Star*. The *Longreach Leader*, in faraway Queensland, carried her photo with a caption reading, "Can Australia do better?" "The Form Divine" moniker seems to have outlasted the others for Beryl since Lillian Roth referred to her as such in her autobiography. Whatever, by mid–December she was back in the East, where she displayed a three-foot-high "model of the Statue of Liberty," naming her "a sculptress" in addition to being "selected as the most beautiful girl of the West."[8]

By New Year's Day in 1923, Beryl was back on stage, this time in Philadelphia at the Adelphi Theatre in "a musical farce, *The Naughty Diana*, said to be an adaptation of a French original." The American

31

version featured songs by Will Ortmann, and with lyrics by Cyrus D. Wood. Beryl played a character named Rose in a cast that included such Broadway veterans as Joseph Allen (1873–1952), Marion Ballou (1870–1939), and Charlie Ruggles (1886–1970). The latter had a long career on both stage and screen. He had been in the original cast of *The Demi-Virgin* and may have been a factor in the young Beryl Halley becoming a cast member. Despite the best efforts of the cast, *Naughty Diana* never made it to Broadway.[9]

Beryl also continued to engage in modeling. Among her papers is a somewhat ragged page torn out of the April 1923 issue of *Harper's Bazaar*. Although uncredited, her full-page image is used in an advertisement for a British firm that manufactured "The Treo Elastic Girdle," which "enables all women ... to enjoy the figure-freedom and dress-distinction that only" their product "imparts."[10]

It soon became apparent that while Beryl continued to support herself by figure modeling, her ultimate goal was to get back on the Broadway stage. Within several weeks she made a major step to achieve that ambition. In the early 1920s, one of the major symbols of New York stage success was the Ziegfeld Girl.

Florenz Ziegfeld, Jr., had earned the sobriquet used in the subtitle of his most recent biography, "Broadway's Greatest Producer." The man himself can be best described as an enigma and a mass of contra-

Alberto Vargas (1896-1982) would become famous for his drawings of "pin-up" girls, but early in his career (1919-1931) he was employed by Florenz Ziegfeld, for whom Vargas painted cast portraits. The Ziegfeld Girl chosen to grace the sheet music for the 1924 *Follies* was Beryl Halley.

3. Norfolk to Broadway, 1920–1924

dictions. Born in Chicago in 1867, the son of a German immigrant professor of classical music, young "Flo" was instead drawn to what one might call the "popular arts." Eschewing the classics, he favored minstrel shows, melodramas, and even burlesque. Yet he aspired to raise the latter to a new level of style and beauty. While he achieved his goal, the man's whole career seemed to be one filled with failures and successes, high and lows, ups and downs. He spent money lavishly on his productions, but he was often on the verge of bankruptcy, with creditors virtually nipping at his heels. The Great Depression—and, ultimately, his death in 1932—put an end to his production "empire," but his legend endured. Even his harshest critics had fond memories of the man who brought a high level of glamour and grandeur to his productions.

In his day, Florenz Ziegfeld produced many Broadway shows featuring a host of memorable stars, including Anna Held, Lillian Loraine, Olive Thomas, Eddie Cantor, Marion Davies, Leon Errol, Will Rogers, Helen Morgan, Ed Wynn, Marilyn Miller, Ann Pennington, Billie Burke, W. C. Fields, and Fanny Brice. While Barbara Stanwyck and Paulette Goddard had brief careers as Ziegfeld Girls, they achieved their legendary status on the screen. Songwriters for Ziegfeld productions included most of the popular composers of the day: Irving Berlin, Jerome Kern, George Gershwin, and Cole Porter, as well as those associated with operettas, such as Rudolph Friml, Victor Herbert, and Sigmund Romberg. Yet today, Ziegfeld is best remembered for his *Follies*, a variety revue that included songs, dances, comedy sketches, tableaus, and—above all—beautiful girls.

While Florenz Ziegfeld produced quality entertainment, he also knew the value of publicity. Almost from the beginning of his career he learned to make the most of that situation. It began with his first successful promotion in creating the image of the strongman Eugen Sandow. It reached new heights in the developing of the iconic Anna Held, his first female star. In her case, the contention was that she maintained her perfect complexion by taking daily baths in milk—forty quarts at a time. Although mostly fiction, it nonetheless created the kind of attention that made Held a major star from the moment she stepped off the boat that brought her from Europe to the United States.

As time passed, the Ziegfeld public-relations machine had pretty much been perfected. Bernard Sobel probably ranked at the top of this pyramid, but others, such as Mark Hellinger, came close. Not only Ziegfeld

Beryl Halley

Girls made good copy; other performers did as well. Their names regularly appeared in the New York City press, and in syndicated columns and wire services that spread tidbits about their lives and their photographs nationwide and beyond. Thus, Beryl Halley managed to get her name and pictures in newspapers nationally almost as much as she had done in Gallia County.

Florenz Ziegfeld loved to be surrounded by attractive women, the more beautiful the better. Naturally, there were questions raised regarding the nature of their relationships with the impresario. Avoiding sensationalism, one can say that he married—sort of—Anna Held, and later, Billie Burke. He had a notorious affair with Lillian Lorraine, which destroyed his relationship with Held. In turn, Lorraine's wild lifestyle eventually wrecked not only her romance with Ziegfeld, but her career as well. Billie and Flo had a daughter, Patricia, who was adored by her father, and in a sense kept the couple together. What other romantic trysts the great producer may have had remain merely subjects of conjecture, although prominent names, like Olive Thomas and Marilyn Miller, are sometimes mentioned. Beyond that, relatively little has appeared in print.

The first *Follies* premiered in 1907, with the principal star being singer Nora Bayes (1880–1928) who, with her husband Jack Norworth (1879–1959), had made "Shine on Harvest Moon," one of the great song hits of the early 20th century. Over the next quarter-century, through 1931 (with the exception of those few years when none were produced), annual editions of the *Follies* ranked among the most popular Broadway attractions. Some productions included spring, summer, or fall versions, with changes in personnel. During certain years (between 1915 and 1921) there were *Midnight Frolics* and/or the *Nine O'Clock Revue* on the rooftop of the New Amsterdam Theatre. Culture historian Lewis A. Erenberg placed these productions in context, "during ... twenty-five years Ziegfeld and his competitors [chiefly Earl Carroll and George White] strove to out produce each other with beautifully mounted productions, each with gorgeous scenery, snappy comedians, and most important, beautiful women, beautifully presented."[11]

While it seems likely that Flo Ziegfeld's own view of beauty changed somewhat over the years, the *Follies* flourished. He expressed his views in the spring of 1923—shortly before the hiring of Beryl Halley—in an interview for the *Brooklyn Daily Eagle*, entitled "Ziegfeld Discusses Girls."

3. Norfolk to Broadway, 1920–1924

He believed it was time to bid "farewell to the flapper and hail to the natural girl." On May 1, Florenz Ziegfeld, Jr., identified as "authority on feminine pulchritude," began the final process of selecting eighteen "new beauties as the spring peach crop of 1923 to further decorate the organization which bears his name."[12]

Ziegfeld went on to explain that of about ten thousand initial applicants, the number had been reduced to 604, then assembled on the stage of the New Amsterdam Theatre. He said, "I have concluded that the girl of the day has gone back to Nature." Getting specific, he said that "your perfect beauty must have well-rounded shoulders, well-shaped [calves], small feet and small ankles, and her legs above all, must be hollowed out from the knees up." He concluded, "That's the kind the great American public [wants to see] ... and that is the kind we comb the beauty market to find ... and that ... we will all be able to present in the 'Follies.'"[13] How close Ziegfeld and his subordinates actually followed all of these standards (or even whether they actually started with ten thousand applicants) cannot be confirmed. What we *do* know is that Beryl Halley made the final cut. Little "Cubby" had come a long way from Bladen Landing via Rio Grande.

A couple of years later, the master producer further elaborated his views in an article carrying his byline in the *New York Morning Telegraph*, the city's leading show business and sports journal, titled "What Makes a Ziegfeld Girl." Either he—or a ghostwriter—opined:

> Beauty, of course, is the most important requirement and the paramount asset of the applicant. When I say that, I mean beauty of face, form, charm and manner, personal magnetism, individuality, grace and poise. These are details that must always be settled before the applicant has demonstrated her ability either to sing or dance. It is not easy to pass the test that qualifies a girl for membership in a Ziegfeld production, but I am frank to say that once she has done so, much of the element of doubt is removed so far as the future success of her career before the footlights is concerned.[14]

Ziegfeld also stressed the long hours of practice and rehearsal involved in the search for as near perfection as possible on stage:

> There is a prevalent impression that once a girl is enlisted under the Ziegfeld standard, her troubles are over and her hard work is ended. What a mistake! Let us hope that for many it does not mean the end of trouble, so far as earning a livelihood is concerned, that it means happy and comfortable home living honestly earned. But there are other troubles ahead for her and plenty of hard work.

Beryl Halley

A Ziegfeld production is no place for a drone or an idler. Often are the times when you who reads these words or just opening your eyes in the morning or are enjoying their breakfast and the early news of the day, that the girls of a Ziegfeld production are busy as bees on the stage of an empty theatre, if indeed they have not already put in an hour or more in striving to come nearer to perfection in that which is expected of them before the footlights. Yes there is plenty of hard work for them in addition to that which they do when they appear, smiling and happy when the curtain goes up. Giving a performance is the least of their worries.[15]

In 1923, one of Ben Ali Haggin's tableaux from *The Midnight Frolic* toured the country with Muriel Stryker portraying Simonetta, based upon the famous Botticelli painting. The Ziegfeld Girls featured in that production included Edna French, Doris Lloyd, Elise Sparrow, and Beryl Halley. Touring from March through July, the girls traveled from coast to coast, and according to the *Daily News*, "showing the famous model in life and death and practically no underwear at all."

Ziegfeld also stressed that Ziegfeld Girls came from "all walks of life."

> The society girl, tired of that life, the school teacher wearied with the duties of the daily grind [is he thinking of Beryl Halley?], the one whose life has heretofore been devoid of purpose, the stenographer [Beryl, again], cashier or even the waitress. Maybe she is a chambermaid, but if she has the necessary talent and qualities a place awaits her in the Ziegfeld ranks.[16]

Cynthia and Sara Brideson note that, in addition to talent, a degree of ladylike behavior was also expected. They wrote that while the "Ziegfeld girls suggested sex and daring," it nonetheless "remained just that suggestion." Like Beryl Halley, many hailed from "provincial towns

3. Norfolk to Broadway, 1920–1924

and rural households." Excessive imbibing, use of illicit drugs, and "generally hedonistic behavior could get you fired. Some never received a second chance, some got but one. Lillian Lorraine (1892–1955), who had been Ziegfeld's mistress and a major figure during the teens, received more chances to reform than any other Ziegfeld girl, but finally wore out her welcome. Upon her passing, she was initially buried in a pauper's grave.[17]

Flo Ziegfeld, in his earlier direction and promotion of his common law wife and first major star Anna Held, beginning in the 1906 production *The Parisian Model*, made "scantily clad women into an art." But as Doris Eaton, known as the longest living of his beauties, had written, "He didn't object to presenting the girls in a sensuous manner." Reckoning and comparing his extravaganzas to a painting of the Renaissance period, she contended that the girls, presumably including her and her sister Mary, as well as Beryl "looked beautiful, not vulgar."[18]

Bernard Sobel once quoted his boss's preferences for his girls. He said "vivacity" counted most, adding that her figure must be almost perfect. "She must not overdo make-up. Her hairdo must conform to her features. She must have plenty of sleep and outdoor exercise. I recommend also instruction in dancing and fencing.... I

Elise Sparrow came from Birmingham, Alabama, as a beauty queen and left New York City in 1925 as the wife of Thomas Yawkey, the longtime owner of the Boston Red Sox. They divorced on November 13, 1944. She would marry Harry Dorsey Watts on December 2 that same year. She signed her picture "To Beryl (pronounced with r-r-r-s), with best wishes." This was no doubt a reference to the difficulty many people had pronouncing her name.

place my first emphasis on the beauty of a girl's ankles. No matter how perfect her dimensions may be, if her ankles are bad, the whole effect is lost because the first feature the audience sees when the curtain rises, is the ankles."[19]

Some years after her Ziegfeld days ended, Beryl explained in a radio interview how she came to be chosen from among the many applicants. She said, "I got my start through [choreographer] Ned Wayburn. He selected me as a show girl. Mr. Ziegfeld saw me at rehearsals and chose me to do all Ben Ali Haggin's tableau posing." Since many of the poses showed girls wearing little (if any) clothing, Beryl said with a laugh in answer to a relevant question comparing it to strip teasing, "No, it wasn't. That was what they called 'art'—at least, Ben Ali Haggin called it art."[20]

Art or not, Ziegfeld Girls set the standard for America's definition of feminine attractiveness for the 1910–1930 period. As Michael Lasser, writing in the *American Scholar* in 1994, explained: "[Flo Ziegfeld] shaped the American perception of female beauty." He further noted that the legendary producer "showed all of us that no one could be as magnificent as a Follies girl."[21]

By the latter half of May, Beryl had been chosen as one of the new "Ziegfeld Beauties" and was immediately sent on a tour with nine other girls. In Atlanta, one of the nine became homesick for New York and was replaced by Frances Thayer, a local girl who had recently won a beauty contest; her mother accompanied her on the trip, which culminated in San Francisco. On May 23, five of the girls paid a visit to the *San Francisco Chronicle*. The year before, Ben Ali Haggin had made tableaux a significant part of the *Follies* and the girls were there to promote one titled "Simonetta," derived from a painting by renaissance master Botticelli. As reported by *Chronicle* columnist George C. Warren, the account of the "Bevy of Pulchritude" reads:

> A quintet of Ziegfeld "Follies" beauties invaded the Chronicle office yesterday, blonde, brunette and Chastain, with Muriel Stryker's lovely dark hair and blue, blue eyes and exquisite profile dominating the show of pulchritude they made. The others were Beryl Halley, Edna French, Frances Thayer, and Elise Sparrow.
>
> They are part of the company of nine divinities who are to present Ben Ali Haggin's tableaux, illustrating the love of Simonetta and Sandro Botticelli, which will be the feature act at the Grenada Theatre next week, commencing Saturday.[22]

3. Norfolk to Broadway, 1920–1924

Warren went on to describe and extract quotations from each of the girls. Muriel Stryker, the exotic dancer and best known of the girls at the time, had relatives in Oakland and had been visiting them. Beryl, described as "very blonde," said, "We've been hunting an apartment to keep house," declaring, "it's so much nicer than living in a hotel." All professed to like San Francisco, although "auburn-haired" Frances Thayer expressed a preference for Los Angeles. Edna French, with "hair that is vividly red," was "quite positive in her liking for San Francisco." Elise Sparrow, Miss Alabama of 1921, created the most interest for her accent, with Warren commenting that her "dialect clings to her and is thick in her talk." The reporter also noted, "Miss Halley, a cosmopolite, likes the place she happens to be most of all until she gets to the next city, but has a preference perhaps for New York."[23]

While the *Chronicle* focused the girl's visit to their office, the Hearst rival *Examiner* looked at another aspect of French, Halley, and Thayer's lifestyles. Apparently, during the December 1922 California visit, the girls appeared in a ninety-minute film *The Enemies of Women* starring the legendary Lionel Barrymore as an exiled Russian prince. Their roles were small and uncredited, and they were likely cast as dancers. The film had been released in April 1923, but the girls were apparently granted a screening during their San Francisco trip. Other small parts were played by the teenaged "It Girl," Clara Bow, in what was only her second film role. Margaret Dumont, who later gained fame for being the target for many of Groucho Marx's comic insults on

Patricia Salmon blazed into New York City in 1923, but her Ziegfeld days blazed out just as quickly. She soon returned to tent shows, participated in dance marathons, and was arrested in 1932 for charges of illegally entering the country. She signed her picture: "To Beryl, with love and best wishes, Paddy."

Beryl Halley

both stage and screen, appeared in the film, as did fellow Ziegfeld Girl Helen Lee Worthing.[24]

Earlier editions of the *Follies* had often played for a week in Atlantic City prior to the official Broadway debut, but this time the *Daily News* reported that it would "Open Cold ... on Monday night Oct. 8." Ziegfeld himself complained that the show was becoming too expensive. Profits of the 1922 revue had been only 1 percent and "production costs" on the current version "exclusive of salaries is $350,000." He announced that this one would be the last. Time would change the legendary producer's mind, or perhaps his comments were just a gimmick to boost ticket sales. If the latter was indeed the case, it worked. O. O. McIntyre in his "New York Day by Day" column of January 19, 1924, predicted as much, saying that "next year Ziggy will be back 'glorifying the American Girl.' The Follies is as much an institution as the seventh inning stretch." McIntyre also pointed out that the day was not far off when the public would tire of exorbitant prices for tickets, a *Follies* seat then cost $22.50. He concluded that instead of attending "the theatre twice a week—a New York idea ... they['ll] go to the movies."[25]

Beryl Halley's first appearance as a Ziegfeld Girl came on October 20, 1923, when the new edition of the *Follies* opened at the New Amsterdam Theatre. The production started some weeks later than usual because the 1922 revue had run longer than planners had anticipated. Beryl had no doubt been in rehearsals for several days, and perhaps weeks prior to the premiere, as the date of her initial contract has not been found among her papers. Critics contended that the show had earlier hit its peak and had started a slow downhill slide. However, the audiences responded positively and the extravaganza ran for a longer-than-usual total of 233 performances. Both Eddie Cantor and Fannie Brice ranked as the most notable cast members. James Reynolds, who had been honored as a costume and set designer for the past three seasons, won his usual acclaim.

In addition to Ms. Halley, another new cast member, sixteen-year-old Lina Basquette, who earlier had ballet training, made her debut starring in a dance number "The Legend of the Drums," set in the Napoleonic Era. Other dance specialties featured the Empire Girls and a specialty titled "Maid of Gold" by the exotic Muriel Stryker—whom Beryl would later term a mentor. (She had been a replacement for Mary Eaton.) Beryl

3. Norfolk to Broadway, 1920–1924

had yet to emerge from the chorus line, but she nonetheless managed to attract her share of attention, as events would demonstrate.[26]

What exactly did Beryl do as a Ziegfeld Girl in the *Follies*? Based on a program for February 1924, we see that the entire cast participated in the opening scene, the highlight of which was the Gene Buck song "Glorifying the Girls." Scene Two featured a song by Marie Dahm, with choral and dance support by Betty Warrington, Helen Lee Worthing, Alice Knowlton, Gladys Coburn, Imogene "Bubbles" Wilson, and Beryl Halley, collectively known as the "Marion Davies Girls." Skipping to Scene Five, a picture and pantomime (a.k.a. tableau) by Ben Ali Haggin, called "La Marquise," with music by Rudolf Friml, was led by Lina Basquette as "The White Marquise," with support by five other girls, including Beryl as the "Marquise of the Bath." Other girls included the aforementioned Coburn, Wilson, and Worthing. The entire cast joined in the Act One finale, which consisted of a song by Brooke Johns. In addition to the regular *Follies* cast, an English choral group, known variously as The Empire Girls (or, as they were known in London, The Tiller Girls) joined in for the closing. Beryl's role in Act Two was seemingly limited to dance routines in "Maid of Honor," another Buck-Friml musical creation, with the lead hoofers being Robert Quinault, Iris Rowe, and Lina Basquette. Among the early Ziegfeld beauties that Beryl counted among her friends, the petite dancer Ann Pennington seems to have been a favorite, and perhaps a role model. The latter began her career

Edna Leedom (October 9, 1896–October 16, 1937) appeared with Beryl in the *Follies* of 1923, 1924, and 1925. Her three prior marriages failed, but on March 9, 1928, she wed Frank Doelger, heir to the Doelger Brewery millions. She left her show business career and gave birth to Frank Jr. Tragically, Edna died at home, from pneumonia, on October 16, 1937.

in Camden, New Jersey, and Philadelphia, soon becoming the toast of Broadway and having some film successes as well. However, whether she went so far as to use Mineralava and Mineralava Face Finish, products she endorsed for removing stage makeup, has not been recorded.[27]

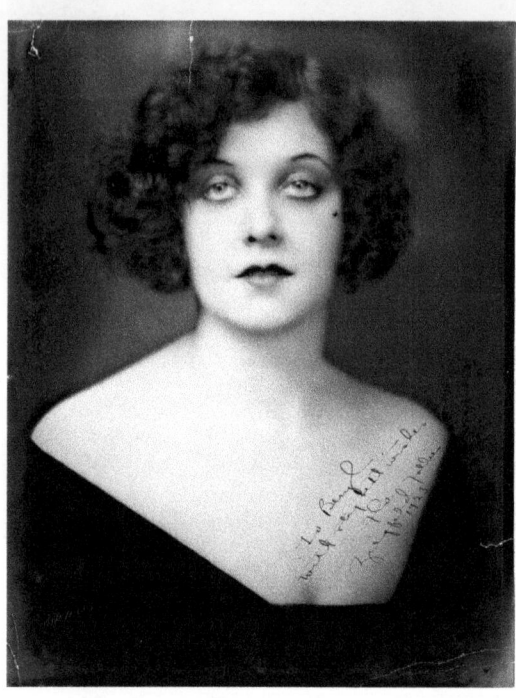

Flo Kennedy appeared in the *Follies* of 1923 and 1925, both featuring Beryl. Her other Broadway credit is the Ziegfeld show *No Foolin'*. She also appeared in a series of magazine ads for Lucky Strike cigarettes along with fellow Ziegfeld member Gladys Glad and Florenz Ziegfeld himself. The native of San Francisco was featured in newspaper articles about beauty secrets of the stars.

Soon after, or perhaps even slightly before the new *Follies* opened, Beryl Halley encountered her first-known serious romantic interest. Among bandleaders in the "Big Apple," Vincent Lopez (1895–1975) ranked second only to Paul Whiteman. Lopez, the son of Portuguese immigrants, was attracted to popular music and by the fall of 1921 played a quality piano and led a seven-piece band, The Kings of Harmony, at the Hotel Statler. (The group would soon increase its number of musicians, becoming a full-fledged orchestra, which only enhanced their popularity and attracted major label phonograph contracts. Over the years several other noted musicians, including Glenn Miller, the Dorsey Brothers, Artie Shaw, and Xavier Cugat, would get their start in his group. Although a single father of a young daughter, Lopez seemed to be an incurable romantic who also "longed to be accepted as a member of high society," and who "wined and dined beautiful show girls continuously."[28]

The Vincent Lopez–Beryl Halley romance began in the fall of 1923, shortly after the famed heavyweight boxing match between champion Jack

3. Norfolk to Broadway, 1920–1924

Dempsey and challenger Luis Firpo. The fight took place on September 13, 1923, with Dempsey winning decisively. Publicist Jim Gillespie arranged for Lopez to present Dempsey with a cup or trophy at the Roseland Hotel. He would also be eligible to go on a double date with Lopez and Dempsey and a pair of Ziegfeld Girls. According to the plan, the Manassa Mauler's date, whom Lopez said had often been billed as "the girl with the most beautiful body in the world," Beryl Halley, and Lopez would escort another "real doll ... a brunette named Estelle Taylor."[29]

During the date at the Roselind Hotel, the two couples went to the Hotel Alamac where, according to Lopez, "Beryl and Estelle were just what the psychiatrist would order for an introverted patient" and also possessed "a lot besides beauty, wit and charm and gaiety." But as the conversation "warmed up," the champ focused more attention on Estelle Taylor. The more Dempsey talked to Taylor, the more Lopez found himself talking with Beryl. She told him that the next day she was going to pose for a statue being made by a noted sculptor, because "Mr. Ziegfeld wants him to do a statue of me."[30]

As the evening wore on, the guys decided to "switch girls for the rest of the night." Vincent and Beryl soon became an item in New York social circles. In his autobiography, the bandleader wrote, "Beryl and I began having so many dates I talked myself into renting a limousine ... to impress" her. The romance would continue for the next year or so. Meanwhile, Lopez increased the size of his orchestra to fifty-six pieces. He also spent himself and his creditors into "dire financial straits." Finally, he decided that his only way out was to take his band to England for a lengthy tour.[31]

Beryl Halley continued to gain favorable publicity. Her picture was increasingly seen in newspapers across the nation. For instance, the March 24, Sunday edition of the *Chicago Tribune* ran a portrait of her made by leading NYC photographer Edward Thayer Monroe. The caption reads: "[Here is] Another reason why men give up their smokes to save $5.50 for a ticket and a front-row seat at the 'Follies.' Show girl de luxe is Beryl Halley. And we'll say she is all of that. Born in Harding's old home state, she comes of English parentage. Formerly a figure model for artists and sculptors. Natural blonde hair and pansy-eyed and doesn't care if she has a career or not."[32]

Ironically, that would be one of the last times for many decades that

Beryl Halley

Ms. Halley would claim an Ohio birthplace. Within the year, she would list it as Kansas City, Missouri, and later, as Kentucky. Undoubtedly, an origin in a center of jazz music or the horse farm country in the bluegrass region looked more impressive than being from Bladen Landing.[33]

Published photographs of pretty girls attracted the attention of a host of admirers, some of whom wrote fan letters. For instance, Ward M. Miller, writing on a Harvard Law School letterhead, said "My Dear Miss Halley, Your picture in the Feb 1 issue of 'Town and Country,' has so excited the admiration of our law club that we seek your advice on how to secure a copy either by legitimate means or by stealth. If you will favor us with a little advice in this regard [our gratitude] will know no bounds." Frederick T. Howard, a student at the Milton Academy in Massachusetts, wrote, "Would you please send an autographed picture to a young chap who would appreciate it very much?" Not all admirers were men. A Marjorie Stewart wrote, "I hope I am not asking too much of you but would you send me one of your personally auto graphed [sic] photographs."[34]

Some fans wanted more than autographed pictures and were quite forward about it. A telegram (punctuation added), from Walter J. Kingsley, reads: "My Wonderful Beryl. I look forward to seeing you in all your radiant loveliness, the queen of all the Ziegfeld beauties, tonight. Dazzle the first nighters with your manifold perfections, each one of which is dear and thrilling to a beauty

Irving Fisher (1886-1959) appeared with Beryl in the *Follies* in 1924 and 1925. His Broadway credits include his work as both a performer and lyricist. As he bore a striking resemblance to Harry Truman, he would occasionally double for the president in public. Fisher was never comfortable with this, saying he was a singer, not an actor. He was also a solid Republican.

3. Norfolk to Broadway, 1920–1924

lover such as [I]." Winfield Scott, Jr., of Fort Worth, Texas, had a friend who had evidently met Beryl some time earlier. He wrote, "I am leaving for New York ... within the next few days and expect to be there for some time, as I intend to rest up.... I am going to discontinue all business for the next two months and frolic around, and I hope I will be fortunate enough to secure you as my playmate while I am visiting in your fair city."[35]

Becoming a Ziegfeld Follies chorus girl and dancer may not have yet been what anyone could term "stardom." However, it did serve as a genuine beginning. Not long afterward, Mark Hellinger, one the more astute reporters on the Broadway scene, would label Beryl Halley as one of the six "most beautiful [actually third]," the others being Kathryn Ray, Dorothy Knapp, Mary Mulhern, Norma Smallwood, and Gladys Glad, respectively. Hellinger, who favored Miss Glad, noted that not *all* could be "most beautiful,"[36]

Meanwhile, back in Gallia County, having almost never mentioned her name in the local press since she left for duty in the U.S. Navy at the end of September 1918, the *Gallipolis Daily Tribune* ran a short article on May 6, 1924, titled "Bladen Girl Attracts Attention":

> Miss Beryl Holley [sic], a native of Bladen, has attracted copsiderable [sic] attention in New York as an outstanding beauty. She is with Ziegfeld's Follies and there is a full page picture of her in the May Red Book. She is a niece of Mr. Sherman Porter, and has been in theatrical work for several years.[37]

In a sense, this short article was a modest announcement that the hometown girl was making it in the big-time.

4

Ziegfeld Girl, 1924–1925

The spring of 1924 must have been a positive one for Beryl Halley. She had signed for a second season with the Ziegfeld *Follies* on June 17. The contract was a standard one, covering such topics as rehearsals, obligations, and responsibilities.[1] While her seventy-dollar-weekly salary may not have placed her remotely close to what a nationally known comic like Will Rogers or a big-name dancer/singer such as Ann Pennington might be receiving, it far surpassed what Beryl's mother and sister were making in Ohio classrooms. In addition, a well-known bandleader was squiring her around the city in a rented limo and spending money he did not have, trying to make an impression on her.

In addition, Beryl's picture had been in the nationally distributed *Redbook* magazine and in newspapers from Washington, D.C., to Australia. Her name and/or photos were beginning to be seen about as often as it once had been in the *Gallipolis Daily Tribune*. When the curtain went up at the New Amsterdam Theatre for the new season of the *Follies* on June 24, Beryl Halley no longer ranked as a "rookie" Ziegfeld Girl.

Fan mail also continued to arrive. S. H. Nickerson of Athens, Georgia, wrote "I saw you in the 'Ziegfeld Follies' a few nights ago and I want to tell you how beautiful you looked as Eve in the 'Beautiful Contest.' You have such a sweet smile.... Wishing you the best of luck from one of your many admirers."[2]

Miss Halley worked in the show for slightly over a month when her bosses sent her and another "glorified American girl" to the British Isles

4. Ziegfeld Girl, 1924–1925

for a month. As early as June, newspapers reported that a theatre organization in England wanted to bring a Ziegfeld show to London. The *Daily News* reported, in "fragmentary statements," that he would stage "two new musical productions," a revue and the popular play *Kid Boots*. Although none of this came to pass, Beryl's trip no doubt had some connection to this desire, and may have been a testing of the waters, so to speak. She departed on the ship *Leviathan* on July 29. To date, no data on her activity in England have surfaced, although she and companion Helen Dobbins may have given some type of performance on August 18. Given the fact that such voyages for pleasure were beyond the means of the average working girl, she was undoubtedly on a Ziegfeld-related public-relations project of some kind.[3] They returned on the *Berengaria*, which departed from Southampton on August 23, with a stop at Cherbourg and arriving back in New York on the 29th. The printed "passenger list" from the ship indicates that the girls traveled in style, with some distinguished shipmates. These included "His Royal Highness, The Prince of Wales," best known at the time as an international playboy, but better known in later years as King Edward VIII, the man who gave up his throne to marry "the woman I love." Other royalty included "H. R. H. Princesse de Bragance (Duchess of Oporto)," of the displaced—since 1910—Portuguese-ruling family. Connected to British royalty through marriage (uncle of Prince Philip, the husband of Queen Elizabeth II) was Lord Louis Mountbatten K.V.C.O., R. N. and Lady Mountbatten, as well as their "Manservant" and "Maid." Lord Mountbatten is perhaps best known as the Last Viceroy of British India and a victim of an Irish Republican Army assassination in 1979.[4] Other Britons of note were "Mr. H. G. Chilton, C. M. G.," who served as "Counsellor of the British Embassy" and "Brig.-Gen. G. F. Trotter," (1871–1945), who held several ranks of knighthood. He had served in both the Boer conflict in South Africa and in World War I. He spent the next fifteen years as Gentleman Usher in the Court of King George V. Last but not least was Captain Alan F. Lascelles (1887–1981), World War I veteran and recipient of the Military Cross. At the time, the British officer was on civilian duty as assistant private secretary to Prince Edward, but later left after a dispute with the Royal; he later served as his private secretary during his short reign, and, even more important, to King George VI. Knighted by His Royal Highness in 1939, Lascalles rendered valuable service to the Crown during the dark days of World

War II. Following the king's death, he enjoyed a long and well-deserved retirement.[5]

Notable Americans from families of wealth and/or power were also represented. One was twelve-year-old John Jacob Astor VI (misidentified as the III on the passenger list), whose father had perished on the *Titanic*. Seven members of the state of Delaware's noted DuPont family, led by Lammot DuPont II (1880–1952), actually had no servants on board. However, the long-distinguished "first family of New Jersey politics," led by George Frelinghuysen, a noted patent attorney and son of Frederick Frelinghuysen (who had served as President Arthur's secretary of state), his wife, and another family member, "Miss Matilda," did have the services of a maid.[6] All in all, the girl from Bladen Landing must have felt some sense of pride to be in such distinguished company.

Back in New York, Beryl found out—if she had not known already—that she was now an official "cover girl." The *National Police Gazette* had been around for nearly eight decades as a controversial and often sensational form of journalism. The weekly's subtitle was "The Leading Illustrated Sporting Journal in the World." From 1876, the leadership of Irish immigrant Richard Kyle Fox made it the leading news magazine for what would later be known as "yellow journalism." Its pink-tinted pages were eagerly read in barber shops, livery stables, billiard parlors, saloons, and other places frequented by males. News concentrated on show business, sports (especially boxing), and detailed crimes both in cities and on the frontier. According to rumor, Fox allegedly told his staff of writers to "write the stuff that the dailies don't dare use! Be as truthful as possible, but a story's a story!" Until photographs became common, Fox kept a staff of sketch artists, saying of his audience, "If they can't read, give them lots of pictures," especially of "muscular pugilists and ... and females in spangled tights." Whatever his strengths and weaknesses, more recent historians have given the colorful editor, owners, and proprietor of the *Police Gazette* credit for being a major force in developing what has become known as the "cult of masculinity." Fox died a millionaire in 1922, and the peak days of his journal had declined somewhat in recent years, but it still had a considerable following. On August 23, 1924, the front cover showed a photo of Beryl Halley, labeled "one of the most queenly of Ziegfeld's 'Follies' Beauties."[7]

Even more appealing was a sheet music cover of Beryl, a watercolor

4. Ziegfeld Girl, 1924–1925

pastel—emphasizing her blonde hair, bright blue eyes, and full red lips—painted by noted Peruvian-born portrait artist Alberto Vargas, and labeled "All Peppered Up."[8] Included were songs from the 1924 *Follies*, with lyrics by Joseph McCarthy and music by Harry Tierney.

Beryl also continued her on-again, off-again romance with bandleader Vincent Lopez, who continued to spend beyond his means in pursuit of the popular Ziegfeld Girl—and perhaps other Broadway beauties as well. By the spring of 1925, as debts began to mount, Lopez decided that the only means of putting his finances on a sound footing was to take his music to Great Britain. By his own account, he had to virtually sneak onto the ship to escape creditors. Prior to launch, Beryl met him for lunch aboard the *Leviathan*. One gets the idea that she was not fully aware of his financial plight. She apparently preferred that he not "bring American jazz to England," as he termed his foreign junket. Lopez, however, believed that Miss Halley had matrimony on her mind. This seemed obvious, as he recalled her asking, "If we could make it together, Vincent, as man and wife, it would be wonderful." Not jumping on her request for a proposal, Beryl came back with a less direct comment: "We'll skip it till you get back. Anyway, we have to think seriously about where we're going, dear.... You and I as two people in love—not Vincent Lopez and his orchestra." She also warned him not to do anything that might "warm ... up" the alleged "quite cold and reserved" English girls.[9]

Lopez spent roughly three months in England, opening at London's Kit Kat Club on May 11. Returning to New York on August 1, 1925, his debts now paid, he and his band were feted at a reception at the Hotel Pennsylvania. He remarked, "Lovely Beryl Halley met me at the pier ... but she missed most of the party ... because of her own show." It seems that her desire for matrimony had faded, possibly due to her learning of his prior indebtedness, and perhaps other romantic encounters. When they met somewhat later at Gray's Drugstore, instead of urging a proposal, she said, "Let's just be friends, Vincent." She further added, "No demands by either of us, except when we really need each other." She also suggested that they could skip the most expensive places. They could even meet "at the Automat."[10]

Lopez reflected on the romance in his autobiography. He wrote: "We saw each other less frequently, and with a bit less intensity." In conclusion, he said, "Our love affair was burning with a smaller though a steadier flame."[11]

Beryl Halley

Apparently, Beryl's employer did not give the couple much encouragement, either. Sometime during this less intense period of their relationship, Beryl arranged for him to meet Ziegfeld at the New Amsterdam Theatre. Lopez, recalling the meeting some thirty-five years later, characterized the great producer as "never the one to make the other person feel comfortable," said, "Oh, you're the one who's been dating Beryl." He added "I have a rule against our girls going out with men from show business," which may have been an implied warning. He added, "They're better off meeting millionaires who want to marry them." Lopez would conclude the meeting by saying that he was neither a millionaire nor did he want to get married.[12] Still, enough rumors were circulating the theatre district to arouse press attention, such as the mention in *Zit's Theatrical Chronicler* on August 8, 1924.

> Vincent Lopez's reported romance with one of Ziegfeld's glorified girls ... has gone on the rocks before it even had a chance to get started. The paramount leader of jazz orchestras said he was not engaged to any of the chorus girls and had no intentions in that direction. "I know nothing about it," was the answer given by Beryl Halley, the girl in the case.[13]

Meanwhile, Beryl continued receiving national press coverage. In December 1924, a photograph by Edward Thayer Monroe appeared with the caption: "Another beauty—Beryl Halley—added to Florenz Ziegfeld's long list in the 'Follies' at the New Amsterdam Theatre, New York."[14]

A likely view of Beryl Halley as a Ziegfeld Girl in the winter of 1924–1925 appears in an essay by literary critic Edmund Wilson, "The Finale at the Follies: Dress Rehearsal." It describes a rehearsal where "Florenz Ziegfeld, who is standing at the front of the house [giving instructions]":

> You've got to get those stockings right. Their garters are out of alignment. There's nothing to the costume but the stockings! ... Darn right! ... A tall girl takes the stage with a flopping sombrero mounts a pedestal and begins to pose.... The show girls—white, green, white, white, black, orange, purple, green, orange, black, white, green. You've got two white ones together. Put somebody between them. You go over on the end, Gladys. Now begin again![15]

Wilson's description details another portion of the rehearsal, this one involving Beryl Halley, although she is not named.

> The girl who is doing the Circassian slave in the number "The Pearl of the East," soft-molded in a fawn-colored robe under which she is almost nude, pale hair smoothed close to her calm little head to accommodate the flooding yellow wig, moves slowly down the house toward a friend. The show girls come in again:

4. Ziegfeld Girl, 1924–1925

one is missing. "Who died?" She appears. "Now do that over.... Say: the girls are all right. It's the lights. I'm explaining to the girls about the lights!"[16]

Although the IMDb contains no listing of it, Beryl apparently appeared in her second motion picture in the summer of 1925. In June, the *Daily News* reported that "Beryl Halley, 'Follies' blonde, will act with Richard Barthelmess in 'The Beautiful City,' his next film." Barthelmess (1894–1963) indeed ranked as among the best-known film personalities of his day. His frequent co-star Lillian Gish proclaimed that he possessed "the most beautiful face of any man who ever went before the camera." Other major stars in *The Beautiful City* included Lillian's younger sister, Dorothy Gish (1898–1968), and William Powell (1892–1984). There seems little doubt that Miss Halley had some role in the production as a post-release review stated: "Later Mr. Barthelmess staged a bang up battle with ... William H. Powell, who appears in the cast along with Dorothy Gish, Frank Puglia, Florence Auer, and Beryl Halley."[17]

Another episode in the Halley saga began in early March of 1925,

when a beauty firm called Dorothy Gray Preparations began an advertising campaign. Among other things, they contended that they could "correct unbecoming droop under [the] chin" and "reduce a double chin." Their early ads contained only pencil sketches or silhouettes, but in May, a "before and

Helen Lee Worthing (January 31, 1905–August 25, 1948) arrived in New York City from Kentucky in 1920, and thus one of the saddest stories of any of the Ziegfeld Girls began. She appeared in the 1923 *Follies* with Beryl, and soon had the attention of Hollywood. She moved to Los Angeles and married Dr. Eugene Nelson, a prominent African American doctor, on June 28, 1927. The mixed-race marriage caused her career to falter, and soon financial, drug, alcohol, and marital problems followed. She died August 25, 1948, in an almost bare room, surrounded by old scrapbooks, alone. An overdose of sleeping pills extinguished forever what once had been a brilliant light. Sadly, she left an estate valued at only $16.18.

Beryl Halley

after" picture depicted Beryl Halley without a "double chin," something she never had.[18]

By October, legal action was forthcoming. In a *New York Daily News* article with an illustration titled "'Wasn't My Chin,' Actress Wails, Asking $75,000."

> Is a double chin worth $75,000? Beryl Halley, who was the Pearl in the tableaux "Pearl of the East" in Ziegfeld's 1925 "Follies," raised this question yesterday when, through her attorney, Eli I. Kreiger of 1482 Broadway, she filed suit in Supreme Court against a 5th Avenue beauty specialist for $75,00 damages.
>
> Miss Halley charged that two of her photographs had been used in advertisements by the beauty specialist, and that in one purporting to be "before," she received beauty treatments falsely as possessing a double chin.
>
> "It was terrible," she said. "Mine was the face that launched a thousand quips. All my friends and acquaintances saw that floppy hanging chin which I never had, and their taunts caused me mental anguish and damaged my good name and reputation."
>
> Miss Halley asked for an injunction against further use of the photographs in question. Dorothy Gray's office declined to comment at present on the double chin.[19]

The case dragged on through the courts for more than three years. However, on November 22, 1928, the press reported that "the final curtain fell ... on Beryl Halley's unmusical comedy 'Before and After.'" By that time, the former Ziegfeld Girl had

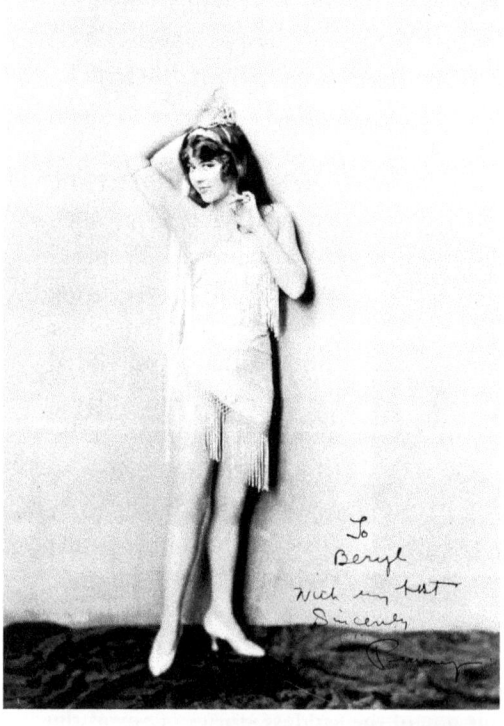

Ann Pennington (1893-1971) was one of Ziegfeld's dancing superstars. She appeared with Beryl in the 1924 *Follies*. "The Girl with the Dimpled Knees" is credited with popularizing the famous dance of the 1920's "The Black Bottom." She signed her picture to Beryl as "Penny," the name she used only with her closest friends.

moved on to Earl Carroll's *Vanities*, where she received a payment of five thousand dollars in damages, considerably less than she had demanded.[20]

Somewhere during her second or third year as a Ziegfeld Girl, Beryl added ballroom dance to her résumé. Chorus girls could always pick up extra money by working after hours in nightclubs, and dance teams could make more for an exhibition than they could from their regular salary.

This dance trend had first gained significant renown about 1912. The attractive young married couple, English-born Vernon Castle (1887–1918) and his American bride Irene Foote Castle (1892–1969), became what the *Dramatic Mirror* called "our supreme ballroom artists, possessing distinction, intelligence, delicacy of the dance, and what is termed in the varieties—class." Although Vernon had been the son of a Birmingham pubkeeper, he attained a university degree in engineering. He came to the States as a dancer when, "in May 1910, he married Irene Foote, the sprightly eighteen-year-old daughter of respectable middle-class parents in New Rochelle." The following summer, the pair journeyed to France where they developed their graceful style at the Café de Paris, to virtually universal acclaim. Back in New York in the fall of 1912, "they made their names almost synonymous with dancing." They appeared in vaudeville, cabarets, on regional tours, and were always popular with fans, many of whom strived to emulate them. Irene Castle, in particular, symbolized a new type of women: tall, slender, short-haired, a trifle rebellious in a sense, yet every inch a lady.

Although the Castles created an image that lasted for decades, their own career as a team proved to be tragically short. Vernon—as a British citizen—enlisted in the Royal Air Force in World War I, became a pilot and a decorated war hero, but subsequently died in a training accident. Irene made patriotic films during the conflict and lived for another half-century. More than twenty years after Vernon's demise, the team's legendary image thrived, re-created in a new bio-picture starring Hollywood's current king and queen of the dance floor, Fred Astaire and Ginger Rogers.[21]

It is not known whether Beryl Halley ever met Irene Castle. It is safe to say that she never saw the Castles dance. However, there can be little doubt that the tall, graceful lady from New Rochelle influenced her. Pages torn from *Harper's Bazaar* demonstrate her affinity for clothing that Irene Castle designed. Beryl and various male dance partners on the nightclub and ballroom circuit over the next few years not only performed some of the Castles' dances, they also incorporated new dance fads into their performances. While none of the Castle emulators ever quite surpassed them, they did, in a sense, glide and walk in the footsteps on the trail that Vernon and Irene had blazed just before the Great War.

The earliest documented example of Beryl as a nightclub dancer took place on November 25, 1925, when she appeared at the "Grand Opening" of the Frivolity at the corner of 52nd Street and Broadway. She was billed as the "Supreme Beauty of [the] Ziegfeld Follies." A review of the club's floor show several days later noted that "undress … is carried [to] the extreme here." The writer added: "Beryl Halley, a stately, shapely woman, is the punch … as anyone with half an eye can see."[22] All one could conclude is that the girl from Bladen had launched her nightclub act with real gusto.

Brooke Johns (1893-1987) appeared with Beryl in *Tangerine* and the *Follies* of 1923. A navy veteran of World War I, he went on to become a star performer for Ziegfeld and in vaudeville. He was billed as "Six-foot-three and Oh! So Different." He signed his picture: "To Beryl, the most beautiful blonde girl in the world—From Brooke the Big Faker—Love and kisses."

5

Palm Beach Nights, The Bunk ... and More, 1926–1927

As the New Year dawned, Beryl Halley had sound reason to view her Broadway career as on track. She had just completed three seasons in the cast of the *Follies* and attained some degree of celebrity status. She also had her share of male escorts, such as the big-spending bandleader Vincent Lopez, who continued to date her on occasion, if with less devotion than the year before. Beryl could also ride horses whenever she so chose and perhaps retain a bit of her rural upbringing.

One item that had the Broadway world abuzz in the early days of 1926 was Flo Ziegfeld's plan for what he termed "Palm Beach Nights." In essence, an entire *Follies*-type revue would be staged in Florida for several weeks. Ziegfeld had sometimes presented plays in other major cities, and even the *Follies* had sometimes played for a week in Atlantic City in what was pretty much a dress rehearsal for the official New York opening a few days later. But "Palm Beach Nights" constituted an extravaganza on a scale like no other. A special train carrying a total of 110 persons of the entire cast and crew to Palm Beach—increasingly seen as a winter playground for the *nouveau riche*—where the premiere was launched at the Montmartre Dinner Theatre on January 12. Ticket purchasers for opening night were expected to happily pay $200 per seat, and by all accounts, they sold out even more quickly than expected.[1]

Press reports varied somewhat, but a more detailed one in the *Palm Beach Post* reads:

> This entertainment has been created especially for Palm Beach, and the entire cast has come here direct from New York.

Beryl Halley

The principals include Harry Fender, Cliff Edwards, Blaney and Farrar, the English singing comediennes; Edmonde Guy and Ernest Van Duren, the French dancers; Demaris Dere, Kathlene Martyn, Morton Downey, Mary Janes, Claire Luce, and Albertina Vitak. Among the glorified beautiful [girls] are Beryl Halley, well known figurante; Beatrice Roberts, Marion Hurley, American Venus, Katherine Burke, Yvonne Grey, Naomi Johnson, Bobby Storey, Mildred Lunnay, and Noel Francis.

The music is by Rudolf Friml and the lyrics are by Gene Buck and Irving Caesar.

Ned Wayburn directed the production.[2]

Edmonde Guy and Ernest Van Duren were a dance team from France. Their exploits ranged from stories of an impending marriage to the revelation that they were brother and sister to a story of kidnapping and intrigue. They came to the United States in 1926 to appear in *Palm Beach Nights*. Edmonde sang "I Will If You Will" and danced a waltz with Ernest. They also became acquainted with Beryl.

The cast of *Palm Beach Nights* consisted of a mixture of veterans and newcomers to Ziegfeld productions. Some of the veterans had not worked for the impresario before. Chief among them was Cliff Edwards, who had gained considerable fame as "Ukelele Ike." He not only had several hit records, but along with Frank Crumit and Wendell Hall "the Red Headed Music Maker," received credit for making the little stringed instrument popular among collegians and the raccoon coat crowd in general. A famed French dance team, Edmonde Guy and Ernest Van Duren, had been imported from Paris, where they demonstrated their skills on the floor, comparable if not superior to the Americans Vernon

5. *Palm Beach Nights, The Bunk* ... and More, 1926–1927

and Irene Castle of recent memory. Reputedly, the pair had been on the verge of marriage when, through a strange quirk of fate, they were revealed to have been actually brother and sister. In California, Art Hickman and His Orchestra had earned a reputation comparable to the bands of Paul Whiteman and Vincent Lopez in New York City. But the Hickman aggregation had not performed much, if at all, on the East Coast. His group also provided dance music during intermissions and for the festivities that followed the stage performance.

Some cast members and background people ranked as newcomers. John Harkrider (1899–1982) began his career as the acclaimed costume designer of *Palm Beach Nights*. Harkrider specialized in the use of feather outfits and spectacular headgear for showgirls, outpacing previous Ziegfeld specialties in this area. He apparently spared no expense when it came to costs of such items as egret feathers. Polly Walker made her debut in the Florida production, singing the song "No Foolin,'" which became the title of the entire production when it opened on Broadway on June 24. Paulette Goddard (originally Pauline Levy) gained her first experience there, and subsequently went on to become one of Hollywood's most celebrated glamour girls for twenty years or so, beginning in 1930. Other lesser figures had their careers begin and end with *Palm Beach Nights*.

Like many Ziegfeld productions, the background of how the show came to be is more complex than one might expect. Flo had often spent winter vacations in Palm Beach and believed the place needed "a shot in the arm." Patricia Ziegfeld later wrote that the wealthy folks of Palm Beach had become bored with one another, "the natural result of being forced to dine with the same people and listen to the same across-the-table talk while eating the same rich food night after night." What *Palm Beach Nights* promised to do was give a degree of entertainment and excitement that was a bit different. Mrs. Ziegfeld (Billie Burke) said supportively, "Flo was right, as he always was; he cared little for convention, but he knew what people liked."

The staging of a production the size of *Palm Beach Nights* needed a location not normally available in the Florida playground city but, as always, Ziegfeld had a plan, one which was fully implemented by opening night. He had earlier acquired a structure, the Palm Beach Supper Club, described as one "that offered nothing distinctive in its design." According to John Harkrider, the wives of two local millionaires, Mrs. Paris Singer—of the sewing machine company—and Mrs. Anthony J. Drexel Biddle—of a Philadelphia banking concern—convinced their husbands to finance the renovation of what had been formerly termed a "barnlike structure ... into such a beautiful place," with the "blue dome of the ceiling ... like a midnight sky." Joseph Urban, who had designed many of the stage settings for the *Follies*, master-minded the transformation of what then became the Club de Montmartre, a dinner theatre. When the production opened, Paris E. Singer and Anthony J. Drexel Biddle, Jr., were credited as presenters along with Ziegfeld, while the ever-steady Ned Wayburn "staged" it.[3]

Singer and Biddle might, on the surface, seem like an unusual pair to finance a risky Ziegfeld production. Paris Singer (1867–1932), a much older man, was the twenty-third of twenty-four children sired by Isaac Singer (1811–1875) who, in addition to his improvements on a machine that helped make sewing easier for housewives, also ranked as a notorious lothario, having his many offspring by several wives. Paris, who moved to Palm Beach in 1918, had earlier survived a well-publicized affair with modern dance pioneer Isadora Duncan that had produced an illegitimate child. Biddle (1897–1961), a World War I officer, had married the decade-older Mary Duke, a North Carolina American Tobacco Company heiress, and was something of a boxing fanatic and outdoorsman. After his Palm Beach days ended, he held several appointments in the New Deal era, including ambassador to

Ernest Van Duren drew this picture of Beryl when they appeared together in *Palm Beach Nights*. After Guy and Van Duren returned to France, their partnership slowly dissolved.

5. *Palm Beach Nights, The Bunk* ... and More, 1926–1927

Poland and Norway. Back in service during World War II, he was later appointed ambassador to Spain by John F. Kennedy, just prior to his death.[4]

Performances began nightly at 10:30 p.m. According to one description, a large silver globe descended from the ceiling and, when lowered to the stage level, exploded. Out of the smoke stepped Claire Luce in a "glittery flapper gown," followed by an opening number called "Hello, Palm Beach," sung by Kathleen Martin, Miss Luce, and twenty-seven other chorus girls, including future star Paulette Goddard. It was succeeded by an acrobatic dance by Julie Steger. Blonde songstress Polly Walker, backed by sixteen girls, did a solo "Tent for Two." Claire Luce, emerging as a major star, wore a Native American costume, adorned with a magnificent feather headdress and carrying a tomahawk, performed her specialty number, "The Broadway Indian." On at least one occasion she supposedly hurled the tomahawk at Paul Whiteman in the orchestra pit. Either the weapon was not as lethal as it looked, or she missed the target![5]

Kathleen Martin appeared in *Palm Beach Nights* with Beryl. She performed a song entitled, "The Only Thing Green About Girls of Today is the Green That Is on Their Hat." This picture was taken at the Royal Poinciana Hotel in Palm Beach, the world's largest resort hotel of the time, with its fourteen hundred employees, 1,081 rooms, and two thousand guests.

Part One continued with Edmonde Guy singing a coquette-like number, "I Will If You Will," after which she and her dance partner, Ernest Van Duren, performed a waltz number. Next up was a comedy skit, titled "The Pest" and featuring Katheryn Penman, Harry Fender, and James Barton. Kathleen Martin sang a song called "Green Hat," with the subtitle, "The

Beryl Halley

Only Thing Green About Girls of Today Is the Green That Is on Their Hat." Sixteen green hat–wearing girls supported Miss Martin. Cliff Edwards then performed some his song hits, followed by Colleen Day singing "When These Charming People Do the Charleston," which introduced Claire Luce and Mary Jane doing a rousing version of the then-popular dance. Then came the intermission, with the Art Hickman Orchestra playing music for those who chose to either dance or just listen.[6]

Harry Fender launched "Part Two," singing "Florida, the Moon and You," which (along with "No Foolin'") constituted the hit songs that came out of the production. Next were the "Goddesses of Feathers," led by Beryl in her character as "The Goddess of the Feather Noff." Others had such names as "Goddess of the White Paradise," "Goddess of the White Peacock," "Goddess of Plumes," "Goddess of the White Argas," "Goddess of the White Pheasant," "Goddess of the White Eagle," "Goddess of the White Ostrich," and "Goddess of the White Cobra Bird." (Ironically, the latter part was played by Katherine Burke, who would replace Beryl on short notice the following January when Ziegfeld fired her from the cast of *Rio Rita* a week before it opened on Broadway.)[7]

The presentation was winding down as Mary Jane performed a "Triple-Time Tap Dance." Then, the

Mary Jane appeared with Beryl in the 1926 production of *Palm Beach Nights*. A native of Pittsburgh, Mary Jane dropped her last name of Kittell for the stage. Her first Broadway appearance was in 1920 at the tender age of eight, in the musical comedy *Jimmie*. She would have seven Broadway shows in all to her credit.

5. Palm Beach Nights, The Bunk ... and More, 1926–1927

English comedy twosome of Norah Blaney and Gwen Farrar did their songs, followed by Harry Fender singing "Old-Fashioned Waltz," assisted by seven "old-fashioned girls," Beryl Halley among them as the "Blue Danubes." Polly Walker was on next, possibly playing a lute while singing "No Foolin'." James Barton then did his dancing comedy act; Guy and Van Duren did a tango; and an ensemble sang the big finale, "Spanish Frolic."[8]

Palm Beach Nights continued to play nightly in the Florida city through March 24, when it closed, only to reopen on Broadway in June. According to the best information available, it had been a success during its Florida run. The *Orlando Sentinel* praised the production: "Every one going to Palm Beach should reserve a table for this brilliant Ziegfeld Revue." A few snags marred the scene, such as when the telephones went "out of order" on February 6, forcing buyers to "get your seats at the Box Office, or at the news stand at your hotel," but did no serious damage. A reviewer in the *New Eve* praised *Palm Beach Nights* as "one of Flo's best," but lamented that it would not be playing on Broadway. Actually it did, as *No Foolin'*, but Ziegfeld's luck ran out in New York, and the run at the Globe Theatre ended after only three months, reportedly losing about thirty thousand dollars.[9]

During the time the

Claire Luce (1903–1989) appeared with Beryl in the 1926 production of *Palm Beach Nights*. Clair appeared as "A Broadway Indian," adorned with a massive headpiece and brandishing a tomahawk. Beryl and Claire were roommates for a time, as indicated by a common address of 237 Madison Avenue and a phone number 9390. Claire also signed as a witness on Beryl's contract with agent George Maines on May 12, 1926.

revue ran in Florida, many of its cast members performed their unofficial duties of getting sufficient attention to get their names in the newspapers, both near and far. Even before arriving in Florida, the French beauty Edmonde Guy was pictured in fancy leather boots and furs with the caption, "She'll Take Furs and all to Palm Beach." Once she got there, Miss Guy seems to have been among those who complained when the Palm Beach town council required females to wear a bit more clothing when going from their hotel rooms to the beach in what the news media termed an "abbreviated costume." Another (less interesting) news item reads: "Charleston dancer Mary Jane received attention for winning a speed boat race."[10]

However, Beryl Halley may have out-distanced the others with her comments on how she loved Palm Beach, but missed the horses in Central Park:

> **"A horse, a horse, my queendom for a horse."**
> Won't someone find a nice prancing steed for Beryl Halley of the "Palm Beach Nights"?
> Miss Halley says that all she misses in Palm Beach is the daily horseback ride that she so much enjoyed back in New York. Let her tell the sad story.
> "I think Palm Beach is just lovely," she says. "The weather is so nice and balmy, just like Coney Island and Long Beach in the summer. People are awfully sweet here, even though most of them have tons of money, and I just love my surf bath every day. And the scenery, all the beautiful palm trees casting their shadows over the streets, and the sunset over Lake Worth—it's all very gorgeous.
> "But why don't they have horses in this town? I can go motoring until I talk like a klaxon and smell like a gas station, and I can ride a bicycle till I'm fit for the six-day races. I can even take an airplane trip once in a while, if I desire to. I've ridden in motor boats, racing cars, bicycles, wheel chairs, seaplanes, and railways, but the one vehicle I love above all, I can't seem to get.
> "When I'm home in New York not a day goes by but I'm out on the bridal path in Central Park 'doing my stuff.' Every handsome mounted policeman nods to me as I go by, and I do believe that the horse himself knows me, even though I only hire him."
> Outside of that, Miss Halley likes Palm Beach fine. Except, she confided, that she misses her favorite hairdresser.[11]

Press releases also made efforts to flatter patrons. Betsy Schuyler, writing for the local *Post*, commented on the "gorgeous apparel" worn by those in the "audience," which "rivals" that of the "performers on stage." She wrote: "Seldom do you see so distinctly glittering an audience." She compared the clothing of the local wealthy wives to those of "Edmonde

5. Palm Beach Nights, The Bunk ... and More, 1926–1927

Guy ... from Paris," who captured much of the attention on stage. In an even longer article, Schuyler listed some of the local attendees by name, such as Mrs. E. T. Stotesbury, who was "regal as a queen in white satin with a wrap of silver cloth collared in sable ... gently falling from her shoulders ... and wearing long white gloves." Three others were named and pictured. Even then, one doubts that the Palm Beach ladies could quite equal Harkrider's new feather costumes or Mlle. Guy's twenty-eight-foot-tall headgear that she wore in one number.[12]

Meanwhile, back in New York, while Beryl awaited the opening of the *Follies of 1926*, which had been renamed *Palm Beach Nights* for the Florida audience, now took another name, *No Foolin'*. A new opportunity arose when she joined the cast of her only notable motion picture venture. Whether the production of *The Broadway Boob* was filmed in California or in the East remains unknown; it was most likely in the vicinity of Fort Lee, New Jersey, where a few silent films were still being made. Glenn Hunter, the principal star, had a bigger reputation on Broadway than in movies. Mildred Ryan had the part of leading lady, while Antrim Short had another key role as Jack Briggs. Beryl Halley, as "Queenie Martine" also played a major part.[13]

The plot centered on Dan Williams, who hails from a small town, from which he departs with a bad reputation. Hoping to do better in New York City, he gets a small part in a Broadway production. From this modest success, his agent creates an overblown tale that he now ranks as a major star, earning three thousand a week. Meanwhile, back in his hometown, his banker father is facing financial ruin and fears a "run" on his bank. In desperation, he turns to what he thinks is his newly wealthy son for help. One review listed among the film's "highlights" to be the "argument between father and son," along with "his return home as a wealthy man." As the plot summary aptly states, "complications ensue," a tale oft-repeated about what happens from exaggerated publicity. Released on April 25, 1926, *The Broadway Boob* quickly fell into the dustbin of cinema history.[14]

Five days after the film's release, a musical play, *The Bunk of 1926*, changed theatres, with some new additions to the cast. This production was largely the brainchild of actor, lyricist, and scriptwriter Gene Lockhart, with a musical score by Percy Waxman. It had opened "off Broadway" at the downtown Herscher Theatre on February 16, where it ran for thirty-eight performances. The production made use of many of the then-current

Beryl Halley

catchphrases and slang terms. The term "bunk," for instance, referred to what might be called "empty talk or blarney" and was a lampoon of "idle conversation."

It then moved to the Broadhurst on April 30, when Beryl and five others were added to the revised cast. Based on contemporary newspaper ads, the new producers must have had reason to believe that "Beryl Halley, America's Most Perfect Beauty" would have considerable audience appeal because her name appeared larger in advertisements than either of the main stars, Lockhart and Dolly Sterling. In addition, an endorsement came from noted drama critic Robert Benchley.[15]

One scene in the play featured Miss Halley, portraying Eve in the Garden of Eden, wearing only a fig leaf, while other "Eves" moved through the crowd, passing out apples to male patrons. As one might expect, the use of nudity created quite a sensation, and on the night of May 10, Beryl found herself under arrest. Will Page, writing about this a few months later, captioned her photo thusly: "Beryl Halley whose appearance as 'Eve' created much excitement on Broadway." The details, of course, were much more complex.[16]

Newspapers across the country printed various versions with a slight variation by the Associated Press. The *St. Louis Post-Dispatch*'s front-page headline reads: "Eve Driven Out of Stage Eden." The front page of the *Elmira Star-Gazette* reads: "Arrest Dancer in Eve Scene." And the *Salt Lake* [City] *Telegram*, also on page one, reads:

> **N. Y. Actress Is Asked to Explain Her Role of Eve;**
> **Beryl Halley Arrested in "Eden" Scene;**
> **Mrs. Al Smith Liked Show**
> Beryl Halley, actress, was ordered to explain in court today her role of Eve at a show attended by Mrs. Alfred E. Smith, wife of the governor.
> Sergeant George ("Hardboiled") Smith and two patrolmen arrested Miss Halley last night in a Garden of Eden scene, in "Bunk of 1926." She had danced under a canvas tree, while smaller Eves danced through the aisles and dropped apples in the laps of men who seemed to want them. Sergeant Smith said Miss Halley was not wearing tights.
> The manager of the Broadhurst Theatre and the stage manager also were arrested.[17]

The next day's court appearance created an equal sensation. As reported in the *Pittsburgh Post-Gazette*, Miss Halley replied:

> "Nude? No! Wore a Leaf!"
> West Side Court being no Garden of Eden, Beryl Halley, the "Eve" dancer in

5. Palm Beach Nights, The Bunk ... and More, 1926–1927

"Bunk of 1926," appeared here today smartly and sufficiently dressed and indignantly denied charges of appearing in an indecent performance Monday night.

Sgt. George Smith and Patrolman Harry Mooney arrested Miss Halley. "It looked to us like she didn't have anything on at all," said Sgt. Smith.

"Why, I did too," replied Miss Halley. "I had on a fig leaf." Graphically, she outlined the size of a fig leaf about five inches in diameter.

"It was so big." She persisted earnestly. "And I also wore a long blonde wig, the brassiere, and a dancing belt."

Magistrate Gordon said he would like to see not only the fig leaf, but the wig, the brassiere, and the dancing belt, and to permit the accused to hunt up all the articles which Sgt. Smith had reported as "missing." The case was adjourned to Friday....

Doggedly sticking to his story, Sgt. Smith said he didn't see any fig leaf.

Ramsey Wallace, producer, and Harry Levy, manager, who were arrested with Miss Halley, also received adjournment. Bail of $500 was continued in each case.

Mrs. Alfred E. Smith, wife of the governor, attended the play. She said she liked it "immensely, immensely." Four clergymen were [also] in the audience.[18]

Not to be outdone, Frederick Boy Stevenson waxed poetic in the *Brooklyn Eagle*:

> **Police arrested—**
> Beryl Halley—
> A Broadway Eve—
> Because They Say—
> She didn't Have On—
> Any clothes—to Speak Of.
> Now Look Out for—
> Raids in the Subways![19]

The continuation of the court proceedings on Friday resulted in a complete victory for "Eve," as reported (with a touch of humor) in the *New York Daily News*:

A new riddle? What's the difference between the picture of a nude woman in an art magazine and a well and almost unclad girl on the stage?

No difference at all, Magistrate Gordon ruled yesterday in West Side Court. And Beryl Halley, dainty Eve dancer, threw him a dazzling smile.

Miss Halley's dance in a Broadway show stirred up a complaint. Police investigated and charged the girl and her managers with indecent exhibition. Gordon visited the show Wednesday night.

"You wore something besides a new fig leaf, didn't you?" he asked the dancer.

"Of course," she answered, "any one looking real close could see I was draped in gauze."

"And I can bring artists to testify the dance was artistic," interposed her attorney.

"Not necessary," said the court. "Case dismissed."[20]

Beryl Halley

Over the next few days, other comments appeared concerning the incident. Leon M. Siler reported in several papers, usually on the Women's Page, under such headlines as "Her Fig Leaf Wins!" Beryl, said Siler, has intentions of suing the New York City Police Department. She also expresses gratitude to Judge Arthur Gordon. She called her presentation "beautiful and refined," pointing that she possessed a degree of dignity and neither smoked nor even sipped cocktails. "I'm glad more for art's sake than for my own," said Miss Halley. Siler also quoted Judge Gordon, saying, "The law does not define lewdness or indecency.... That must depend upon the setting, the scenic portrayal and, in large measure, upon the custom and modes of the community."[21]

While Beryl had won her battle for artistic expression, *The Bunk of 1926* was not faring nearly as well. A group called "New York's Play Jury" deemed the presentation as "being objectionable from the viewpoint of public morals." Reviewing the play's history, it first premiered at the Heckscher Theatre at the corner of Fifth Avenue and 104th Street. It ran there for a month, where it was considered "innocent." Then, two other producers took it over, moved it to the Broadhurst, made changes and "almost overnight it became one of the breeziest ... revues." Since Actors' Equity had a contract requiring that they abide by decisions of the play jury, *The Bunk of 1926* closed, at least for the time being.[22]

However, that did not end the story. Producer Ramsay Wallace was back in court within hours, arguing that members of the "play jury," eight of whom were named in the "social register, had taken it upon "themselves to decide arbitrarily [what the public] shall see and approve." He noted that "the show has been proven clean because Beryl Halley, a dancer, was ... released upon her proving to the satisfaction of the court that she really did wear some clothing."[23]

The Wallace appeal received a temporary reprieve from New York Supreme Court Judge Aaron Levy, who issued an injunction preventing the lower court order from being enforced until a new hearing was held the following Monday, the *Daily News* reported. Accordingly, the play reopened on June 9.[24] Whether or not Beryl remained in the cast is uncertain. What *did* transpire was a series of editorials from several newspapers about censorship. One of the best, and most thoughtful, of these commentaries appeared in the *Harvard Crimson* on June 10—repeated below in its entirety—under the title "Naughty Niceties."

5. *Palm Beach Nights, The Bunk* ... and More, 1926–1927

Systems of censorship possess a peculiar fallibility, an inconsistency which often glitters in the public press. By the very nature of their task, the suppression of obscenity, boards of censors are confronted with a psychological difficulty which is well-nigh insurmountable. An acute mind can trace delicate touches of sensuality, deep into literature.

Because of differing perceptions, censors are ever incurring either the enmity of reformers or the vindictiveness of liberals. Particularly in criticism of the stage, whose shadier products receive a wide advertising in diversity in interpreting the niceties of naughtiness apt to appear. The latest disturbance comes from "The Bunk of 1926," which a citizens' play jury has banned from the New York stage. Judging from the published accounts, it would seem that the jurors had decided somewhat hastily and without complete realization of the effect of their action.

Although one can scarcely doubt that the bad taste of the title is carried through the whole revue, "The Bunk" appears to merit some fate better than suppression. Its off-stage prototype is at worst punished with a tolerens yawa [*sic*]. The citizens' jury, which has the unofficial backing of the District Attorney and the support of the Actors' Equity Association, might better have directed that the performance be denuded of suggestiveness. The present decree, as admitted by some of the censors themselves, smacks of that arbitrary bureaucracy which is essential to avoid.

The private system of censorship, in spite of occasional lapses such as the present, has worked well since it draws support from the actors themselves. The board of suppression has at least an understanding of the problems of playwrights. For this reason, the play jury is infinitely more desirable than a miscellaneous panel of up-right but ill-informed moralists.

Now that the second thought of several jurors has recommended a policy of moderation, the citizen censorship will no doubt operate with an increased sense of proportion. The frauds of the future may be permitted a tolerant existence because "The Bunk of 1926" has become a Freudian martyr.[25]

Another criticism took the form of an attack on the decision of Paul Dulzell, the acting executive secretary of the Actors' Equity Association who had endorsed the decision of the play jury. In a letter/editorial by Burns Mantle, he argued that "Clean Stage or Dirty Stage, It Is Really Up to the Actor," to decide what material is, or is not, proper. Since the actors whose livelihood as well as his professional moral code should be able to say: "We hold our profession in too high [of] respect to appear in this play or that revue." Writing from a nearly six-decade historical perspective, Samuel Leiter reflected: "'Bunk of 1926' had become the center of a controversy when some of its material proved salacious to the police, who ordered the show shut down. An injunction was granted allowing the revue to stay open, but before further action could be taken, the show closed for lack of ticket sales."[26]

Beryl Halley

Amid all the controversy over the show, other significant events in the life of Beryl Halley were taking place. On May 12, she signed a new management contract with George H. Maines, a press representative, through 1928. The contract, likely a standard one, would give Maines half the money she received through sale of pictures, portraits, and artwork. Generally speaking, she would pay him 10 percent of her earnings and sign no appearance contracts without his approval. The contract was witnessed by Beryl's friend, fellow Ziegfeld Girl and occasional roommate Claire Luce.[27]

Ernest Linenkamp (1885–1956), a noted Viennese "artist and seeker after the world's most beautiful women," named Beryl "The Venus of the Twentieth Century." He declared that "she is capable of inspiring the highest art."[28] Needless to say, these phrases would be included in press items referencing Miss Halley over the next several months.

In early November, Beryl ranked among those interviewed in a symposium on the subject held by the Hearst paper, the *New York American*, of what men felt most attracted to in the opposite sex. The differing viewpoint for "greater charm" favored either "bewitching eyes and a provocative mouth" or "shapely legs [and ankles]." The whole controversy evolved from a 102-year-old physician, Dr. Marie Degollere Davenport, who had said in Washington: "Girls, cultivate your legs above your mind. They are your most important asset. They count over education, intellect and culture." The Associated Press reported that Davenport's "displaying a pair of trim ankles in explanation of her winning a husband 47 years her junior." Ziegfeld beauty Ann Pennington partly disagreed, saying, "It's only in the dancing world that legs are a girl's best asset."[29]

Beryl Halley, a Pennington protégée, argued that "for the flapper type, legs count most." She added that "all men love a pretty ankle," while "a girl who isn't good looking otherwise can have lots of admirers by wearing dainty pumps over silk stockinged legs and showing them." Frances Alda said that legs were important but that in "the olden days ... beauties held their admirers by mystery and subtle charm." Another female physician opted for "a sweet smile, a provocative mouth [and] a pair of soft veiled eyes" as more important. Like virtually almost all symposiums, no conclusion ever took place.[30]

The Bunk of 1926 soon closed, with the only lasting memory Beryl's fig leaf episode. Even though she was not in the cast of *No Foolin'*, she

5. Palm Beach Nights, The Bunk ... and More, 1926–1927

remained in good standing with the Ziegfeld organization. And, as usual, The Great Ziegfeld had already begun looking forward to his next endeavor. This called for building his own theatre on Fifty-Fourth Street. Josef Urban already had plans and construction underway. Ziegfeld had long complained to Charles Dillingham that Abraham Erlanger often made more money than he as producer of those venues he staged at the New Amsterdam. As usual, "Ziggy" needed an angel, and had found one in the person of media giant William Randolph Hearst. The latter remembered that Ziegfeld helped launch the show business career of Marion Davies, who had become the newspaper tycoon's mistress. Urban's project was reported to hold a total of eight hundred persons on the ground floor, and 1688 "on the upper." The prediction of an early November completion also proved premature. When finished, the actual theatre seated only 1,638, but it still ranked as one of the larger venues in the district. The initial production, however, remained as planned, a musical-comedy with a Hispanic-American theme—*Rio Rita*.[31]

Once the controversy over the "fig leaf" calmed down, Beryl Halley was reported to be going abroad. News reports said that "Beryl Halley, stage beauty who was in 'Bunk of 1926,' will make appearances in Europe under the direction of Arthur Klein, with Paris as her first stop." However, to date, no evidence has been uncovered to confirm that this trip ever took place. Beryl did, however, continue to fill open spots in her calendar with night club work. In October, she was reported dancing at the Silver Slipper, one of the best clubs in the theatre district, where the management advertised her as "the World's Most Perfect beauty."[32]

By October 22, the press reported that "Ziegfeld will pick sixty dancers for 'Rio Rita' this week." The Four Yacht Club Boys would sing. Other parts would go to the comedy team of Bert Wheeler and Robert Woolsey. The title role would go to a relative newcomer of English background, named Ethelind Terry, with J. Harold Murray as the male lead. Promoted from the chorus line were Ada May Weeks, who would appear in the role of "Dolly, a cabaret girl," and Beryl Halley, cast as "Montezuma's Daughter."[33]

Meanwhile, on December 9, an elaborate cornerstone-laying ceremony took place at the yet-to-be-completed Ziegfeld Theatre, with Beryl Halley among the attendees. Others included Gladys Glad, architect Joe Urban, Billie Burke (Mrs. Ziegfeld), her ten-year-old daughter Patricia

Beryl Halley

Ziegfeld, Ada Mae Weeks, Marion Benda, and the leading musical-comedy star Marilyn Miller.[34] Much, if not most, of the structure, with the exception of the façade, had already been finished. Completion was expected by February 1, 1927, with *Rio Rita* to premiere the following evening.

Like many Ziegfeld productions, *Rio Rita* was set to play a week at the Colonel Theatre in Boston in late December and another week in early January in Philadelphia. The cast departed by train for New England on the 26th. Simultaneously, Dan Healy, a Ziegfeld male dancer, would be joining the cast of *Betsy* at the New Amsterdam on December 28. Beryl Halley joined Healy in a series of dance routines at the Silver Slipper Club beginning on December 29. Ads read: "An Entirely New Gorgeous Revue Headed by Beryl Halley, America's Most Perfect Beauty, [with] Dan Healy [and] Dolly Sterling."[35]

Obviously, Beryl could not be in New York and Boston at the same time. It seems likely that this circumstance may have led to serious discontent between "America's Most Perfect Beauty" and her main employer.

In the short run, however, no visible tensions had been detected. On January 2, a quarter-page photo in the *Morning Telegraph* with a full-length shot of "Beryl Halley, Twentieth Century Venus with Flo Ziegfeld's 'Rio Rita'" kept New Yorkers prepared for the coming hits. *Rio Rita* opened

Bunny Hill signed her picture to Beryl "with love and best wishes always, Oct. 25–26." Bunny has no Broadway credits, and seems to be one of the more than fifteen thousand women Ziegfeld auditioned for the *Follies*, of whom just over three thousand were chosen. Bunny seems to have made a living by dancing in clubs in New York City. The *Brooklyn Daily Eagle* of March 16, 1929, refers to her as a "night-hut terpist," a word derived from the Greek Muse of Dance, Terpsichore.

5. Palm Beach Nights, The Bunk ... and More, 1926–1927

at the Forrest on December 10, with a cast that included "Gladys Glad, America's Foremost Beauty, and Beryl Halley, America's Venus." The run in Philly had been expected to last two weeks, and the New York opening to be on January 24. However, reports from the City of Brotherly Love suggested that the play was proving so popular there, outpacing such prior hits as *Sunny* and *Sally*, that it "may play a third week in Philadelphia."[36]

Within days, however, a Broadway bombshell dropped. Apparently, either because of the Silver Slipper appearance, or some other unspecified reason, Beryl Halley had antagonized her boss and found herself "fired." She threatened a lawsuit.[37]

A new chapter in her life as a former "Ziegfeld Girl" was about to begin.

Ada May Weeks (March 8, 1896–April 25, 1978) was billed without her last name. She was in *Rio Rita* as well as other venues and was known as "America's Comedienne." The picture she inscribed for Beryl includes an early version of a "smiley face." After being temporarily ill, an ad in the *Daily News* of February 21, 1927, touted the "Reappearance of Ada-May in the All-Star Cast of *Rio Rita*, the greatest musical comedy of all time!" From 1924 to 1933, she was married to millionaire big game hunter and sportsman Wilson Potter. The divorce came after they had not seen each other for two years.

6

The Bladen Beauty's "Big Apple," or Beryl Halley's New York City

The New York City—with 5.6 million people—in which Beryl Halley settled in 1921 ranked as vastly different from Bladen, Rio Grande, or Gallipolis, where she had spent her formative years. It was almost as different from Columbus (237,000), where she sometimes visited; Youngstown (132,000), where her sister taught school; or Norfolk (115,000), where she spent her U.S. Navy days as a stenographer. From its earliest days as a tiny Dutch village—with 270 people in 1628—on the southern tip of Manhattan Island at the mouth of the Hudson River, New York in nearly three centuries' time had become one of the three premier cities on the planet. In 1898, the city of Brooklyn (a.k.a. Kings County), on the western end of Long Island, became a part of New York City as did much of Queens County to the north of Brooklyn and the Bronx, which was on the mainland, and Staten Island (or Richmond County). This, in 1900, gave New York City a total population of 3,437,202. Still over half of these were wedged onto Manhattan Island, with another million-plus in Brooklyn.[1]

From its earliest days, even when it was New Amsterdam, New York City had a cosmopolitan atmosphere. Early observers tended to see this in religious terms as much as ethnicity. One person in 1643, wrote, "Besides the Calvinists [which included Dutch Reformed and Presbyterians] there are in the Colony, Catholics, English Puritans, Lutherans, Anabaptists [Mennonites], etc." Slavery also existed from early days. By the time of the first U.S. census in 1790, New York City had 33,131 persons,

6. The Bladen Beauty's "Big Apple"

and by 1810, its 96,373 people enabled New York to replace Philadelphia as the nation's largest city. By 1875, New York's population exceeded one million.

From the late 1840s, famine in Ireland and economic and political upheavals in the German states fueled massive numbers of immigrants, many of whom settled in New York City. In addition, continued rural-urban migration, and a smaller natural increase, led to even more growth. In the 1880s, a new wave of immigrants—Italian and Jewish (German, Polish, and Russian) foreign-born—began to settle in New York City.

A city of over five million people had its share of problems involving crime, transportation, water, noise, and sanitation. Some problems were solved through the passage of time, attrition, and technological innovation. For instance, in 1900, city planners worried about the problems of a million horses who dropped about fifty pounds of manure and urine each, six days a week, on city streets. Luckily, this problem was solved by the automobile, which would eventually create new problems.

As popular historian David Wallace states in his book *Capital of the World*: "The 1920s were, simply speaking, the most transformative and probably the most exciting decade in American history. Sometimes known as the Big Apple, Metropolis, or Gotham, New York had also become a world center of finance, education, and culture. All this was supported by the vast array of commerce that provided the economic underpinning that made this demographic behemoth possible." He further elaborates that New York City was "setting the pace for American and global change."[2]

By 1920 or 1921, when Beryl Halley first saw N.Y.C., with its large population of immigrants and first- and second-generation Americans, the city's politicians could brag with considerable honesty that New York had more Irish people than any city on the globe, more Italians than any city but Rome, and more Germans—many of them Jewish—than any place but Berlin. By 1930, the African American populace had climbed to more than a quarter-million, concentrated largely in the upper Manhattan section known as Harlem. Jobs were plentiful and a wide variety of service industries catered to workers' innumerable needs.[3]

While New York had its share—if not more than its share—of poverty, crime, slums, and social tension, the city also had a large concentration of upper-middle-class and wealthy folk who supported such cultural forms as museums, libraries, and theatres. Sporting events, such as baseball, had seen growth in New York before spreading to other locales. All classes of people could enjoy the games of three major league baseball teams (Yankees, Giants, and Dodgers). The game as a whole bounced back from the scandal of 1919 to achieve more popularity than ever. The American League Yankees—after years of mediocrity as the Highlanders—began a period of dominance, winning six championships in the decade with a number of stars led by long-ball-hitting George "Babe" Ruth. Other household names, like Lou Gehrig and Tony Lazzeri, had legions of fans, along with their ace pitchers Waite Hoyt and Herb Pennock. The National League Giants may have been less colorful but took four pennants in a row (1921–1924), and three world championships. Their leading players included such future Hall of Famers as Frankie Frisch, Travis Jackson, and Fred Lindstrom. Over on Long Island, the Brooklyn Dodgers won their league in 1920 before falling into the middling ranks, but had a great outfielder in Zack Wheat, a quality pitcher in Burleigh Grimes, as well as the colorful Floyd "Babe" Herman to excite their faithful fans.[4]

Boxing, always a popular sport in New York, came out of the shadows, to become more widely accepted and celebrated under the watchful eye of William Muldoon and the New York State Boxing Commission. Rivals in the ring, Jack Dempsey and Gene Tunney both had scads of fans in the heavyweight division. For those who preferred smaller pugilists, Mickey Walker (welterweight and, later, middleweight) and Benny Leonard (lightweight) gained wide recognition.[5]

While the National Football League did not command the attention it would in later decades, the New York Giants dated from 1925. College teams still grabbed the most attention.

New Yorkers could cheer for such home teams as Columbia or Fordham. However, the dominant sports hero of the gridiron came not from New York but Illinois, in the person of Harold "Red" Grange, who also paved the way for big-time football.[6]

Among other sports, golf may have ranked as most notable. While New York City residents did not dominate the sport, its increasing popularity was felt in the American metropolis as much, if not more, than elsewhere. In earlier decades, its association with "the Upper Four Hundred," had now become that of "the Upper Four Million," in the words of sports historian Benjamin Rader. New York businessmen flocked to either the country club courses, or the less exclusive public ones at which anyone

6. The Bladen Beauty's "Big Apple"

could play for a fee, hoping to become the next Walter Hagan or Bobby Jones. In addition, more and more women—as in tennis—were indulging in golf.[7]

For the literary minded, New York was the center of the publishing industry and, if few of the literati spent a great deal of their lives there, they certainly wrote about it more than any other place. For instance, the great F. Scott Fitzgerald (1892–1940), Minnesota born, spent more time in Europe and California than New York, but *The Great Gatsby* (1924) and many of his short stories take place either in a New York or Long Island setting. He did live in suburban Great Neck for a time and apparently based many of his characters on people there. Since much of his writing has a focus on the newly rich and what he saw as their decadence, the culture he saw there provided him with plenty of inspiration.[8]

Other literary figures also lived at least part of their lives in the American Metropolis. Edith Wharton (1862–1937) became the first woman to be awarded the Pulitzer Prize for literature with *The Age of Innocence* (1920), although it was actually written when she lived in Provence. Eugene O'Neill (1888–1953), considered by many as America's greatest playwright, was born there. More long-lasting with a mass audience, Anita Loos wrote *Gentlemen Prefer Blondes* (1925), the third film version of which in 1953 made Marilyn Monroe the ultimate sex symbol of the mid-century.[9]

Another literary phase associated with New York in the Roaring Twenties was "the Harlem Renaissance," or the "New Negro Renaissance." Among the major literary figures associated with this movement were Langston Hughes, Claude McKay, Countee Cullen, Zora Neale Huston, George Schuyler, and James Weldon Johnson. All, in their way, helped elevate serious interest in African American writers to new heights.[10]

If the great literary figures did not always linger in the Big Apple, the great drama and literary critics did. The more noted of these formed part of a group of seven known as the "Round Table" which met with regularity at the Algonquin Hotel. Members included Robert Benchley, *New Yorker* founder-editor Harold Ross, Robert Sherwood, *Times* critic Alexander Woollcott, and perhaps the wittiest of all—Dorothy Parker. At times they engaged in writing fiction and screenplays, but they primarily wrote about the works of others.[11]

In addition to the serious literature of the time, New York City held a place in mass-market fiction. Although many of the popular detective novels of the day had a London, San Francisco, or Los Angeles setting, New York also came in for its share. Willard Wright, using the pseudonym "S. S. Van Dine," created "Philo Vance," an eccentric, snobbish, but well-educated "man about town" who solved sensational crimes as illustrated in *The Benson Murder Case* (1926) and *The Canary Murder Case* (1927), the top sellers in the field up to that time. The Vance novels remained popular into the thirties but, at the end of the of the twenties, a new fictional creation began to generate serious buzz. Frederic Dannay and Manfred Lee developed a young adult son of a New York police detective who helped his father solve seemingly impossible crimes. Beginning with *The Roman Hat Mystery* (1929), "Ellery Queen" would soon take his place among a long list of fictional detective heroes.[12]

A variety of other writings came out of New York City in the twenties. One was the mass-market news magazine *Time*, a weekly, founded in March 1923 by Briton Hedden (1898–1929) and Henry Luce (1898–1967), a pair of young Yale alumni who designed their magazine to inform "busy men" of what was going on in the world. Luce later—in 1936—started another, the heavily illustrated *Life*, both of which made him a giant in the publishing field. It also led to the creation of a phrase, once common in academe, "*Time*'s for people that can't think; *Life*'s for people who can't read." Luce was also the husband of actress-playwright Claire Booth Luce (not to be confused with Beryl's friend Claire Luce). Herald Ross (1892–1951) started the *New Yorker* in 1925, as a "reflection of metropolitan life," with emphasis on "gaiety, wit and satire." With progressive cartoonists like James Thurber on the writing staff, it slowly gained an audience and thrived, although on a more modest scale than the publications of Luce.[13]

Even more closely tied to the entertainment world than the *New Yorker* came with what David Wallace termed "Gossip Journalism." He credited Walter Winchell (1897–1972) with being the virtual king within the trade, and not restricted to show business. There were others, such as Louella Parsons (1893–1972), who started at the *New York Morning Telegraph*, a sports show business publication, before being syndicated by the Hearst papers. Parsons had a rival in the floridly behatted Hedda Hopper (1890–1966). As filmdom ultimately replaced Broadway as the entertainment center, all of these folks moved west. More than the others, Winchell's career declined in the sixties, as did his credibility.[14]

Stage productions, vaudeville, and the burgeoning film industry dom-

6. The Bladen Beauty's "Big Apple"

inated mass entertainment in 1920, but another innovation showed remarkable growth, and like the phonograph record, its impact was strictly auditory. In 1912, a young Russian-Jewish immigrant named David Sarnoff (1891–1971), who worked for the Marconi Wireless Telegraph Company, made his first appearance on the national stage when he picked up distress signals from a sinking ship, the *Titanic*. While Sarnoff's communiqués did nothing to help the victims perishing in the mid–Atlantic, it did assist in spreading awareness of the disaster. Sarnoff ranked among the first to see "the potential of radio as a point-to-mass-audience rather than a one-person to one-person medium."[15]

Within a few years, others took part in the development of commercial radio, from those of the Westinghouse Corporation who opened station KDKA in Pittsburgh, to Cincinnati's Powel Crosley who did for radio what Henry Ford did for the automobile (i.e., manufacture them at a price the average person could afford). Sarnoff continued, forming the Radio Corporation of America (RCA), which in 1929 bought the Victor Talking Machine Company as well a piece of the motion picture industry in Radio-Keith-Orpheum (R-K-O). By forming hookups, several radio stations could play the same news and entertainment programs. Sarnoff's firm, the National Broadcasting Company, also went into television at a later time. Although his main interest was in electronics and technology, his influence on entertainment—especially through radio—remained immense.[16]

Although Los Angeles would become the center of the film industry, it had not yet replaced Broadway as the center of celebrity culture. Broadway stars could still be cultural icons in 1921, but that would prove less true as the advent of sound motion pictures relegated stage stars to a distant second in America's search for heroes in an increasingly consumer-based culture. Those who were big on Broadway in the 1920s and retained their fame did so through motion pictures, network radio, and, in a few instances, television.

The cultural change in New York City resulted from circumstances resulting from two unlikely events. The first was the passage of the Eighteenth Amendment to the U.S. Constitution in 1919, followed by the passage of the Volstead Act by Congress, of which enforcement began in 1921. The amendment culminated decades of advocacy from temperance groups concentrated in much of the mainstream forces of rural Protestant America. A Presbyterian minister in Seattle, looking at alcohol-related social problems, noted that "the saloon ... takes your sweet, innocent daughter, robs her of her virtue, and transforms her into a brazen, wanton harlot." As popular evangelist Billy Sunday spoke joyously at the time of its enactment: "The reign of tears is over.... The slums will soon be only a memory." He predicted that "we will turn our prisons into factories and our jails into warehouses." Sunday's eloquence derived from the assumption—not entirely untrue—that urban poverty resulted in large part from drunken fathers who neglected their families, sometimes leading to further degradation and even death from alcohol-induced negligence.[17]

Although it has been pointed out that per-capita consumption of alcohol actually declined during the 1920s, it was also true that widespread violation of the Prohibition laws also characterized the decade. This was especially true in large urban centers, such as Chicago and New York City, where the law enjoyed minimal popular support in the first place. As former president and chief justice William Howard Taft had predicted, "Those who think that an era of clean living and clear thinking is at hand are living in a fool's paradise." As the wise judge further explained, passage had been achieved "against the views and practices of a majority of people who live in many of the large cities." Coming from a city with a large population of beer-loving Germans, Taft understood the problems better than most, concluding that "the business of manufacturing alcohol, liquor and beer will go out of the hands of law-abiding members of the community and will be transferred to the quasi-criminal classes."[18]

As predicted, the "quasi-criminal classes" not only took up the business, so did the big-time criminals. The dominant force moving into this vacuum was a relatively hitherto confined criminal element of Italians—mostly immigrants—earlier known by such terms as the Black Hand, but more commonly as the Mafia. This organization of Sicilians had migrated to America in the 1880s, along with tens and hundreds of thousands of Italian immigrants simply interested in improving their poverty-laden lives. For the most part, the Black Hand in those early years concentrated on extracting protection money from Italian immigrants. Notably vulnerable were those who might run a small business, such as groceries or saloons in their neighborhoods. For the most part outside of these ethnic enclaves, few knew or cared of their existence. Those who did generally kept quiet out of fear.[19]

The general public first became aware of the Black Hand due to an

6. The Bladen Beauty's "Big Apple"

1890 incident in New Orleans. Police Chief David Hennessy was murdered on October 30, blaming it with his last words on "dagoes," a familiar epithet for Italians. Several suspects soon found themselves arrested and jailed. A mob of citizens then broke into the jail and lynched several inmates. After that, awareness of the Black Hand in other cities with large Italian populations became more common.

The first serious efforts to deal with this criminal outfit dated from the early 1900s in New York. Under the guidance of a city police officer of Italian birth, Guiseppe "Joseph" Petrosino, an "Italian Squad" within the larger department endeavored—with considerable success—to put the Black Hand out of business. Petrosino went so far as to go to Sicily and establish cooperating connections with the police there. Unfortunately, he was assassinated for his trouble in March 1909. However, the work of the New York police in their efforts to stamp out the criminal organization continued unabated.

Mafia families, although sometimes considered to be a tightly knit organization, were also sub-divided into different crime "families." Sometimes they tended to wage war on one another.

For instance, the dominant figure early in the century had been Joseph Morello (1867–1930), soon followed by Joe Masseria (1886–1931). He acquired a rival, Salvatore Maranzano (1886–1931), who had emigrated from Sicily in 1925. By the end of 1931, through clever manipulation, Charles "Lucky" Luciano had managed to eliminate both, and take control.

Prohibition and the efforts of thirsty New Yorkers to "wet their whistles" provided a golden opportunity for nightclub and "speakeasy" owners to enter into a new business. "Underworld" figures soon moved in to fulfill that need. Thus, underworld figures—mostly Mafia—and nightclub owners formed an uneasy alliance. Even if the clubs were properly licensed, whether through bribery or some other means, large quantities of illegal beverages almost always seemed to be available. Consciously or unconsciously, the entertainers who worked on Broadway and in the clubs became linked in this somewhat, at best, shady activity. According to Burton Peretti in his authoritative study *Nightclub City*, "The Silver Slipper [was] the most successful club to be operated openly by organized crime figures."[20] Located (at least sometimes) at 1500 Broadway (it moved more than once), but always in the theatre district, this club was one that employed Beryl Halley as a dancer several times.

Beryl Halley

One observer noted three major criminal classes profiteering from the illegal liquor-nightclub scene. In addition to the aforementioned Mafia, the oldest were the Irish gangsters, typified by Owney Madden, formerly of the Hell's Kitchen Gopher gang, and organizer of hijacking illegal shipments of booze from Canada. Madden not only had a part-ownership in the Silver Slipper, he also owned the most popular of the Harlem nightspots, the Cotton Club. Finally, there was the Jewish element, the most prominent example being gambler Arnold Rothstein, the supposed "fixer" of the 1919 World Series. Rothstein's assassination, on November 4, 1928, would set in motion events that brought about the downfall of several persons, including some in the city government.

The modern nightclub, as it evolved in New York City during Prohibition, originated in 1922, thanks to an Irish-American businessman-hustler named Larry Fay. A former taxi-driver who initially made notable sums of money moving Canadian whiskey into the city, expanded his business to owning numerous cabs and then leased a space on West 45th Street, called Club El Fey. He hired an ill-tempered immigrant from Swedish Lapland, Nils Thor Granlund, to manage it for him. Throughout the decade, Granlund would be in charge of running different clubs and hiring the entertainment. Soon, other clubs opened, some with, some without, and some partially under mob ownership or control. Although Granlund himself was presumably honest, he had a liberal view of some of those for whom he worked, believing that gangsters were "essentially just a tough breed of businessmen."[21]

Clubs usually operated on tight profit margins, as high expenses characterized most of them. Adding significantly to the cost were such high-priced headline acts as Clayton, Jackson, and (Jimmy) Durante, as many as a dozen dancers, and eight-piece orchestras. Waiters, cashiers, bartenders, kitchen help, and doormen were another factor, as was the renting of space from building owners. As a result, most clubs had *couvert*, or cover, charges to keep them running. In addition to numerous clubs in the Broadway theatre district, a few prestigious clubs also thrived in Harlem. Ironically, the ones that became best known—such as Connie's Inn and the Cotton Club (a Madden investment), and Ed Small's Paradise had black entertainers with white owners, but maintained policies that admitted only white customers, and "appealed to a white vision of Harlem life."[22]

6. The Bladen Beauty's "Big Apple"

The entertainment in the clubs in the theatre district usually began at about 10:30 or 11:00 at night. This coincided with times when the shows were ending and the patrons could then fill the clubs for a few drinks before going home. By the same token, the moonlighting entertainers could go to their second jobs, performing in floor shows. If there was a second set, it might begin about 1:00 or 1:30 a.m. Clubs that remained open after three might have what Burton Peretti termed "impromptu" amusement.[23]

Since Beryl Halley, as far as can be ascertained, worked at the Silver Slipper more than elsewhere, it deserves special attention. Nils Granlund, who managed, remodeled, and hired the entertainment, recalled in the mid-fifties:

> Broadway night life reached its peak in the Silver Slipper. Never before or since has anything surpassed it. Its career stands as the most fabulous portion of that free-swinging era. It was the most incredible, the most exciting of all the plush saloons of the Prohibition period. And it launched more stars than any similar springboard in the history of entertainment.
> The boys gave me a free hand with the Silver Slipper.... I scouted the country for the prettiest girls I could find, and I decked them out in the finest costumes anyone ever saw.[24]

Granlund may have been overstating the role he played in making stars out of Ray Bolger, Imogene Coca, Jimmy Durante, Ruby Keeler, George Raft, and Ginger Rogers (all of whom were well-known at the time of his writing), but he undoubtedly had some part in their success.

For Beryl, her "Big Apple" life focused on the Broadway theatre district, which, by 1917, consisted of fifteen major venues, with a few more to be constructed prior to the Great Depression. The Palace Theatre, at 47th and Broadway, with 1,743 seats, primarily catered to the big-name vaudeville acts, but the others hosted a variety of musical comedies, dramas, and revues. Some of these venues also had "roof gardens," where presentations were made in warmer weather. From 1913 until the completion his own new Ziegfeld Theatre, with 1,638 seats, opened in 1927, most of the *Follies* took place at the New Amsterdam Theatre, which seated 1,702 and was located on West 42nd Street, half-a-block from Broadway. Other Ziegfeld productions took place in such show places as the Globe, the Casino, the Century, and even the houses of his rivals, the Shuberts and Earl Carroll.[25]

The theatre district, as it existed in the twenties, had earned that renown only over the past quarter-century. As the Brideson Sisters have pointed out: "In 1896, Broadway was not yet considered the cross roads of the show business world." Quality of productions varied from low to middling, until six (predominantly) Jewish theatre owners "introduced cohesion and efficiency" to the system, uplifting the situation. The six originally constituted Abraham Erlanger (1859–1930), Charles Frohman (1856–1915, who perished on the *Lusitania*), Raphael "Al" Hayman (1847–1917), Marcus Klaw (1858–1936), Samuel Nixon (1848–1918), and J. Fred Zimmerman (1843–1925). They created the Theatrical Syndicate early in 1896, which, in their case, did not necessarily imply a negative term. While many of these original founders had died before Beryl Halley ever arrived on Broadway, let alone left Gallia County, their legacy lived on until interrupted by the Great Depression. By the end of 1926, Will Page identified what he termed the "Big Six" who controlled Broadway. Abraham Erlanger remained from the originals, but the others were new. Charles Dillingham, Florenz Ziegfeld of the *Follies*, George White of the *Scandals*, Earl Carroll of the *Vanities*, and Jacob J. Shubert now ranked as the dominant figures. Marcus Klaw was still around as something of a successor to Frohman, but the outsider Shubert had gained major status, even if he was not quite in the club. As Page phrased it, they were in charge of "gorgeous girl exhibitions."[26]

Still, like many business combinations of that era, the syndicate demonstrated tendencies toward trust and monopoly. Without their approval, it became virtually impossible to mount a show or for a performer to get a job. Later, in 1896, three brothers—Am, Lee, and Jacob Shubert—obtained their own theatre and challenged the trust. Thereafter, they co-existed in an uneasy rivalry. Ziegfeld, for the most part, worked with the syndicate, although not always smoothly. Since New York City had a large Jewish population, Yiddish comedy and comedians increasingly began to supplant the previously dominant Irish comedy teams. In essence, such pairs as Joe Weber and Lew Fields (the latter name Anglicized from Moses Schoenfeld), immigrant Jews from Poland, had begun to replace older teams like Edward Harrigan and Tony Hart. As Jewish people accounted for half the number of theatregoers, this new trend was good for business.[27]

After his early successes presenting Anna Held, Florenz Ziegfeld had become a force that could not be ignored, whether the syndicate theatre owners did, or did not, wholeheartedly embrace his maverick style of operations. Besides, if they objected to some of his tactics, he could defect to the rival Shuberts, which he nearly did on one occasion, signing a contract with them. He later violated the contract; this resulted in a lawsuit which he lost, but in the long run it strengthened his position with the syndicate.[28]

According to Granlund, the stock market crash and the repeal of Prohibition had less impact on the decline of the "speak-easy [and nightclub] business" than commonly supposed. He says they "were dying out by the end of the 1920s for the simple reason that they were choking the geese that laid their golden eggs." Rephrased, he pointed out that customers increasingly got wise and developed "an awareness of what a racket the cabaret business really was."[29] No doubt the vanishing of their own surplus funds also played a part in their newfound awareness.

After the stock market crash in late October 1929, followed by a declining economy, profound changes took place in the nightclub and Broadway theatre district. In short, the supply of money for entertainment and extravagant expenditures diminished sharply. While night spots and New York theatre survived—as did drinking and crime—the ensuing decade would be markedly different.

For better or worse, the motion picture industry had far outpaced live theatre during the twenties. In terms of dollars expended in ticket sales: in 1921, movie sales were $301 million, while those of live theatre were $81 million. By 1929, the respective numbers were $720 million versus $127 million. Theatre ticket sales, both on Broadway and for other live productions, peaked in 1927 at $195 million, declining thereafter. While the coming depression hurt every aspect of the economy, vaudeville virtually died, and even on Broadway, it never again matched the windfall it had in the "roaring" decade.[30]

The 1930s brought changes in the political culture of the Big Apple as well. The twenties had been personified by state senator turned mayor James J. "Jimmy" Walker, nicknamed "Beau James," for his "Let the Good Times Roll" attitude. Investigations, led by former Judge Samuel Seabury, brought about Walker's resignation on September 1, 1932. After an interregnum, a maverick Republican, sometimes allied with Socialists, old Bull Moose Progressives, and New Dealers would symbolize the next decade. Fiorello LaGuardia might seem like an odd mixture of contrasts. He was half–Italian, half–Jewish, Protestant, and a Freemason who drank sparingly but opposed Prohibition. Nicknamed "The Little Flower," he had a touch of puritanism in his makeup, yet was not a prude. In the words of nightclub historian Burton Peretti, "Mayor LaGuardia attempted to reform civic life in the contexts of social policy, leisure, and nightlife."[31]

None of what happened in New York City in the twenties should be interpreted as what necessarily happened in the entire United States, although events there were reflected throughout the country to some degree. As one noted historian has pointed out, most people were not reflecting on what F. Scott Fitzgerald wrote about. Although his first novel sold well, never in his lifetime did his work appear on a best-seller list. The masses were more likely to read the works of Zane Gray, Gene Stratton-Porter, or one of the popular mystery writers of the time. Many, in fact, were too busy trying to make a living. While numerous folks may have been violating the Prohibition laws, nearly as many were quietly abiding by them.[32]

Beryl Halley, who began to receive national attention from the time she appeared in *Tangerine,* and even more when she became a Ziegfeld Girl, seems to have found her place in the world of New York easier than those who were "spoiled by success." Nashville, Hollywood, and the New York stage are adrift with those who self-destructed as a result of their newfound stardom. Tragic examples of this involve two of Beryl's contemporaries. Marion Strasmick, also known as Marion "Kiki" Roberts, worked at the Silver Slipper and in the production of *Whoopee!* She then became involved with the notorious gangster Jack "Legs" Diamond (1897–1931), which cost her both jobs. When Diamond was shot by a rival, she was found weeping over his prostrate form. She claimed that she had learned her lesson, but took up with him again after his recovery. Then, in December 1931, he met his death in her apartment. Except for brief notoriety, her career was ruined; after 1937, no one knows what became of her.

Another Diamond girlfriend at the Silver Slipper, Gracie Carroll, came to an even more tragic end. The latter witnessed two murders and, to ensure there would be no living witnesses, gangsters placed her feet in a tub of concrete, after which she was dumped in either the East, or the Hudson, River. Since no trace of her had been found, it is not known if she was fatally shot first.[33]

6. The Bladen Beauty's "Big Apple"

An unknown girl from a farm community with a high school diploma, a year of college, and a year of rural school teaching under her belt, Beryl Halley never attained the celebrity heights that the above threesome did; neither did she suffer the fall. The girl from Bladen apparently seemed to accept her Ziegfeld fame effortlessly, and when advancing age—meaning past thirty—and the Great Depression ended her stage career—she also went effortlessly back into stenography, marriage, and motherhood.

7

The World She Left Behind, or Gallia County in Prosperity and Depression

Song lyrics can sometimes make a point better than other explanations. An example is "Rollin' Down the Mountain." Written in 1932 by Arthur Lippman, Manning Sherwin, and Harry Richman and published by the Crawford Music Company, the song tells the story of a young girl named Nancy Brown, who was escorted up the hill by various types of men. Each time "she came rollin' down the mountain," but finally she meets "a city slicker, who had hundred dollar bills, came ridin in his auto to the West Virginia hills." Nancy marries him and is off to the city, leaving the West Virginia hills far behind her.[1]

Although not a girl from West Virginia, Beryl Halley was a product of the same Appalachian culture as the mythical Nancy Brown. This comical little song, and the actual life experience of Beryl Halley, typifies the historic struggle between the urban and rural sides of life. The same time Beryl moved to New York City was also a benchmark in American population trends. The 1920 census was the first such survey to demonstrate that a majority of Americans resided in urban rather than rural areas. The face of the American population was changing, and a shift in cultural norms and mores was occurring, to the delight of some and the chagrin of others.[2]

William Giddings Sibley was a native of Racine, Ohio. He was a graduate of Marietta College in 1881, and ventured into the newspaper business in Gallipolis. In 1890, he became the owner of the weekly *Gallipolis Trib-*

7. The World She Left Behind

une and soon changed it to a daily paper. He would eventually write a daily column, "Along the Highway," for the *Chicago Journal of Commerce*.[3]

Never an urbanite, Sibley preferred the rural setting of Gallipolis and Gallia County; he would simply mail his columns to Chicago. On Saturday, November 6, 1920, Sibley penned the following editorial in his *Gallipolis Daily Tribune*. It offered an idyllic, if whimsical, view of the changing American population:

> The farmer gets up these glorious November mornings ... lowers his bulk beside the breakfast table and busies himself with hot biscuits, yellow butter, ham and eggs, hot coffee, and just as likely as not a huge wedge of cold pie. He is glad he is where he is with what he has, surrounded by broad fields and wooded hills. He likes his occupation and his location in the scheme of things.
>
> An hour later, maybe two, the city dweller deserts his virtuous couch, takes his morning shave and bath, breakfasts daintily on orange juice, egg, bacon, toast and coffee, and then hoofs it to car or train. He rides to his street, dodges his way in a dingy atmosphere of blue gasoline fumes between lofty buildings to his place of business, and begins his day's work. He thrills to the urge of the city, the ambition to acquire wealth, and loves the gloomy walls that surround him. Proud of his position, keen to climb higher and higher in his commercial rating, life is worth living to him. Opportunity surrounds him. Big achievement beckons him on. He is thankful that he has a firm foothold in his city. No tangled woodlands for him, thank you. Nor smiling fields, nor rising suns, nor lowing cattle. He has no use for a barn or a kitchen meal. Certainly not. The farm life is all very well and very necessary, to be sure; the rural scenes are tranquil, of course; but give him the hustle and bustle of the city, if you please. Nor does the farmer want the city man's life. What, go through his days dodging devil wagons, clutching his pocketbook, and being penned up under electric lights when the sun shines? Not any of that for him.
>
> But slowly, surely, the lure of city gold and city lights is pulling the majority. Ten years ago our rural majority in the United States was seven millions. Now it has turned into an urban majority of four millions. It is not an altogether happy sign of the times. It is well that more men and women trod the soil than the pavements—that the plain life of the farm, with its wholesome delights, should steady and please the masses of the people.[4]

The population of Gallia County in 1920 was 23,311. By 1930, that figure actually decreased to 23,050. By the 1940 census, Gallia County had grown to a population of 24,930.[5] In a county comprised of 471 square miles, that is forty-nine people per square mile. When compared to New York City, the mind is staggered by the world Beryl left and the world she came to inhabit. The 1930 population of New York City was 6,930,446, all contained in an area of 302 square miles. The total of New York's population density of 22,948 people per square mile, as opposed to Gallia

County's forty-nine people per square mile, may well qualify as the major difference in the argument of urban versus rural.

An interesting factor enters into play when discussing Gallia County's population loss from 1920 to 1930. As stated in the *Gallipolis Daily Tribune* on May 29, 1930, in a page-one article titled, "Detailed Census Figures Show Loss in County," there was a continued infrastructure problem that existed and would continue to for several more years. One sentence stands out in this article: "Gains will be noted particularly in townships where there are few mud roads while those townships still in the mud, almost invariably show declines in population."[6]

During a visit to his home county in 1926, Oscar Eagle, born in Raccoon Township, Broadway actor, producer, and director, was asked about important improvements in Gallia County. "The last time I drove through to Gallipolis, I nearly wrecked my car," he said, "but this time I found no better roads than right here in Gallia County." Eagle went on to state that only a few days before he had seen within a thirty-minute period, "a fine Minerva car carrying a Maryland license, a Cadillac with an Oklahoma tag, and still another large car bearing the license of a far distant state."[7]

The story about the mud roads and the improvement of roadways marks the other physical difference in Beryl's old home and the new one. In addition to the population differential, the infrastructure was a major difference. The typical city dweller in 1930 would have been a twenty-six-year-old male. He would live in an apartment complete with a flush toilet, running water, and electricity. He would hold a job, working for another person or company, earning as much as a hundred dollars a month. A telephone was a common item. He would listen to the radio at night, and on the weekend take in a movie. Despite Prohibition, he would still have the occasional drink. He would be driving a car of his own, purchased on the installment plan. He would marry a girl three years his junior. She would quit her job to have the first child, and the family would dream of eventually having a home of their own.[8]

The person living in Beryl's old world of Gallia County would have the same dreams, desires, and aspirations as the city dweller, but the remoteness of the area and small population would guarantee that the changes would occur, only in a much slower fashion. As late as 1931, newspaper ads still stated: "Those needing wagons, buggies, farm machinery, or general blacksmithing done, bring it to T. T. Rutherford and Sons Auto

7. The World She Left Behind

and Wagon Repair Shop below fair ground, between River Road and old street car line."[9] The use of draft animals in farming and logging would continue into the 1940s.

In the 1930 census, Gallia County showed a net loss of 154 farms since 1920. However, the average farm was 91.3 acres in 1930, a growth in acreage per farm of 1.7 acres over 1920. Of the 2,769 farms in Gallia County in 1930, 2,210 were operated by the owners, fifteen were under the guidance of a manager, and 544 were handled by tenants, an increase of one hundred such cases over 1920. Lands classified as pasture had increased by seven thousand acres, wood pastures had increased by fifteen thousand, and woodland pasture had increased by four thousand. This was a reflection of agricultural practices and trends.[10]

In terms of economic growth, the construction of paved highways and the construction of a bridge across the Ohio River had a greater effect on the area than had the railroad's growth on breaking down the rural isolation.[11] The terrible conditions of the roadways can be seen in two simple lines from the *Gallipolis Daily Tribune*. On July 22, 1920, a news brief reported that "Huntington business men propose to place a ferry at the end of the paved road about 20 miles north of Huntington."[12] The distance from Huntington to Gallipolis is about forty miles. And this blurb from December 16, 1920 states that improvements must be made to "improve road between county paved road and city pavement because it becomes almost impassable in winter."[13] By 1928, the situation of the roadways had only been exacerbated. The existing, poorly built roads were rebuilt, and new highways—one a north and south route, the other east-west—were constructed.

"THRONGS HERE FOR BRIDGE OPENING," declared the headline of the *Gallipolis Daily Tribune* of Tuesday, May 29, 1928. The lead story began: "On the eve of one of the biggest celebrations ever known in the city's history, Gallipolis was preparing to be host to thousands of visitors coming here for the dedication of the Silver Bridge, [the] new million dollar highway span connecting Gallipolis and Pt. Pleasant, W.Va." The Silver Bridge, so named because of the paint used on it, would not only connect these two towns but would also complete a direct path for Columbus, Ohio, and Charleston, West Virginia. It was of such significance to the entire region that it would be nicknamed "Gateway to the South."[14]

Perhaps the final word on the improved roadway system in southeastern Ohio may be found in an article that originally appeared in the *Telegram*, the newspaper in nearby Wellston, Ohio, which was reprinted in the *Gallipolis Daily Tribune* of Friday, February 25, 1938. The headline invokes the name of Beryl Halley's alma mater: "R. Grande College Made Accessible by New Highways." The article states: "Rio Grande is not so remote as it once was. When traffic used to ride on steel rails, it was five miles or more overland to Bidwell, the nearest station on the Pumpkin Vine route. Now a state highway passes right by the campus, and any energetic student can thumb a ride to Gallipolis or Jackson, and points beyond, with little delay."[15]

The telephone also experienced a surge of use in Beryl's old world, just as it did in her new one. In 1916, telephone service had extended to Rio Grande, as evidenced in this line from the 1916 catalog: "Upon arrival at Oak Hill, students should call by telephone one of these gentlemen, or the President of the College."[16] Telephone use had grown so much by 1920 that labor unrest extended to the telephone operators—women—who went on strike at Pomeroy and Middleport.[17] By 1931, the city of Gallipolis had 1,219 telephones in use. That number dropped to 1,053 in 1933 at the height of the Great Depression, but reached an all-time high of use (to that time) of 1,245 in 1939. The Ohio Bell Telephone Company that year announced a plan to spend $14 million for expansion and improvement to meet the expected growth of use.[18]

Technology also spread to the area of entertainment in Beryl's old world. After the first commercial radio broadcast of station KDKA, in Pittsburgh, on November 2, 1920, radio rapidly expanded as a primary source of entertainment and information. By October 31, 1923, a listener in Gallipolis could pull in WOR from Newark, KDKA from Pittsburgh, WAEF from New York, WMC from Memphis, WHAS from Louisville, WDAP from Chicago, WGY from Schenectady, WDAF from Kansas City, WCX from Detroit, WTAM from Cleveland, and WOS from Jefferson City, Missouri.[19]

"Moving pictures" had been seen in Gallipolis since December 1905, and soon became a local mainstay. For a dime, sights of the world and films from Hollywood and New York were available. The boundary of distance was beginning to lessen, not just with the physical roadways but with electronic media. By 1929, the Gallipolis Theatre was a steady advertiser in the local paper, but movie theatres in Huntington and Wellston

7. The World She Left Behind

also competed for the moviegoers' money.[20] The last great barrier fell on January 15, 1930, when the Gallipolis Theatre showed *In the Headlines*, the first all-"talkie" movie shown in that city. It was followed by the film debut of Sophie Tucker in the production of *Honky Tonk*.[21]

The greatest equalizer of Beryl's new and old worlds was the energy to power these breakthroughs. A story exists that a Tennessee farmer stood to testify at a church revival. "Brothers and sisters, I want to tell you this," he said dramatically. "The greatest thing on earth to have is the love of God in your heart—and the next greatest thing is to have electricity in your house!"[22]

Cities and towns in southeast Ohio had electricity available, but through the 1930s the lack of electricity caused rural dwellers to live much as their ancestors had in the 1880s. In 1931, fewer than half the farms in Ohio were electrified.[23] Electrification meant running hot and cold water could be provided by pumps; washing machines, flat irons, and refrigerators made the workday chores of a housewife easier; electricity could power feed grinders and milking machines; and the availability of light at the flick of a switch changed the daylight-to-dark pattern of life on the farm.[24]

On May 11, 1933, President Franklin Roosevelt issued an executive order creating the Rural Electrification System (REA). Under this system, local electrical cooperatives were created to work with the REA to expand services.[25] On September 3, 1938, a group of local residents founded the Buckeye Rural Electric Cooperative. The early work of extending power lines into the remote areas was done by hand, using mules and horses to drag poles and electric lines up and down the steep terrain and to ford the many streams and creeks.[26] In spite of the efforts to electrify, it would be well into the 1950s before some areas had electricity. As late as 1952, one of the conditions put forth by a prospective bride was that the house must have electricity and running water before the anxious groom would hear "I do."[27]

Socially and politically, the time of the 1920s and 1930s was influenced by three forces that acted upon American society—Prohibition, the reemergence of the Ku Klux Klan, and the Great Depression. Each shared similarities and differences in Beryl's two worlds. A song from 1930 about Prohibition being a failure made the point.[28]

When Prohibition went into effect, John F. Kramer, the first commissioner, proclaimed: "This law will be obeyed in cities, large and small, and in villages, and where [if] it is not obeyed it will be enforced. The law says that liquor to be used as a beverage must not be manufactured. We shall see that it is not manufactured. Nor sold, nor given away, nor hauled in anything on the surface of the earth or under the earth or in the air."[29]

The lofty goals and words of Commissioner Kramer were never met, and in all likelihood never could have been. From the first day to the last, Prohibition was doomed to failure. The reactions to it were at times comical, at times tragic, and always predictable. The thirteen years, ten months, and nineteen days of Prohibition were chronicled a total of 259 times in the *Gallipolis Daily Tribune*—185 times for the word "Moonshine" and seventy-four times for the word "Bootlegger."[30]

The first incident in Gallia County of Prohibition violations occurred on August 7, 1920. Three half-gallon mason jars filled with "moonshine" were confiscated by Sheriff H. W. Sowards after a car with three West Virginia men crashed into a tree. The men were described as more or less "tead up," and after the booze was confiscated, the men were sent home "much saddened" over the loss.[31] It would prove to be the first of many such incidents.

The next incident was much more serious, and foreshadowed other dangerous events. In nearby Meigs County on August 30, officials went to the home of a man named Jim Barnett, described as "colored." A homemade still was confiscated, but Mr. Barnett escaped over the hill, barefooted, bareheaded, and coatless. On September 1, officers returned to the Barnett home. Upon the approach of the officers, Barnett opened fire with a .45 caliber revolver. Mrs. Barnett also opened fire, only with a Springfield army rifle. She was soon captured, but Mr. Barnett escaped again. A still was confiscated.[32]

Antagonism towards law enforcement grew to the point that Charles Dale, the local game warden, sent a letter to the *Tribune* on August 15, 1921, stating: "I also wish to make it plain that I will enforce the Game Laws to the letter until September 15, on that day I go out of office, not to take up the enforcement of the Prohibition Laws, but to work at my trade as a Bricklayer. Now you fellows that are worrying so much about me being a Prohibition Officer can rest assured that I am not connected with this branch of the Law in any manner."[33]

"Pity Me" is a small collection of houses set squarely on the Gallia-

7. The World She Left Behind

Meigs county line.[34] It also seems to have been a site of much bootlegging activity. An article headlined, "No Offense Intended to a Big Meigs County Industry," was followed with a long description of a diatribe filled with seventeen uses of "blanket blank" unleashed by a moonshining resident of "Pity Me," also referred to as a "Village of Sin." The aggrieved whiskey maker said, "There is so many bootleggers in Gallipolis that they have cut the price so low that a decent bootlegger can't make a living there." The article further states that one would often hear "Let's go to Gallipolis, where we can buy some cheap whiskey."[35]

On a far less humorless note, the *Gallipolis Daily Tribune* of Thursday, January 1, 1925, reported that a constable in bordering Jackson County had been sentenced to five years in the penitentiary for manufacturing distilled liquor. The man had been a constable for sixteen years, and had a wife and nine children. He was the fifth man sentenced to the penitentiary, or a reformatory, that year.[36]

On July 29, 1925, the home of the town marshal in nearby Chesapeake was dynamited by two men. The marshal had been active in the prosecution of bootleggers and moonshine liquor distillers.[37] A barn owned by a Gallia County Commissioner, active in the pursuit of moonshiners, was dynamited after the commissioner received an anonymous letter, warning that his barn would be burned.[38]

"Pity Me" would once again be in the news on June 21, 1926. A local "flapper" was arrested when she was inebriated and out for a ride with a married man. The irate wife forced the car to stop in the middle of the road. She proceeded to beat up her husband, until the "flapper" got out and entered the fray. The wife pressed charges, and the "flapper" was fined $25 and costs and sentenced to six months in the county jail.[39]

There followed yearly raids of stills and the arrests of the moonshiners. Side-by-side articles appeared on the front page of the *Gallipolis Daily Tribune* for January 15, 1929, one marking the celebration of "Temperance Day," when two hours on Friday would be set aside in the schools for instruction in temperance and respect for the law. The adjoining article was headlined, "Reformatory Can't Hold Her, Woman Bootlegger Tells 'Em." Nell Judson, of nearby Athens County, had pleaded guilty to charges of bootlegging because "she had to earn money to keep her children in school." She escaped and was recaptured only after she emptied a six-shot revolver in the direction of a deputy.[40]

Beryl Halley

> Oh, at the next election, I'm sure you all will see,
> We'll have light wines and good old beer in 1933,
> And if we do not get it, I'm tellin' you and you,
> We'll make our own liquor, and drink our old home brew.[41]

The great social experiment of Prohibition clearly failed. The situation degenerated to the point that a return to the whipping post was advocated,[42] and a judge lectured a forty-six-year-old female bootlegger, an expectant mother of ten, on the virtues of birth control before sentencing her to fifteen days in jail.[43] The official end of Prohibition was quietly marked in Gallia County by a simple ad in the paper on Saturday, March 10, 1934. It read simply: "Wines and Beer—Vince's Place, Court Street, Phone 50."[44]

The 1915 revival of the Anti-Reconstruction Ku Klux Klan took on a partly different focus in the 20th century, proclaiming patriotic ideals, but expressing intolerance towards Roman Catholics and Jews, particularly in Northern states. Still, there were some who could find humor in their "hooded Americanism":

> The night was dark and dreary
> And the air was full of sleet
> The old man joined the Ku Klux [Klan]
> And ma, she lost her sheet.[45]

The Ku Klux Klan experienced considerable influence of sorts in the twenties. Millions of American men and women donned sheets and marched through the streets of American towns and cities. In the time period of 1923 to 1926, Gallia County experienced open Klan activity. This revival was almost benign, if it is possible to say that about a widely recognized group that historically had relied on fear and terror. The resurgence of the Klan took the form of fraternal orders not unlike the Masons, Odd Fellows, and various other groups.[46]

In 1925 and 1926, in the Fraternity Bulletin of *The Gallipolis Daily Tribune*, meeting times would be posted for the Masons, the Knights of Pythias, Modern Woodmen of America, the Improved Order of Redmen, the American Legion, Daughters of the American Revolution, and the Ku Klux Klan. The Klan notices were short and cryptic, such as "Did you get your pitchfork?"[47] "Ku Klux Klansmen take notice,"[48] and "April Meetings First Degree, Educational Business, Second Degree."[49]

A brief paragraph in the April 28, 1923, *Gallipolis Daily Tribune*

7. *The World She Left Behind*

stated: "The Ku Klux Klan presented a local organization Friday evening, we understand, with a new membership of about 60 to add to a membership of about 50 which had previously taken in. just what their plans are for local improvement are not made public."[50] That brief paragraph was obviously enough to make the locals wary and watchful.

Sunday, May 13, 1923, brought a general alarm to many residents of Gallipolis. A number of people saw the Ku Klux Klan cross, red and about two feet long, on the north face of the town clock. Upon closer inspection on Monday, it turned out that what had been seen was the trap door leading to the roof. It had blown open at some time in the night. "All the various things people thought about the Klan making an effort to intimidate County Officials were entirely wrong."[51]

A crowd estimated at about two thousand to twenty-five hundred gathered at the Fair Grounds on Thursday, September 20, 1923, to see about two hundred citizens officially join the Ku Klux Klan. The ceremony was performed in front of the grandstand in the light of three burning crosses. A parade of about one hundred robed Klansmen, including the Hamden–McArthur Klan band, marched through downtown Gallipolis.[52]

Cross burnings would sometimes be publicized. Such an event was scheduled for Friday, July 31, 1925, commemorating the death of attorney William Jennings Bryan, one-time Democratic presidential hopeful, and defender of old-time religion.[53] After this, no other Klan activity would be noted for nearly three years.

The last mention of the Klan during this period occurred in June of 1928. The Klan was sponsoring a social with free ice cream and cake. All were invited.[54] With this event, the Ku Klux Klan receded out of the public view in Gallipolis and Gallia County.

Not long afterward, economic concerns became dominant:

> I went to the bank to borrow some money,
> I tell you right now, didn't find it funny,
> The banker said he had none to loan,
> Get your old hat and pull out home.
> For all we got's gone, all we got's gone.[55]

The front page of the *Gallipolis Daily Tribune* of October 30, 1929, had no large headlines. Notice was made of preparations for the funeral of Senator Theodore Burton; mud roads were blamed for abandoned farms; the best football game of the season was expected on Friday, pitting

Beryl Halley

Gallipolis against a strong Nelsonville team at 3:00—admission 50 cents for adults, 25 cents for children. The weather was predicted to be rainy and colder, and there was no mention of Wall Street or the crashing market.[56]

"Black Tuesday" had marked the beginning of The Great Depression. Its effects would soon encompass every aspect of American life, and no city, state, or region of the country would escape unscathed. Beryl's old world would suffer, perhaps not as much as her new one, but the rural life could not avoid its own economic challenges.

A letter to the editor of Friday, April 6, 1934, by an anonymous writer simply identified as "A. GALIPOT," may provide the best insight into the effects of the Depression in Gallipolis, as well as any rural area. Among the writer's more cogent points:

> Everybody seems to agree on one thing and that is, that the cause of the depression is unemployment of labor, and that no cure or recovery can possibly take place unless people can earn wages.
>
> Sometime ago we had a machine shop that employed 20 to 30 people, two furniture factories that gave work to approximately 150 to 175 men, a small chair factory that employed 8 or 10. Three brick yards and a tile works that had jobs for 40 to 50 people. These industries all ran steadily and while they didn't pay the biggest wages in the world ... they gave employment to about 250 men. None of the above industries are here now.
>
> In addition to these mentioned, we had three flour mills, three stave foundries, and three or four bakeries that ran steadily and gave work to 60 or 80 people every day. We now have two mills, one foundry, and one bakery.
>
> We used to patronize our two local tailors who each employed 6 to 8 workmen at good wages, but that business died out with the others and is quit also.
>
> Is there any other wonder that there is a depression in Gallipolis when so many people have been thrown out of work?
>
> Good times will never return until people get back to work, and the beginning of the real prosperity will start at the bottom and climb up. Not start at the top and come down. The great buying power of this nation rests in people who dwell in towns the size of Gallipolis, and there is never going to be any real honest to God return of good times until people in the thousands of places like Gallipolis have a few dollars to spend.[57]

A. GALIPOT, in all his anonymity, was quite the economic prophet! "Beauty in the flesh continues to rule the world," Florenz Ziegfeld stated in 1929, and it expresses how the new world had opened for Beryl. On May 29, 1929, the editor of the *Gallipolis Daily Tribune* chose to take Mr. Ziegfeld to task. This may be a perfect reflection of Beryl's old-versus-new world. To quote the *Tribune*:

7. The World She Left Behind

So, we think it true that the realm of feminine beauty is the home that a woman possessing it finds in a husband her dearest happiness, and in her children her greatest joy in life. Certainly we do not regard the display of a beautiful woman's flesh on the stage for a salary, as a ruling power in world's affairs, or as likely to yield her the happiness and security that family life gives. Nor do we incline to believe Mr. Ziegfield [sic] harbors any such notion. He is a dealer in feminine beauty for public exhibition, to be stared at and gloated over by the imagination of men who pay to see it and so possess it only with their eyes and during a performance of the Follies.[58]

It would seem that the writer did not hold "the Great Ziegfeld" in the same regard as did the New York crowd, even to the point of misspelling his name. While an edition of the *Follies* would never get close to southeastern Ohio, shows of a similar nature did play the area and to large crowds that offered a warm reception to the dancing beauties.

In May 1923, a touring company billed as "Happy Hal Kiter and his Musi-gal Mardi Gras" played the Gallipolis Theatre and was well received. The show featured "a dainty dancing chorus that sings more than half the time, dances most of the time, and looks pretty all the time." All seats were reserved, and the theatregoer could pay thirty-five cents, fifty cents, or seventy-five cents for a show that started "at 8:15 sharp!"[59]

An unusual item appeared in the *Gallipolis Daily Tribune* on Friday, August 6, 1926. An article on fashion featured Katherine Burke, who was, coincidentally, the girl who would take Beryl's place in *Rio Rita*. As stated, "Katherine Burke, the most shapely of the girls in the Ziegfeld forces, and the only one who poses absolutely in the nude in the new 'Ziegfeld Review,' advises all women and girls to wear corsets of the modern comfortable sort." Burke is quoted as saying, "Put on a corset. It will brace vital organs and mould your form gently. I am never without mine except when I am on the stage. I don't want to be thin and puny or fat and flabby."[60] (Incidentally, there is no indication as to the increase of corset wearing among the females of Gallia County.)

The first movie adaptation of a Ziegfeld production to play in Gallipolis was the silent film *Kid Boots*, in October of 1926. Eddie Cantor played the starring role, supported by Clara Bow, Billie Dove, and Lawrence Gray. The movie had just opened in New York City on October 9, and played in Gallipolis on the 14th.[61]

Ziegfeld may have been the master promoter of the *Follies* and revues, but several other notable personalities produced similar entertainments.

97

Beryl Halley

Among Ziegfeld's competitors, one of the most successful was George White. *The George White Scandals* ran on Broadway from 1919 to 1929, with the exception of 1927.[62] White took the show on the road that year, and Gallipolis was one of the stops. Within two days of the announcement, and before the first advertisements appeared, more than a hundred applicants for main-floor seats had been received by the Gallipolis Theatre.[63]

The first ad appeared on February 28. Billed as "The Supreme Musical Attraction" and the "World's Greatest Show," a special notice appeared that informed the public that the free list was suspended and no babies would be allowed in the audience.[64] On March 3, the prices for tickets were announced, and far exceeded what the homefolks were accustomed to paying. Tickets sold for $1.10, $2.20, and $3.30, including War Tax.[65]

The Saturday showing was warmly received by a large audience. The show proved to be all that was advertised. "Graceful dancers, beautiful scenery, and effective work of the chorus pleased even the hardened theatregoers who are accustomed to going to the larger cities for their theatrical experience." Coincidently, the story just above the account of the *Scandals* was a report on the message of a local evangelist headlined: "Evangelist Warns of the Devil Awaiting: Selfishness, Lust, and Commercialized Sin Condemned."[66]

Perhaps nothing else personified Beryl's old world and new world as did her alma mater, Rio Grande College. The college was slow to change, partially because of its relative isolation, partially because of economics, and partially by its philosophy of education.[67] Horace Houf, an ordained Baptist minister, arrived in 1923 to serve as the president of the school. From 1876 to 1923, a span of forty-seven years, four men had served as president. In the seventeen-year period starting with the arrival of Houf until 1940, four men held the office. Ruth Houf, Horace's wife, would later reflect upon the school when they arrived: "There were no sororities or fraternities—or dancing," she said. "There were parties and pranks and jolly times shared by students, professors, and towns people as well. Mr. and Mrs. Howard Gross gave the college its first radio. There was great excitement and much noise, but only now and then a word or scrap of a sentence could be understood. Perhaps with a regular electric current the reception could have been much better, but only generators furnished electricity in Rio Grande then, and very few people had them. For lighting, people mainly used oil lamps or acetylene gas. Fire was a terrible hazard

7. The World She Left Behind

in those days as there was no public water system. The fire department was a bucket brigade. Improved roads ... led into Rio Grande later in 1923."[68]

The "Fifty Golden Years" of Rio Grande College were marked on June 7 and 8, 1926, by a historical pageant written and directed by Chestora McDonald Carr. Carr taught elocution and drama at Rio Grande from 1901 to 1929, and in 1932. She also directed programs, plays, and other pageants, but only during the spring term. The rest of the time she toured on the Chautauqua circuit, specializing in the mimicry of birds, winter winds, and frontier preachers.[69]

The two-day production was massive in its undertaking. The eleven episodes of the history and seven episodes of the college activities involved students, faculty, trustees, and the townspeople. Over five hundred individuals were involved, beginning with "The Forest Primeval" to "The Spirit of 1861" to "The Shades of Night." Graduation ceremonies occurred on the second day.[70]

The tickets sold for a dollar apiece, and the parking was free. The *Gallipolis Daily Tribune* of June 12 reported: "Thousands See Pageant Celebrating Fiftieth Year." The trustees also voted to erect a new classroom building.[71]

The new building would be named Anniversary Hall. The cost of $100,000 was covered by donations, and the result was the third building on campus. It would be dedicated on Homecoming Day, October 22, 1927. The three-story brick building had the architectural style of elementary schools built in that era.[72]

In 1928, Willard Bartlett assumed the presidency of Rio Grande College. Among the first actions of the new presidency was moving to junior college status. No longer would Rio Grande be a four-year college; only the first two years would be offered. Partially as a reaction to educational trends and partially as an economic move, faculty, students, alumni, and townspeople mainly detested this junior college idea. Bartlett would leave to pursue a doctorate in 1931. It would be 1941 before Rio Grande once again granted a four-year degree.[73]

Enrollment would suffer because of the ill-advised move to junior college status and from the effects of the Great Depression. Enrollment went from 217 in 1931 to fewer than two hundred students from 1934 to 1939. The minutes of the Board of Trustees meetings reflect the economic hardship of this period. In 1931, there was a discussion of financial woes and a possible merger with Cedarville College; in 1934, there was discussion of the need to raise money to pay the faculty; and, in 1935. there was active discussion of moving the entire school to Ironton, Ohio, or Charleston, West Virginia.[74]

November 19, 1937, marked the day that many felt could be the death knell of the entire institution. Venerable old Atwood Hall, the original building, burned to the ground. Nothing was salvaged. The air of gloom settled over the campus that early Saturday morning. With a stubborn resistance, under the direction of President William Lewis, the school would struggle onwards. Amazingly, all classes were held on Monday, and students carried on with their studies.[75]

An interesting side note had occurred in 1930. Beryl must have smiled if she had heard the news. The Board of Trustees had approved dancing on campus on December 28, 1929. When students returned from the Christmas holiday, they discovered that they could now dance on campus. This solved the concern that "the college town, it is pointed out, provides no diversions for young people. With the ban against dancing on the campus the students have been going elsewhere, some of which have been rather questionable in their character, it is asserted."[76] The irony of the situation would not have been lost on Beryl, for it turned out that there had never been a definite prohibition of dancing on campus: it was simply a precedent that had been accepted as fact.

As the period of 1920–1940 drew to a close, southeastern Ohio had undergone slow but radical changes in the way of economics and lifestyle. A good reflection of the time can be found in a letter by LaRue Habercom, a student from 1935 to 1937. Dated 1986, the letter reads in part:

> Rio was under church auspices then—its motto "the School That Studies the Student" ... there was a large plaque on the campus so stating Rio was a bastion of complete male chauvinism rules for male students were practically nonexistent (no one—but no one—was allowed to smoke on campus.) Girls were not supposed to smoke at all—nor to drink (some of us did.)
>
> Girls were allowed three dates a week ... one on a week night ... two on week ends. On non-date nights curfew was 9 o'clock ... date night curfew was 10 o'clock with an occasional until 11 o'clock permitted.
>
> Social life centered around mixers, tea dances, formal dances, sororities, fraternities, clubs, and dating. There were three favorite spots around Rio for couples—Indian Creek Bridge, Lover's Hill, and the lily pond behind the Rio school. Should that pond ever be drained, there will be found at the bottom a half-empty pint of sloe gin tossed there on a June night in 1936.

7. The World She Left Behind

>   Clubs were the Dramatic Club, Press Club, CCA (College Christian Association—there were no Jews on campus ... plenty of atheists.)
>   Few students had cars and, though hitchhiking for girls was strictly a no-no (honored in the breach), we were guilty of it—never thumbing alone, of course.
>   The restaurant across from Davis Cottage ... owned and operated by "Mom" Sayres, was the place to go for the best sticky buns and hamburgers.... Mom let us all go on the cuff if we had to ... and most of us had to [at] one time or another ... we listened to the radio over there (they were forbidden in the dorm).
>   you were mattered not a damn ... it was what you were. I learned more about human nature than I could have ever learned any place else.[77]

In many ways, it seems LaRue Habercom and Beryl Halley were quite similar: increasingly, throughout the years of 1920–1940, Beryl's old world of southeastern Ohio and her new world of New York were becoming more and more alike.

8

Life After the *Follies*, 1927–1929

Beryl Halley's initial reaction to her sudden dismissal from the Ziegfeld organization could best be described as unabashed anger. Legal recourse came in a close second. According to reporter Grace Cutler, Ziegfeld (or his proxy) "told her in so many [words] to park her gold headdress and leave the show." That the removal came without just cause was indicated by the fact that her name remained on the marquee in Philadelphia and in the printed program when someone else played her part. This, in more modern terminology, constituted a form of "identity theft." Ironically, Katherine Burke, a friend and colleague from *Palm Beach Nights*, now took the role of Montezuma's Daughter. According to reports, Beryl sought $100,000 in damages. Although no notice appeared in her hometown newspaper, the not-far-distant *Chillicothe Gazette* carried a photo bearing the caption: "Beryl Halley didn't marry a millionaire before she left the 'Follies,' so she's suing Ziegfeld for $100,000 because he fired her."[1]

Ziegfeld, never a shrinking violet when it came to giving the media an earful, soon offered his own verbal retaliation. He thought a $100,000 lawsuit bordered on the ridiculous. According to his explanation, Miss Halley left *Rio Rita* voluntarily, perhaps a reference to her absence from the show in Boston. He said, "She was never more than a chorus girl for me," before adding: "Her name was never in lights nor in front of the theatre in any way." Throwing fuel on the fire, Ziegfeld concluded, "As for Miss Burke—she's so much more beautiful than Miss Halley there's no comparison." The latter comment might seem rankingly hypocritical from

8. Life After the Follies, 1927–1929

one whose publicity machine had only days earlier tagged her as "America's Venus." The following day, the ad for *Rio Rita* listed Katherine Burke as "America's Venus." A similar situation continued when the production moved on to Baltimore.[2]

Strangely enough, the entire controversy vanished from public view almost as quickly as it had developed. It seems likely that if Beryl had missed shows in Boston without prior authorization, this placed her in violation of her contract and therefore subject to dismissal. Perhaps she mistakenly thought that she had her boss's approval. One suspects that an out-of-court settlement put an end to the matter without fanfare. Some evidence also suggests that Beryl may have gotten back in "Ziegfeld's good graces by the end of the year."

The "Glorified American Ziegfeld Girl" did not remain unemployed for long. When the cast of *Rio Rita* left Philadelphia for Broadway, the replacement at the Forrest was a variety revue known as *Rufus LeMaire's Affairs*, produced by Rufus LeMaire (1895–1950), one of the less successful Ziegfeld imitators, headed by Charlotte Greenwood (1890–1978) and bandleader vocalist Ted Lewis (1890–1971). The former, a tall Philadelphia native, was best known as an "eccentric acrobatic dancer ... noted for her high kick." *Time* commented that the show was "full of crudely ridiculous skits, awkward clowning (by Charlotte Greenwood), amazing absurdities (by Lester Allen), pretty chorus girls [and] striking ensembles." Her husband, Marion Broomes, had composed the music. Ted Lewis was best known for the song "When My Baby Smiles at Me" and his catchphrase, "Is Everybody Happy?" Like Beryl Halley, he too hailed from southern Ohio, where he was born in Circleville as Theodore Friedman. Another major figure, comedian Lester Allen (1889–1949) had worked for *George White's Scandals*. By the time *LeMaire's Affairs* arrived at Broadway's Majestic Theatre on March 28, Beryl Halley had joined the cast.[3]

The former Ziegfeld star would have plenty of reasons to feel at home in *Affairs*. Other Ziegfeld alums in the cast included Peggy Fears (1903–1994), and the dance team of Mitty and Tillio. Most significant for Beryl was former Follies sidekick Lina Basquette, who had temporarily left the stage to marry Sam Warner of the movie studio family. But after the birth of her daughter, Lina had returned for a brief period as among "the World's Greatest Dancing Stars."[4]

Despite fairly decent reviews, *Affairs* ran just eight weeks, closing on

Beryl Halley

May 19 after fifty-six performances. According to one report, it lost $100,000. At about the same time *LeMaire's Affairs* opened, an investigative news report took a look at the income of Broadway showgirls, mostly those who worked in nightclubs. It concluded that such work resulted in the girls making double (or more) than the salaries they earned through their stage work, taking the dubious position that the "nightclub must pay her twice as much as she earns in the show for her late-hour service." This, then, helps to "increase the girl's popularity ... [and] she becomes what is known in New York as a 'personality.'"[5]

The report goes on to read:

> Take the case of Beryl Halley! Miss Hawley [*sic*] entered the musical comedy field as a showgirl. She received about $50 a week for her services. Then she received an offer to appear in a nightclub. She did! Her particular type of good looks, together with her very daring attire, made such a deep impression on the nightclub revelers that Beryl Halley became a "name." The nightclub was obliged to pay her $200 a week for two hours a night.
>
> Later she was snatched up by no less than Flo Ziegfeld. From him she received another $250 a week, and though a temperamental disagreement ended her contract with him, Miss Halley today can earn $400 to $600 a week without any special effort.[6]

This report, while containing some grains of truth, is also error laden. While Beryl started out in *Tangerine*, perhaps at $50 a week, it is doubtful that she really became a "name" until she became a Ziegfeld Girl. Her second-year contract called for only a $70 weekly salary. Nightclub work frequently was not a nightly engagement, but may have been available only two or three nights weekly. Sometimes, when the girls were not working on the stage, they still might be working in clubs, which likely constituted their sole source of income. Furthermore, rehearsal time paid nothing unless extended for more than four weeks, which producers undoubtedly worked strenuously to avoid.

While Beryl may have been taking in much from nightclub work, she was soon cast in a new play, *Half a Widow*. Beryl, in a more dramatic role, played the character of June Love. The production, set in France during World War I, was said to be a romantic musical. According to reports, producer Wally Gluck had been trying to get the show on Broadway for several years. The principal role went to Halford Young as a U.S. Army captain who marries a young French girl, Babette, "a French inn-keeper's charming daughter," played by Gertrude Lang. Babette's motives, incidentally, are not exactly pure. She believes her American husband will be killed in battle, allowing her to collect his life insurance money and marry her true love, a French soldier. Captain Bob Everett, it turns out, survives the war and Babette decides to stay with him.[7]

A preview was held in August at the Sam S. Shubert Theatre in New Haven before opening on September 12 at the Waldorf, on Broadway. Rehearsals suggested that *Half a Widow* had some racy scenes and received mixed reviews. On the plus side, the *Morning World* called it "excruciatingly funny," with "solemn clowning and eccentric tap dancing" that "brought down the house." The *Herald Tribune* called if "full of good humor, pleasant songs, pretty faces, and nimble dancing." The *Morning Telegraph* said the "music is joy and has the lilt and fancy." Most upbeat of all, the *Brooklyn Eagle* opined that "the chorus is excellently trained and with possibly one exception, the most effective that has appeared in Manhattan for several years. The music is tuneful and sufficiently reminiscent to be both catchy and a bit stirring."[8]

Other reviewers were less kind. One called it "Half a Wiggle." George Jean Nathan dismissed it as "a deadly stupid hoof and yodel show." Another said, "Interest in it after its production was as minimal as that preceding it." Even before it closed after sixteen performances, Burns Mantle of the *Daily News* said in his pre-obituary that *Half a Widow* "had a much more interesting past than present."[9]

In another sense, *Half a Widow* may have been lucky to remain on stage as long as it did. At one point, the unpaid cast refused to perform until they received their wages. After one missed night, tobacco heir R. J. Reynolds, Jr., stepped forth as backer and coughed up $25,000 to pay for the "failed" production to run until its demise, shortly afterward. Despite his best efforts, Walter J. Gluck had a short career as a Broadway producer.[10]

Several weeks later, evidence surfaced in the press that Beryl had resolved her problems with Ziegfeld. The *Daily News* made a brief note in early December that "after a long absence from the stage, Beryl Halley has rejoined the 'Rio Rita' cast." Apparently, she remained through the show's relocation from the New Amsterdam to the Lyric on December 26, and through its closing on March 11, 1928. As her *Rio Rita* days wound down, the *Daily News* reported: "Beryl Halley, of 'Rio Rita,' has decided to change" her name "to Arden Stuart."

Beryl Halley

An undated clipping in her belongings reads that Beryl "at the Lyric Theatre, New York, no longer answers to that label. She has changed her name to Arden Stuart." The *News* credited her decision to confusion "because her name is always mispronounced."[11] This was hardly new, as both names had been that way almost from her birth in Gallia County. The first name being like either "Berr-ill" or "Burl," while the surname was either "Halley" or "Holley" (even her brother's tombstone spells it "Holley").

The name change evidently proved temporary and only one other reference to an Arden Stuart has been located—and one cannot be certain that it refers to the same person as Beryl Halley. A book by Adela Rogers St. Johns, titled *The Single Standard*, addressed the question as to whether both men and women should be judged "by a single moral standard." It includes a case study of "Arden Stuart," probably not her real name. Stuart had lived her life up to that point by the traditional single standard, but would soon be making a decision whether to abandon or keep it. According to St. Johns,

> Arden Stuart is not the aggressive modern woman who thinks solely of a career and "freedom." Nor is she a promiscuous butterfly accepting everything as it comes. She is an extraordinarily attractive girl, and her family is an old established one, her mother a conservative society matron. [If this *is* Beryl, it is true by the standards of rural Ohio.]
>
> Imbued with an intense love of life hating "half-gods, half-loves, half-measures" wanting the cup to be full, whatever it's full of, Arden has the courage to believe in [living] according to the single standard.[12]

Seemingly, Beryl Halley decided that the name she had possessed since birth was more marketable than the new one, as that was how she will be billed in her next Broadway show.

During her second stint with *Rio Rita*, Beryl attracted considerable press attention for her participation in a scientific experiment involving Dr. William Marston, a member of the psychology faculty at Columbia known for his pioneering work with lie detector tests. The *Daily News* ran an article on a forthcoming experiment comparing brunettes and blondes, which was scheduled for January 30, 1928. The *New York Times* ran a lengthy article concerning the results. Marston conducted his "laboratory" at the Embassy Theatre, as follows:

> By elaborate and allegedly delicate instruments known in scientific circles as the sphygmonianometer and the pneumograph, by charts and graphs, and by the

8. Life After the Follies, 1927–1929

simpler expedient of holding hands, Dr. William Marston, a lecturer on psychology at Columbia University, proved yesterday in the presence of a staff of coy press agents, camera men, motion picture operators and columnists that brunettes react far more violently to amatory stimuli than blondes.[13]

Marston showed several hundred feet of film of love scenes from two films, both starring Greta Garbo and John Gilbert, then considered Hollywood's steamiest love team. Using his instruments to determine whether blondes or brunettes, when "subjected to the sensory stimuli," showed more inner emotion to the scenes, the scientist concluded that "in each test the brunettes won—or lost— as the Puritan would insist."[14]

The three blondes in the experiment were Beryl Halley, from *Rio Rita*; Claudia Dell, from *The Three Musketeers*; and Rose Gallagher, a blonde, from *Show Boat*. The brunettes were Jean Ackerman, from *Rosalie*; Peggy Udell, from *Show Boat*; and Patsy O'Day, from *Rosalie*. The entire sextet all worked in Ziegfeld productions at the time. Marston pointed out that the equipment measured changes in respiration and blood pressure, however minute they might be. He concluded that brunettes "enjoyed the thrill of pursuit," but blondes "preferred the more passive enjoyment of being kissed." According to Marston, the girl who displayed the largest extreme variation of highs and lows in the measurements was Beryl's partner Peggy Udell. Numerous onlookers and reporters witnessed the experiments, but

Lucille Fay LeSuer (March 23, 1908– May 10, 1977) was a dancer from Texas who made her way to New York City in the early 1920s. Lucille had two Broadway appearances in 1924: *The Passing Show of 1924* and *Innocent Eyes*. Her looks and talent attracted the attention of MGM officials, and with a name change to Joan Crawford, she became one of the giants of Hollywood. Beryl had this early picture of Joan from her days at MGM, but it is unsigned and undated.

Beryl Halley

one "bright lad," on leaving the theatre, was quoted as saying, "Well, there was a big bunch there all right, but you couldn't see the crowd for the press agents."[15]

Beryl Halley probably did nightclub dancing or perhaps a combination of some club or revue work over the next two or three months. Even before *Rio Rita* closed, the *Brooklyn Eagle* reported on March 15, that "tonight a new revel premieres at the Silver Slipper," where "Beryl (The Beautiful) Halley heads the cast of 27 people, including blondes." The reporter further commented that "eleven thousand dollars was spent for the costumes alone, which is a lot of money, considering as Alkali Ike would say that there don't appear to be none concluding 'Wait till you see.'"[16] (Alkali Ike was a prospector in Texas who later became a comical movie character.)

Much of Beryl's nightclub employment up to this point took place at the Silver Slipper, which, despite its underworld connections, hired numerous respectable and well-known entertainers, including Jimmy Durante, Morton Downey, Sr., and, a little later, Fred Astaire and Ginger Rogers. George Raft, an actor and dancer who seemed to be a "bridge figure" between the entertainment world and the mob, often hung out there. Most likely, the Silver Slipper was where Beryl made the acquaintance of Owney Madden, a noted gangster once described by Mae West as "sweet … but oh so mean."[17]

In spite of Prohibition and frequent raids by "dry officers," enforcement could be quite relaxed at other times, especially on New Year's Eve. On December 31, 1927, the *Times* ran a lengthy piece that began: "It will be a big and costly party tonight when the latest addition to the family of years arrive." Going on to anticipate relative safety from "dry" raids because "Major Chester P. Mills, prohibition director, left last night to spend the week-end at his home in Connecticut and said his men contemplated no raids tonight." In addition, Mayor Jimmy Walker issued a dispensation, allowing the clubs to remain open until 8 a.m.[18]

Nightclub operators prepared to let the good times roll—and rake in bigger profits. As a result, most clubs increased their "couvert [i.e., cover] charges" accordingly, and "Liquor is on Hand at Swollen Prices." Some places such as the "Club Anatole" had a charge as high as forty dollars. Texas Guinan's charged "$25, and many of the others, including the Casa Lopez, had but $15."[19]

8. Life After the Follies, 1927–1929

A dry-raid-free New Year's weekend did not necessarily mean an overall relaxation of Prohibition laws. Texas Guinan's various places would continue to be subjected to periodic raids. The second-place honors apparently went to those associated with Helen Morgan (1900–1941), who had first made a name for herself in Chicago. Miss Morgan was a torch singer who sang while perched on a grand piano. She became a virtual overnight Broadway star in the role of Julie in Ziegfeld's production of *Show Boat*, beginning in December 1927. According to the *Daily News*, Morgan had since become so famous that dry officers could gain the most publicity by making raids on her establishments. They answered their own question, "Why Helen?" thusly: "The wise boys say that the government is looking for some first class publicity, and next to Texas Guinan, Helen is the best bet."[20]

In August 1928, Beryl returned to Broadway as one of the principal features in *Earl Carroll's Vanities of 1928*. Carroll had initiated his variety revue in 1923. Of all the Ziegfeld rivals in variety revues, those of Earl Carroll and George White (of the *Scandals*) came closest to matching his popularity. Flo had little respect for either and especially detested Carroll, calling one of his productions "one of the filthiest things ever seen in New York," an opinion echoed by a number of critics at the time. Carroll held a different opinion, of course. One story goes that he thrived because patrons who could not afford *Follies* tickets often settled for the *Vanities*. Furthermore, many of the same performers worked for both men—as well as for George White—over the years.[21]

Earl Carroll possessed a more unsavory reputation than Ziegfeld or White, although how deserved this may have been is open to debate. His only biographer to date, Ken Murray, titled his book *The Body Merchant*. He quoted Carroll, who apparently wrote the following in an uncompleted autobiography, about his work as a producer:

> Girls are a commodity the same as bananas, pork chops, or a lot in a suburban development. They are the most fundamental of all commodities. Girls like to admire beautiful girls, and men unquestionably do, and they will all pay for this pleasure. Of course, this leads to my making money, thus satisfying my material as well as artistic desire.[22]

Like him or hate him, Earl Carroll had led an atypical life in the thirty-five years before Beryl went to work for him. A Pittsburgh native, he finished high school at seventeen, where he had spent much time hanging

Beryl Halley

around, and sometimes working, in area theatres. Desiring to see the world, he took a job as a cabin boy on a ship bound for Manila, in the Philippines. From there he journeyed to British Hong Kong, then to China where he sold Bibles, and visited some other foreign lands before returning home upon learning of his father's death. Both before and after World War I, he wrote song lyrics on Tin Pan Alley. Becoming an airplane pilot after enlisting in the service, he married a French girl while on overseas duty, but his marriage soon failed and he returned to New York after his discharge. With a little luck and financial support, he staged his first *Vanities* revue in 1923, which ran for 204 performances.[23]

Beryl Halley's personal opinion of Earl Carroll—who had spent six months in Atlanta Federal Prison in 1927 for violation of Prohibition laws—was not recorded. But the promise of a successful run in the *Vanities* looked more hopeful than that of either *Rufus LeMaire's Affairs*, *Half a Widow*, or the brief notoriety that came with *The Bunk of 1926*. Besides, it did not seem unusual for girls to shift from the *Follies* or the *Scandals* to the *Vanities*. In addition, her salary had jumped to $200 weekly, more than twice what she was earning with Ziegfeld only four years earlier. At any rate, the press seemed celebratory regarding both the return of the *Vanities* and Beryl's return to the Broadway stage.

> Saint Earl of 7th Ave. will stage a comeback tomorrow night after two years where he plants his seventh edition of "Vanities" at the Carroll theatre with a regiment of American beauties ranging from Miss Hohokus to Miss Western Hemisphere. Among the shapely ladies who will exhibit their professional talents are Dorothy Knapp..., called the most beautiful girl in the world, including the Scandinavian, and Beryl Halley, modestly known as the American Venus. Some of the bewitching houris are drawing as much as $325 a week, for Mr. Carroll believes in supporting them in the Hispano-Suizas and duplex apartments to which they have become accustomed.[24]

According to a lengthy piece by Burns Mantle in the *Daily News*, Carroll's recruitment of acts for his new *Vanities* had agitated "the Beauty Market" by paying girls more than did either Ziegfeld or George White. He claimed that some girls signed by Earl later, tore up their contracts after being pressured by their old bosses.[25] Whatever transpired, "Saint Earl" still managed to assemble a competent cast for his revue.

If that were not enough, other former Ziegfeld associates were on the Earl Carroll payroll. These included Louise Brooks, Ray Dooley, W. C. Fields, and Dorothy Knapp who took "a shine" to the producer (and vice-

8. Life After the Follies, 1927–1929

versa). Beryl would also be working under the same roof with her occasional boyfriend and escort, Vincent Lopez, who would be in charge of the music.[26]

The *Daily News* had positive things to say about the sketch performed by W. C. Fields in which he gave an "imitation of five Scotchmen in a British railway carriage." He also won plaudits for "praying for strength when, attired as Brigham Young in flaming red pajamas, he knelt beside the bedside of ten or twelve palpitating wives." One of the wives, "Beryl Halley, who became famous for nude posings, will not pose for any Vanities photographs any more unless fully clothed."[27]

In addition to veteran performers like Fields, newcomers who became Halley's friends also joined the cast, such as future Ziegfeld Girl Faith Bacon. Another future

Film director Malcolm St. Clair (May 17, 1897–June 1, 1952) signed this picture "To Beryl, Best Luck to You Always," in 1930.

star, an eighteen-year-old, up-and-coming songstress named Lillian Roth, considered Beryl a mentor. Lillian recalled over a quarter-century later: "I had the 'Vanities' to thank for Beryl Halley, 'the Form Divine,' one of Mr. Carroll's featured show girls. [When] she took me under her wing, I weighed 135 pounds. Beryl who was my height [5'3"] weighed only 118. The reason for the difference wasn't hard to find." Roth went on to explain that she put her maid on a special assignment: "Every few hours she vanished in the direction of the corner soda fountain and returned with a hot fudge sundae or a banana split, buried in whipped cream."[28]

One day, Beryl came into her dressing room, watched briefly as the singer devoured one of her sundaes, then said, "Lillian, you disgust me." She went on to say that she thought the eighteen-year-old had leading

Beryl Halley

lady potential if she would slim down. Lillian retorted "flicking a blob of whipped cream off [her] nose that she was just a singer—like the hefty Sophie Tucker and Belle Baker—that Earl Carroll had the girls like her 'to be beautiful.'" Beryl said, "Take a good look in the mirror." You could be more "if you wouldn't stuff yourself like a little pig."[29]

Roth decided to take her mentor's advice and "went on a diet under" Beryl's "guidance" of "apples, oranges and lamb chops." Before many weeks had passed, the food intake, together with a "vibrating machine for the girls" that Carroll had installed in the rehearsal room, Lillian's weight equaled that of Beryl's. And, sure enough, within a couple of years' time she had indeed become a leading lady. A little later, unfortunately, she developed a serious drinking problem which virtually destroyed her career and almost her life. Finally, she got her problems under control, rejuvenated her career primarily as a nightclub singer, and wrote a best-selling autobiography, *I'll Cry Tomorrow* (1954).[30]

The *Vanities* ran for some two hundred performances before closing on February 2, 1929. Reflecting on the significance of the last edition in the decade, Samuel Leiter pointed to the comedy of the veteran Fields and a Broadway newcomer, the "stuttering comedian Joe Frisco." Another highlight came from "an array of gorgeous corybantes [that] included many beauty-contest winners, from Miss Universe to Miss Brooklyn, and Carroll boasted that the girls earned the highest salary of any similar entertainers in the history of the theatre. Much flesh was shown, and Dorothy Knapp and Beryl Halley were the two most prominent exhibitors of it."[31] The *Vanities* would subsequently run for four more seasons over the next eleven years, but that would be Beryl Halley's only season with Carroll. In fact, as far as can be determined, it would be her last appearance in a Broadway production.

Beryl's dancing career, however, continued for a time. On February 23, in partnership with Richard Varell, and advertised as "formerly of Ziegfeld Follies ... in High Class Ballroom Dancing" Beryl opened at the Nixon Restaurant in Pittsburgh. Local celebrity "Dick Ware, Master of Ceremonies," billed sometimes as "The Boy with a Million Friends" and "Harry Hoffman and His Orchestra," rounded out the bill. Halley and Varell did two shows nightly, at 7:30 and 11:30. Respective dinner and supper were also served at those times. This program apparently continued for four weeks, as the press reported in mid–March: "Richard Varell

8. Life After the Follies, 1927–1929

and Beryl Halley, who came to the Nixon café from the Amsterdam Theatre, New York, with their classical ballroom dance numbers, will continue this week "with Harry Hoffman and his orchestra" and "Dick Ware as master of ceremonies."[32]

Similar opportunities came knocking. In July, the Stockton Hotel in Sea Girt, New Jersey, opened their new ballroom with a crowd of "approximately 1,000," including Garden State Governor Morgan F. Larson among the well-wishers, and exhibitions consisting of "specialty dances [that] were given by Miss Beryl Halley, dance star of 'Rio Rita,' and her partner Richard Nardell [sic]." Another appearance took place in August at a Veteran Wireless Operators Association banquet in the Yacht Room in the Hotel Astor, where "Berl [sic] Halley, dancer, and other Broadway and radio stars will be present to provide entertainment for the assemblage."[33]

Beryl also branched out into the medium of radio, which had barely existed when she first came to New York. Station WOR, in Newark, New Jersey, first carried a notice in their daily logs for *Beryl Halley, a Beauty Chat*, a five-minute program at 11:30 a.m. Sometimes called *Beryl Halley's Beauty Tips*, the program continued well into the following year.[34]

A common belief was that many Ziegfeld Girls married millionaires. While a handful did, the theory was largely a myth. Once reaching their expiration date at

After her involvement with *Earl Carroll's Vanities of 1928*, Beryl moved on as a featured dancer in clubs on the East Coast. She is pictured here with frequent dance partner Richard Varell.

Beryl Halley

age thirty, many showgirls began to think of new careers (or husbands) to pay their bills. Bernice Ackerman fell into this category. The beauty from Kansas had gone on to be a co-star in the Marx Brothers stage-version of *Animal Crackers*. On December 9, 1928, she married a commercial artist, Lester Martin, in a ceremony at the Barbizon Club, with the Marx Brothers as witnesses. Beryl Halley remained single for a few more years, but when she did marry, Bernice Ackerman would be her witness and matron of honor.[35]

By 1930, Beryl was serving as a dance hostess at the Club Plaza in the Plaza Hotel in New York City. As the Great Depression settled over the United States, she would soon be working primarily as a stenographer and private secretary.

Historian Lewis Erenberg notes that "chorus girls were symbols of the single working urban woman." Yet the myth of the glorified Ziegfeld Girl usually did not fit their original dream. While a few married into wealth and lived happily ever after, most did not. In spite of the glamour of their jobs, the hours were long, rehearsals paid nothing, and marriage actually served as their best hope for long-range stability. Once you passed thirty, your days of glorification were numbered—unless you had some special talent, such as singing or performing comedy.

Dancing in a chorus line could get you only so far.[36] In 1928, no one thought much about the state of the economy, but that too would change and hang over Broadway like the proverbial dark cloud.

8. Life After the Follies, 1927–1929

In October, Walter Winchell reported in his widely read column that something of a renewal of the Halley-Lopez romance was taking place. Ironically, that would be the last press mention of the two in the same sentence. Before October ended, other events would bring about changes that would profoundly impact not only the Broadway scene, but all of America.[37]

9

Surviving the Depression, 1929–1933

The stock market crash, while dramatic enough on its own terms, did not mean the populace woke up the following morning to say, "We are now in the Great Depression." However, it did signal the start of what developed over the next several months, and did not improve much over the next several years. From a stock market high of 452, it fell to 224 by November 13. With slight fluctuation, it hit its lowest, at 58, on July 8, 1932.[1]

Since through most of 1929 the economy had been strong, average unemployment for the year was only 3.2 percent. It had been under 3 percent for the first ten months. However, for 1930, the average rate climbed to 5 percent. In 1933, it had been estimated at 24.9 percent. Manufacturing declined, farm prices fell, and national income declined, and with some fluctuations, overall conditions remained at near-misery level. Such consumer items as books and phonograph records were now considered luxury items, beyond the means of the average American. In politics, the national Republican sweep of 1928 turned into something quite different in 1930 and 1932. President Herbert Hoover, initially thought of as the engineer and technocrat who could keep the country running smoothly, soon became the brunt of jokes. For instance, shack and shanty towns on vacant spaces or on the outskirts of cities became known as "Hoovervilles"; empty pockets turned inside-out were called "Hoover flags." Even with agricultural commodities selling cheaply, many town dwellers had little cash to buy food, even at reduced prices. Since many persons could no

9. Surviving the Depression, 1929–1933

longer pay property taxes, local governments, generally responsible for helping the needy, had no funds. Charities had their resources strained to—or even beyond—their breaking point. City dwellers, dependent on non-existent wages, and those already at the bottom of the economic scale, tended to take the hardest hits. Country boys who had moved to the city lost their jobs and moved back to the farm, but at least they did not starve, even if a diet of potatoes and turnips was not especially appealing. At first, entertainers tried to build up confidence with songs like "Happy Days Are Here Again" in 1930, but by November 1932, the defining song of the time became "Brother, Can You Spare a Dime?"[2]

For Beryl Halley, the once-plentiful jobs in shows, clubs, and the occasional movie became more sporadic. In addition to a declining economy, her age was increasingly becoming a factor. Richard Masseck in "About New York," noted, "Show girls, such as Joyce Hawley, Beryl Halley and Dorothy Knapp, have their big years before people begin asking what became of them, but it's harder for a dancing team to cause even momentary sensation."[3]

The bottom had still not yet dropped out when the November issue of *The Dance Magazine* went to press. Among the key features, it contained an illustrated article on a new arrangement of the foxtrot called "The Rhythm Glide." Illustrating this were eight photographs of Beryl and dance partner Barry Nordell (who may or may not have been the same person as Charles Varell and Richard Nardell) demonstrating the dance.[4]

On April 17, 1930, the one-time Broadway girl began an engagement at a club, possibly in Brooklyn. Weekly columnist Rian James noted in the *Eagle* that he had gone "to the Dome on 8th St., for the premiere of Beryl Halley, who looks swell in a new hair comb, and Ray Sadler, and to find the crowd both small and dull."[5] A year or two earlier, she would have packed the place, but conditions had changed.

A couple of deaths in 1930 likely affected Beryl, but there is no way to measure their impact. Back in Gallia County, Samuel Halley passed away from pneumonia on February 26. He was eulogized as "a highly respected citizen" with two surviving daughters "Beryl of New York and Cecil [sic] of Youngstown." Whether Beryl attended the funeral or even sent flowers is not known. As he died without leaving a will, she received one-third of his estate. Although hardly wealthy, Sam Halley owned some World War I bonds valued at about $4,500, a house and lot in Eureka

Beryl Halley

valued at $1,200, and "notes, etc.," bringing his total worth to $9,510. Assuming that Melissa and Paul continued to occupy the Eureka property, any outstanding debts were paid out of this. Melissa now served as Paul's guardian as he had been ruled "incompetent." His share became part of a trust fund, although he received from it five dollars weekly. Cecile and Beryl each received a third of the remainder, which may have been somewhat more than her $1,500 share from the war bonds. Beryl signed the document, and as there is no witness signature, she may very well have returned to sign it.[6]

A few months later, Ernst VanDuren, the celebrated European dance partner of Edmonde Guy and portrait artist, took his own life, an incident that received worldwide press coverage. Beryl held onto the Van Duren portrait until she died. (Today, it adorns an honored spot on a wall in the University of Rio Grande Archives.)[7]

Beryl may have spent much of 1930 on the road, as efforts to locate her in the 1930 Census have not been found. She may have been working outside of New York and missed the census enumerators. In August, Mark Barron, in his "A New Yorker at Large" column, asked the question: "And whatever became of Beryl Halley, who won fame by wearing only a fig leaf in 'Bare Facts of 1926' [sic]? She was hailed as Broadway's most beautiful showgirl and her picture was in every newspaper. But she took her scrapbook of clippings and disappeared."[8]

Barron thought she had vanished, but that was hardly the case. The king of "celebrity gossip," and "dirt digging," Walter Winchell, located her in Atlantic City some weeks later. He wrote: "Beryl Halley, once America's Venus, [is] ballrooming with a partner in Evelyn Nesbitt's night shack in Atlantic City." Nesbitt, a chorus girl in the early decades of the 20th century, was a figure in the love triangle that involved her eccentric millionaire husband Harry Thaw and lothario architect Stanford White, which ended with the latter's death in 1906. Nesbitt's notoriety lasted for a quarter-century. Beryl's stay there lasted for several weeks as Winchell continued a month later with: "BERYL HALLEY, whom Ziegfeld once billed as America's Venus, says the title stamped her merely as a beautiful femme and 'that isn't enough.' ... Now, there is something to cope with. But Beryl has been Laying 'Em Cold with her dancing at Evelyn Nesbitt's jernt [i.e., joint] in Atlantic City."[9] So, for at least a year after the crash, Beryl Halley remained prominent as a showgirl—she was simply a less active one.

9. Surviving the Depression, 1929–1933

If the deepening decline in the economy posed tough times for Beryl, it proved even more challenging for her former employer. This derived largely from the fact he had so much more to lose—and he did. The "Great Ziegfeld" had always been a gambler and a risk taker. Although at times he had lost thousands of dollars in a night at the casino tables, his wife's threat to leave in February 1924 managed to curtail—but not entirely eliminate—this habit.

On the other hand, risk taking was a prerequisite for Broadway producers. Ziegfeld had acquired—justly so—a reputation as the greatest showman of his time. This all but guaranteed that he could find financial backers for his projects (very little of his own schemes were backed with his own money). Some of the biggest successes in the theatre district had been his: *The Pink Lady* (1911–1912), *Sally* (1920–1922), *Kid Boots* (1923–1925), *Rio Rita* (1927–1928), *Show Boat* (1927–1928), *Rosalie* (1928), and most of the annual *Follies* (1907–1931), could all be called hits. *Whoopee!* (1928–1929), still playing at the time of the crash, did quite well, starring the reliable Eddie Cantor, and elevating Ruth Etting to major stardom. Although *Rio Rita* had been a real financial success, yielding a half-million dollars in profits, many of the hits failed to make much money because of their high production costs. Other Ziegfeld productions could be deemed modest successes.

The producer also had his share of box-office flops: *Miss 1917*, which, despite good reviews and such stars as Marion Davies and Irene Castle, could not be saved; *By Pigeon Post* lasted through only twenty-five shows in 1918; *Smiles* (1930–1931), had a line of stars that included Adele and Fred Astaire, Eddie Foy, Jr., and Marilyn Miller (who, in all fairness, had severe health problems throughout the run), but failed to last two months. Other failed productions ranged from *The Rescuing Angel* (1917) to *Betsy* (1926).

In 1927, Flo also began investing in the stock market, where, after the crash, many of his investments vanished. A merger with Hollywood mogul Sam Goldwyn did not work out very well. By mid–1932, his credit and confidence gone, Ziegfeld's health broke down. His wife, Billie Burke (1885–1970), a noted stage and film actress in her own right, used most of her own savings to keep her husband's ventures afloat, albeit without success.

Florenz Ziegfeld passed away on July 22, 1932. His safe contained two five-dollar bills, while only one of several bank accounts had anything in it: $2,773.05, in the Citizen's Bank in White Plains. His widow, a strong-willed survivor, continued on with a distinguished career as a "feather-brained, twittery comedienne" in such films as *Dinner at Eight* (1933), *Topper* (1937) and *Topper Returns* (1941). Her best-known role was as "Glinda, the good fairy," in *The Wizard of Oz* (1939). This enabled Billie and daughter Patricia to live a comfortable if modest lifestyle, and pay off most of the family debts. She retired in 1960. The widow Ziegfeld did not manage to save Burkeley Crest, the estate at Hastings-on-Hudson, where they had lived in the glory days. It sold at auction in 1940 for less than 20 percent of what it had cost to build.[10]

Ziegfeld's principal rival, Earl Carroll, despite numerous setbacks, weathered the storm of the Great Depression. He did make at least one glaring mistake by starring his new girlfriend, Dorothy Knapp (a close friend of Beryl's), in what would have been his biggest production yet. *Fioretta* told the story of an Italian peasant girl who loves a count. The problem for the production stemmed from the fact that Knapp was not a singer. The presence of other Ziegfeld alums, the ever-popular Fanny Brice and Leon Errol, was not enough to save it. Badly panned by critics from day one, it closed after 111 performances and lost an estimated $300,000 to $350,000, the biggest loss in Broadway history up to that time. Carroll's romance with Knapp also ended and he found a new girlfriend in another showgirl, Beryl Wallace, with whom he remained until his death in 1948.[11]

Undeterred by the failure of *Fioretta*, Carroll and the *Vanities* had a successful season in 1930, running for 204 shows. However, both 1931 and 1932 proved to be failures as the depression had deepened. Although the 1931 edition ran for four hundred performances, Carroll dropped the ticket prices so much that it still lost money. The latter revue closed after eighty-seven performances. It did, however, introduce to the public Milton Berle and Bob Hope.[12]

Economic decline continued to have an impact on the Broadway scene. Cleaning up some of the "off-color" shows seems to have been one such change. An Associated Press report by Mark Barron contended: "Broadway has solved its own censorship problems." The former "scarlet pathway to Babylon five years ago now is suffused with purity, sweetness and lightness," causing "the reformers [to] have relaxed their sentinel duty upon the theatre." Citing as evidence, he noted that the most popular play

9. Surviving the Depression, 1929–1933

of 1930, *The Green Pastures*, had a biblical theme. There was also the "drama of literature's sweetest romance," *The Barretts of Wimpole Street*. Barron concluded that Broadway "has become spotless."[13]

Not much information surfaced on Beryl Halley in 1931 until December, at which time she was spotted at Nils Granlund's Hollywood Restaurant. The latter had given up on nightclub management and opened a first-class establishment at 44th and Broadway, which he ironically named after the theatre world's film rival. The *Daily News* noted that "Beryl Halley's body [is] now subbing for Marian Martin's at the Hollywood restaurant…. Miss Halley, who used to do nudes for Carroll and Ziegfeld and who hasn't been seen around these parts for a year, was called in to do nudes for Miss Martin, who has a cold."[14]

While there were no more lengthy accounts of Beryl's showgirl activities, she still rated mentions now and then. For instance, in an interview with former Ziegfeld press agent Bernard Sobel he discussed a favorite topic when the *Follies* came up for discussion, female legs. Sobel named his top ten, which included Beryl Halley among the leading Ziegfeld Girls.

Others on the list included the most famous of all, Marilyn Miller; Beryl's friend Flo Kennedy; fellow *Palm Beach Nights* co-star Edmonde Guy; and Katherine Burke, who took Beryl's spot in *Rio Rita* when Ziegfeld terminated her in Philadelphia.[15]

The death of Flo Ziegfeld brought out memories of his famed *Follies* from past years. Mark Barron recalled—somewhat inaccurately—that:

> Beryl Halley was another to encounter trouble with the police censors when she appeared as Eve in a revue in 1926. A patrolman charged that her costume consisted only of a fig leaf.
> Miss Halley went into obscurity for a time, but soon Ziegfeld brought her back to the footlights as the girl with the most perfect figure. The stage had not been too kind to her, however, and today she is a stenographer.[16]

Barron must have had a faulty memory since Beryl had worked for Ziegfeld both *before* and *after* the "fig leaf" incident. It also omitted the fact that her case had been dismissed in court. Another press notice came in a gossip column in the *Daily News* that "Beryl Halley and that medico have turned up the heat."[17] Apparently her off-and-on romance with Vincent Lopez had faded and she was now dating a physician. That seems to have been the last time her name appeared in the metropolitan media for 1932.

Beryl Halley

Ziegfeld also received attention back in Gallia County, Ohio, where the *Tribune* reported that "his death has shocked and saddened the theatrical world." The local paper also recalled: "Beryl Halley is the girl referred to, and the other names as typically Ziegfeldian are Gladys Glad and Dorothy Knapp. Beryl was born and reared at Bladen. She is a daughter of the late Samuel Halley and her mother is a sister of Col. J. S. Porter of Lexington, Ky. Bernard Sobel, the producer's press agent—O. O. McIntyre was Ziegfeld's press agent for a year or more about a decade ago—says: 'The typical Ziegfeld Girl is tall, statuesque, with a well rounded figure and extreme perfection of line and face. Ziegfeld disliked the flapper type and the over-dieted girl.'"[18]

Eight days later, the *Tribune* waxed eloquent again on their local connection to the Broadway legend. Their writer said that "of all the American beauties 'glorified' by the late Florenz Ziegfeld, Beryl Halley, born in Bladen and educated at Rio Grande, is acclaimed as 'the girl with the most perfect figure, by New York dramatic writers.'" The *Tribune* also stated that although Beryl Halley may have then been working as a "stenographer," other Ziegfeld Girls had fallen on even more difficult times. The leading example, Imogene "Bubbles" Wilson, touted as "the most beautiful glorified girl ever," "plunged into the scandal" that ruined her own and Frank Tinney's Broadway careers, followed by "a long exile in France and Germany." The paper concluded that "ill luck continues to pursue ... Bubbles." The other unfortunate, Jessie Reed, married twice to what she thought "were wealthy men, only to learn both times that her husbands were poor," but became the first Follies star whose daughter became a second-generation Ziegfeld Girl.[19]

The mention earlier that Beryl had abandoned her show business career took place the following February, when O. O. McIntyre offered a confirmation of what Barron wrote seven months before, briefly noting that "Beryl Halley, once a Ziegfeld beauty from Gallipolis, O., has become a private secretary."[20]

Whether young ladies work as stenographers or private secretaries, they do not make the entertainment pages, gossip columns, or society sections. Thus did Beryl Halley virtually vanish from the Broadway scene. The next time she attracted any attention came a few months later, when she walked down the aisle.

10

Marriage and the Ziegfeld Girls Club, 1933–1941

Beryl Halley's press drought came to a sudden end in October 1933, when the *New York Daily Mirror* ran an article headlined "Beauty Secretly Weds." A few days later, a page-one piece in her hometown *Tribune* read: "Beryl Halley, This County's Most Famous Beauty, Weds." Outside of the New York theatre district and Gallia County, Ohio, most people were too busy either working or looking for a job in the depressed economy to pay much attention, but in those two locales, it did constitute as news.[1]

The *Tribune*, quoting the *Mirror*, related the story:

> Beryl Halley, former Ziegfeld dancer … said goodbye to the stage and all that sort of thing Sept. 30, it was learned yesterday (Tuesday) when she became the bride of Chester O. Falkenhainer.
> Falkenhainer, an executive of the Travelers Insurance Co., and the dancer were married in the Ridgewood, N. J. Methodist Episcopal Church. The ceremony was attended only by Bernice Ackerman as matron-of-honor and A. V. Kerr as best man. For several months, Beryl has not been seen on Broadway but has been occupied mysteriously. She won't say how.[2]

The *Tribune* reminded readers that the former Miss Halley was a Bladen native, whose mother still lived there; that she had attended Rio Grande College, and gone to New York, where she became "famous overnight [an exaggeration]." Bernice Ackerman, Beryl's witness, was herself a one-time Ziegfeld Girl, originally from Kansas, while Archibald V. Kerr, a longtime Falkenhainer friend and sometime roommate, also worked in insurance.[3]

Chester O. Falkenhainer was an Algona, Iowa, native, born July 28, 1900, and like Beryl, a World War I veteran, but of the U. S. Marine Corps.

Beryl Halley

His family had been part of the great migration of persons who left the German states for the U.S.A. in the 1840s as a result of the economic and political upheavals. While a large share of these migrants settled in such Midwestern cities as Cincinnati, Milwaukee, and St. Louis, many others settled in more rural areas, from Ohio to Iowa. He finished high school in 1917. Attending college, he obtained a B.S. degree from Columbia University in 1922. During the summer months, he seemingly worked for a shipping firm—A. H. Bull & Co.—that operated between New York City and a variety of locales, ranging from Porto Rica, Santo Domingo, and a variety of West African, Mediterranean, and Black Sea ports. In 1930, the census enumerator listed him and Kerr as residing at Apartment 9, 130 Wark Place, in Manhattan, and employed in the field of insurance. From time to time in the 1930s, Chester spoke at his alma mater on various facets of the insurance business. He eventually rose to the post of branch manager of Banker's Life Insurance (later Principal Financial Group) in New York City. In 1938, he was named "as #2 in the country in writing new business."[4]

A native of Iowa, Chester Otto Falkenhainer would serve in the Marine Corps in World War 1. He graduated from Columbia University and went on to become a successful insurance executive. On September 30, 1933, he married Beryl Halley in the Methodist Episcopal Church of Ridgewood, New Jersey. Thus began a relationship that would run the gamut from bliss to distress.

Son Chet has no idea how his parents met. But if Beryl had engaged in office work, it seems likely that they met somewhere in connection with his job. Although the bridegroom was three years younger than his bride, he apparently did not know that as Beryl had—in typical showgirl fashion—reduced her age.

10. Marriage and the Ziegfeld Girls Club, 1933–1941

Following their nuptials, not much more was heard from the Falkenhainers for a time. They settled into a residence at 400 East 57th Street. In 1935, the couple took a vacation in Bermuda via the ship *Monarch* of Bermuda. Later that year, the couple relocated to 17 East 38th Street. Still, her name popped up in occasional news columns in "'Round About New York." George Tucker wondered what had happened to Beryl Halley, the girl "wearing nothing but a [fig] leaf ... billed as the girl with the most perfect [figure] in the world." Tucker wrote, "I don't know where she is today, but for a while, after her brief hour before the footlights [actually most of the 1920s], she earned her living in New York as a stenographer."[5] Nonetheless Beryl's Ziegfeld connections would never disappear, nor would her legendary employer.

Florenz Ziegfeld had hardly been laid to rest before a wave of what might be termed "*Follies* nostalgia" hit the entertainment world, not just on Broadway and in Hollywood, but elsewhere. With the authorization of Billie Burke, new editions of the *Follies* were presented at the Winter Garden Theatre in both 1934 and 1936. Metro-Goldwyn-Mayer had been at work on a major bio-picture to be titled *The Great Ziegfeld*, budgeted at $2 million, and released in April 1936. The picture received reams of publicity, attracted large audiences, received four Academy Award nominations, and won in two categories: Best Picture, and Best Actress (Luise Rainer, for her portrayal of Anna Held). William Powell played Ziegfeld, and Myrna Loy essayed Billie Burke. Yet to many critics, it fell short of really capturing the man and his productions.[6]

Among the fallout from *The Great Ziegfeld* came the organization of a club made up of former "Glorified Girls." It eventually took the name "Ziegfeld Girls Club," but early notices called it the "Follies Alumnae," and its stated objective was to provide assistance to Ziegfeld Girls who had fallen on hard times (after all, the nation was still experiencing an economic downturn). One newspaper called it "a unique society ... comprised of 'glorified girls' who had appeared in one or more of the late producer's revues." Billie Burke gave her approval to the group, and former press agent Bernard Sobel promoted their activities.[7]

Beryl Halley Falkenhainer played a significant role in the activities of the club and served as their secretary for a number of years. One activity they sponsored that first year was a dance to help the "destitute ex–'Follies' girls." To attract more ticket buyers, they announced that Fanny Brice and

Beryl Halley

After the death of Florenz Ziegfeld, the Ziegfeld Girls Club was formed. Beryl would be active in the club, serving as secretary for a number of years. In this picture of the club members, Beryl is seated in the front row, sixth from the left.

Jack Pearl (best known for his comic character Baron Munchausen) would be among the attendees. Spokesperson Caryl Bergman pointed out that "many former Ziegfeld Girls are down and out," adding "we'll be glad to help them, both with money and [in finding them] positions."[8]

A bigger project consisted of a tour of some nine cities in which they presented a *Follies*-like program in large theatres from Detroit, Michigan, to Montreal, Quebec. The revues ran for up to a week at some locales, but most were one-nighters. They opened at the Michigan Theatre on August 12 as *The "Glorified" Follies of 1936*, in which "a bevy of former Florenz Ziegfeld beauties appear together with several topline vaudeville acts."[9]

From Detroit, the glorified girls went to Pittsburgh, where they opened on the 28th. The eight identified Ziegfeld Girls were Beryl Halley,

10. Marriage and the Ziegfeld Girls Club, 1933–1941

Helen Gates, Anita Rice, Christine Sepl, Josephine Russo, Judy Stewart, Bettie MacDonald, and Lenore Masso. The entire cast numbered forty.[10]

The troupe may have taken off a few days before they opened at the RKO in Boston, where they received more publicity. In the New England metropolis, their show was augmented by the addition of the Three Stooges (Larry Fine, Moe Howard, and Jerry "Curly" Howard) to their act. One of the girls identified by name was Caryl Bergman, who had understudied Marilyn Miller (Miller had died on April 7, 1936, from her long-troubling sinus problems), and sang some of the songs from her hit shows. Although the anonymous reviewer showed himself to be a fan of the Stooges above all others, he had to conclude, "All in all, it is a splendid, fast-paced and well-rounded show."[11]

On October 21, in the "Rubber City of Akron the 'Glorified Follies of 1936' offered a reply to the recurring question, 'What became of Ziegfeld's girls?'" The *Beacon Journal* reported:

> A group of them ... are to be seen this coming amusement week at Loew's.... Among those in Akron for this show will be Beryl Halley, known as the "American Venus"; Bettie McDonald of "Whoopee!"; Josephine Russo of "Rio Rita"; Glada Cummings of "Show Boat"; Lenore Masso of "Hot Cha"; Rosamond Du Bose of "The Three Musketeers" and Christine Sepl [or Cepl] of "Simple Simon."
>
> Caryl Bergman, in several Ziegfeld [productions], will present hits from "Sally" and "Rosalie," assisted by Dan McCarthay. Charles Carllile, from radio networks, is in the star singing role with the new company. Also in the troupe are Ondee Odette, Bob Easton, Ruby Lane, Robert Pitkin and the Chester Hale trained chorus.[12]

After opening night, the same newspaper supplied an upbeat review:

> Riding a crest of the interest the screen has revived in ... Ziegfeld ... a group of show girls ... glorified by the great one himself took the stage at Loew's.... Before smartly lighted sets of bright design, a well costumed company presents a pleasing hour-long revue.... If you remember names from the Ziegfeld programs of yesteryears the presentation of Beryl Halley [and numerous others] as show girls will add glamour to the parades.[13]

From Akron, *The Glorified Follies of 1936* moved on to the Lyric Theatre in Indianapolis for a week, with pretty much the same cast. Then, on November 6, the group opened at the Schubert in Cincinnati, where Beryl was the subject of a solo photo in the *Enquirer* prior to the opening, calling her a "decorated damsel" who "goes in for feathers." A later feature erroneously stated: "A real veteran under the Ziegfeld banner is Beryl Halley, a Chicago charmer in a half-dozen of the noted glorifier's revues."[14]

Beryl Halley

The next stop on the tour to Dayton ranked as only a short distance up the highway from Cincinnati. Betty Kern, reviewing the show as presented in the Colonial, said that it "moved along with [a] smoothness that is rarely seen on this vaudeville stage." She added, "The 16 girls in the line work in complete harmony and rhythm, and as for the beautiful girls who do the parading they have nice features and shapely bodies." In addition to complimenting comedian Hal Sherman, vocalist Charles Carlile, and the team of Bob Easton "and his midget friend Ondee Odette," Kern concluded, "There is nothing offensive about any part of the production."[15]

On Thanksgiving week, the show moved on to Chicago, where it played at the RKO Palace. Virginia Dixon and Glada Cummings were added to the cast by this time as Gates and Rice had dropped out somewhere along the way. But Beryl and the others still hung on, although they may have been tiring by this time. In Montreal at Loew's by mid–December, the tour wound up before Christmas. The girls were doing three shows daily, at 3:15, 6:15, and 9:15. At every location the revue shared the theatre with a motion picture, which must have served as a reminder that vaudeville acts and touring Broadway shows, not unlike the Old Gray Mare, "ain't like she used to be."[16]

While some of the Glorified Girls were on the road show, others carried on their cause in N.Y.C. They had a scheduled meeting on September 14 at the Ziegfeld Theatre, but because of those on the tour, the *Daily News* doubted "if any of the girls show up." They remained active, however, scheduling a benefit lunch at Leon and Eddie's restaurant and knowing that celebrities would attract more guests, noting that "Fannie Brice, Evelyn Law, Eddie Cantor and other former Ziegfeld stars are scheduled to attend." Phil M. Daly, writing in *The Film Daily* in January 1937, commented that the "success of the Ziegfeld Girls Club offers striking proof of the constructive benefits to materialize of something that started more or less as a promotional stunt."[17]

The Club girls—just as they did during their halcyon days—found ways to get their names in the papers (probably with assists from Bernard Sobel). One way was spotlighting the contented life of club president Dorothy Brown (Fox), who had become the typical happy homemaker. Miss Brown had been in the 1924 *Follies*, served as an understudy for Billie Burke, and had a part in *Louie XIV* before marrying linen salesman John J. Fox in December 1925. She later returned and had a part in

10. Marriage and the Ziegfeld Girls Club, 1933–1941

Whoopee! before leaving the stage for the final time. With two children, seven-year-old Phoebe and five-year-old Norman, "the contented Flatbush housewife ... moves with the grace of a dancer [in both her] tastily furnished dining room [and] the spotless yellow and white kitchen." Mrs. Fox pointed out that from the proceeds of their June dance, "the club put a chorus girl [who was] down on her luck, back on her feet and fitted her up with a new job—which she got." In closing, President Fox recalled that she had once turned down a motion picture contract because "I couldn't give up Brooklyn, my babies, and my husband."[18]

The girls had their first anniversary reunion in April 1937. It may still have had a charitable purpose, but the Associated Press treated it more as a social event. It pointed out that the club had about two hundred members and that many of the now-married *Follies* alumni brought their children, especially daughters, with them. Those quoted tended toward recalling incidents "from the good old days of ten to twenty years earlier when they were younger and more glorified, or tell old stories about how one girl had called in sick when she was really eloping with her boyfriend."[19]

Meanwhile, Beryl appeared on WOR Radio to plug a fundraiser dance for needy former Ziegfeld Girls. While she joked around a bit, she still emphasized the charitable aspect of the Ziegfeld Girls Club. The former dancer also mentioned that most of the housework in the Falkenhainer home was done by the maid.[20]

A page-long feature in the Sunday supplement of the *Atlanta Constitution* put the focus back on helping the less fortunate among them. Adorned with pictures of Marjorie Levoe and Joan Burgess pushing their young toddlers in baby carriages, it also featured a head-and-shoulder shot of Paulette Goddard—then emerging as one of Hollywood's top glamour queens. But the main emphasis of the article dealt with the plight of "when Mary Nolan [a.k.a. Imogene "Bubbles" Wilson], sick, broken and unwanted, lay delirious on the cot of her cheap room but a few weeks ago," only to be rescued (temporarily, at least) by the Ziegfeld Girls Club. The article implied that other girls had been assisted by the club, but gave no names, as most obviously preferred to remain anonymous.[21]

The piece went on to describe others who had attended a recent meeting at which "Beryl Halley arrived, bundled up in silver foxes, a gift from her wealthy husband Chet Falkenhainer." Other attendees included Louise Andrews, Eileen Wenzel, Marian Martin, Betty Real, Vera Milton, Gypsy

Beryl Halley

Rose Lee, Francis Hartigan (from 1909), Cherry Preiser (still a teenager), and Ruth Etting, not yet thirty and still a star. The officers listed Helen (or Dorothy) Brown Fox as president, and Beryl as vice president (her post as secretary would come later). They also talked about the Hollywood chapter, with Virginia Bruce as president, and Hazel Forbes, Paulette Goddard, Harriet Hoctor, Ruby Keeler, and Ethel Shutta as notable members. In conclusion, it reads, "The girls are loyal to their luckless sisters."[22]

Articles continued to promote former Ziegfeld Girls as contented in domestic matrimony. The *New York Mirror* featured several in a Magazine Section piece. Noting that many had married well, the Social Register still followed a practice of excluding them and their spouses. Among those happily wed were Carolyn Nunder, Phyllis Haver, Mary Duncan, Ruth Taylor, and Blanche Satchell. And there was this mention:

> Stroll down the garden of lovely ladies, and you'll see what we're driving at. Ever hear of Beryl Halley? Probably not. Beryl was one of the first "Follies" beauties. Beryl won quite a place among the sensations in a daring show called "Bunk of 1926" [which was not a Ziegfeld Production].
>
> Well, sir, she married an insurance man, Chester O. Falkenhainer, four years ago, and is happily and not unprominently married, to be sure. The Falkenhainers do not aspire to be upper-bracket social peers, but they furnish a good example of the normality of actress-into-society-housewife transition.[23]

On or about the third of August, Beryl had some company from the old home in Ohio. The *Gallipolis Tribune* carried a brief notice: "Mrs. Melissa Halley and daughter Cecile are visiting their daughter and sister Beryl in New York City."[24] With the possible exception of Beryl, who may have come home when her father's estate was being settled, this could have been the only direct contact with her mother since leaving Ohio to enter the navy.

Continuing with their fundraising in November, the club had a drawing for a Gruen Curvex watch that had been donated and to which "proceeds went to the club fund for needy members." Dorothy Brown Fox and Lenore Masso were pictured in press notices, with the latter seemingly modeling the watch on her wrist. At their next meeting, Beryl and Anita Rice Yorks "offered a toast to the donor" of the timepiece. The club also continued helping troubled "sisters," one of whom was Laverge Lambert, who had been "a victim of the bombings in Shanghai" when Japanese planes attacked the city in 1937. She then fled to the Philippines, where she "was reported desperately wounded and destitute." Club secretary

10. Marriage and the Ziegfeld Girls Club, 1933–1941

Beryl contacted American Consul Henry Day, who reported that Lambert was lodged in a Manila hotel.[25]

In the fall of 1938, *Variety* noted that "Beryl Halley, one of the club's leaders, was operated on for appendicitis recently but has recovered." Beryl's problems apparently ranked as less important than those faced that autumn by Ruth Etting. The latter was involved in a love triangle that also involved her ex-husband, mobster Martin "Moe the Gimp" Snyder, and pianist Myrl Alderman, Etting's paramour. Snyder shot and wounded Alderman, and Etting faced a torrent of bad publicity. The club sent her a thirty-nine-word telegram offering moral support. Beryl, still hospitalized from her own operation, "vowed that Ruth Etting would never lack friends as long as the Ziegfeld Girls' club is in existence."[26] (Etting survived the scandal, married Alderman, retired to Colorado, and later sold her story to Hollywood. The resulting biopic, *Love Me or Leave Me*, starred Doris Day as Etting, James Cagney as Snyder, and Cameron Mitchell as Alderman. Ironically, Snyder outlived both, dying in 1981.)

In December 1938, the club moved beyond the Etting controversies to sponsor a luncheon honoring Patricia Ziegfeld, the now-grown daughter of Florenz Ziegfeld and Billie Burke. In addition to Beryl and the usual group, those attending included Faith Bacon, Neva Lynn, and Eileen Wenzel. The following April, the club sponsored a "Ziegfeld Ball," with Beryl as its primary organizer. Ned Wayburn heaped a great deal of praise on the event, saying to Beryl that "the success of the affair reflects great credit upon you." He added that "your splendid executive ability and always gracious manner ... are 'ace high.'" He also hoped to be able "to have three programs" for future meetings.[27]

In May 1940, Alice Hughes in her "A Woman's New York" column wrote a favorable editorial about their recent ball, co-emceed by Eddie Cantor and George Jessel. She further commented, "Ask father if he remembers Beryl Halley, Agnes Franey and Dorothy Brown Fox." She added "They were all there" and that "proceeds went to the less lucky Ziegfeld beauts who are ill and needy."[28]

The Federal Census of 1940 shows the Falkenhainer Family living at 137 East 38th Street in Manhattan in a rented residence at $125 monthly, where they had been since 1935. Chester was employed as an insurance manager at an annual salary of five thousand dollars. Beryl reported that she had not worked in the previous year and received no income, which suggests that all of her work for the Ziegfeld Girls Club had been on a volunteer basis. In essence, they were living comfortably but not extravagantly. Beryl apparently danced in costume at the 1940 reunion, as a belated photo of her doing so appeared in the *Daily News* in 1947.[29] In the next couple of years, the family, enlarged by one, would depart "the Big Apple" for the suburbs. For the time being, however, they still resided not far from the theatre district.

The spring 1941 annual ball honored Billie Burke, the photos of whom showed a still-glamorous woman. One press release, by Geraldine Smith of the *Philadelphia Inquirer*, offered a sour note by pointing out that some girls either chose not to attend, or indeed were not welcome, Lillian Lorraine chief among them. Another girl, who had married the disgraced lawyer of mobster Dutch Shultz, was also unwelcome. On the other hand, the now-retired Adele Astaire seems to have simply moved on, while Ann Pennington was busy as a dance instructor. Beryl Halley received but scant mention in the article, although she did appear in one photograph. However, her activity in the club slowed down, partly because, on July 22, 1941, she gave birth to Chester Otto Falkenhainer, Jr. Henceforth, her life took a new turn.[30]

Beryl remained out of the limelight for several years. The last evidence of any show business activity took place only days following the Pearl Harbor attack, on December 7, 1941. Back in Ohio, her hometown paper noted: "The former Beryl Halley, Gallia County girl who became famous as a beauty in Zegfeld's [sic] Follies was heard last night in the radio program 'Battle of the Sexes.'" Apparently, Beryl and three other former Ziegfeld Girls—Mary Alice Rice, Billie Aland Hoagland, and Pearl Harris—comprised one of the two competing teams on the popular show. The *Tribune* further stated, "Some years ago she married C. O. Falkenhainer of New York City." Ironically, it would appear that Beryl Halley ended her show business career in a manner similar to the way it had begun two decades before. She played a supporting position to the better-known duo of Frank Crumit and Julia Sanderson. Thereafter, her life would be dominated by marriage, motherhood, and a career as a legal secretary that endured much longer than her career as an entertainer.[31]

11
New York to Texas, 1941–1953

World War II had just been declared when Beryl Halley made her entertainment exit per a guest appearance on network radio in *Battle of the Sexes*. Chester Falkenhainer had passed forty, and with a wife and newborn son seemed unlikely to be called in defense of the country. While the bloody conflict raged in North Africa, Europe, Southeast Asia, and various Pacific Isles, Chester, Beryl, and little Chet remained on the home front in Greater New York City.

Chester Falkenhainer received a promotion with his insurance company employer that enabled his family to relocate to the suburbs. No later than September 1943, they had moved to 10 Eton Crest in Manhasset, part of western Nassau County, near the somewhat better-known city of Great Neck. The town was about forty minutes by rapid transit from Grand Central Station. This was at a time when increasing numbers of city dwellers were seeking the open spaces no longer available in the crowded inner city.

On September 16, 1943, the Executive Committee of the Actor's Fund of America elected Beryl Halley Falkenhainer to a Life Membership. Although unspecified, this honor seems to have been based on her financial contributions to the fund. Along with her notice of election, the former Ziegfeld Girl received a membership card and an embossed certificate. The letter closed with the comment that "the Actor's Fund appreciates your great interest in this charitable work."[1]

Even though Bernard Sobel had left Flo Ziegfeld's employ when the

Beryl Halley

Master could no longer pay him in the winter of 1931–1932, he still managed to push anything connected with the *Follies* and their legendary producer whenever he had the opportunity. In the winter of 1945–1946, Sobel again wrote about the Ziegfeld Girls in *Stage Pictorial* magazine. He turned his spotlight on a number of former Ziegfeld beauties, including the "alluring Gypsy Rose Lee"; Paulette Goddard, then at the pinnacle of her movie career; style expert Mary Alice Rice; advertising executive Gertrude Vanderbilt; magazine writer Louise Baer; and frequent club leader Dorothy Brown Fox.[2]

Sobel gave nearly as much, if not more, attention to Ohio-born Beryl Halley, with so much "exquisite symmetry and distinction" for tableaux, of whom he wrote:

> Beryl Halley was one selected for this apostrophe to beauty, a distinction that brought her [a] high salary, fame and eventual stardom. But mere symmetry did not content Beryl. She wanted to use her mind and talents, prove that she could do much more than stand motionless before an audience. So she studied dancing and soon had engagements in important nightclubs as a ballroom artiste.
>
> "Beryl has made good," declared the boosting Ziegfeld girls, but by this time Beryl had already deserted the dressing room and become a private secretary. Miraculously she learned the seemingly intransigeant [sic] art of letter-writing and became expert in turning out commercial and social correspondence. Competent and well-poised, she did noteworthy work on important assignments.
>
> However, Beryl was not to remain long in the business world. She met one day, a young fellow named C. O. Falkenheiner [sic], a handsome male specimen, duplicate to her own physical perfection, taller, blonder, finely featured and a stalwart go-getter. After several years of married life, the two were joined by an infant son. He came later than most offsprings do, but he does them full credit, lusty and tow-haired, he is destined to be the perfect offspring.[3]

An accompanying photograph of mother and son bore the caption: "The exquisite Beryl Halley was excitingly lovely to look at when she posed daringly in some of Eve's most bewitching adornments. Now she's Mrs. Chester O. Falkenheiner [sic] and very happy indeed with her husband and Junior."[4]

A few months after the Sobel article appeared, Cecile and Beryl's old high school and college friend Helen Martin paid a several-day visit from her home in Little Rock, Arkansas, to visit friends in Ohio generally and to Gallia County in particular. Although the twelve-page letter is undated, the visit took place in late June 1946, and the letter written a few days after the Fourth of July to her twin-brother Hollis's wife in Royal Oak,

11. New York to Texas, 1941–1953

Michigan. Helen visited a number of people in the area and discusses them in considerable detail. Of interest to this study are her visits with Beryl's cousin J. Sherman "Jim" Porter, then working for the *Daily Tribune* and its weekly, *Gallia Times*; Melissa Porter Halley; and Cecile Halley, who was visiting her mother in Eureka from her home in Youngstown.

Relevant excerpts from the letter, with spelling corrected, follow:

> While I was talking to [Ruth Richards at the *Times* office], I asked if Jim Porter was at the office and she said he had gone home to work. Told her about being a friend of Cecile's, and wondered if he would know whether she was home, etc. So she called his house for me, told him what I wanted and he said—"That is who I am talking to now!" So away we went to Jim Porter's house, and there were both Cecile and her mother, and Cecile was tickled pink to see me and of course there was nothing wrong except that she just didn't write. Said she doesn't write to anyone anymore. Anyway, we had a nice visit and she promised to come out to Rio on Monday p.m. Think it was a stunner to her to find I was in Gallia Co. and had expected to leave without seeing her. Mrs. Halley doesn't look much different, but is getting feeble. Cecile had her hair a little yellower and outside of that hasn't changed much. She was leaving the 1st of July for New York to visit Beryl, and she and Beryl were going somewhere in Canada together. Then she will be back to Ohio during August and Beryl and her husband are going to Banff [National Park Iin Alberta] for the month of August. Three cheers for Beryl, but I still like her [feigning jealousy] as much. Poor Mrs. Halley said how much she would like to see that grandchild and I think it is pitiful that Cecile doesn't take her mother over there, and we all recognize that the reason doesn't lie with Cecile, and her refusal to take her mother—so that leaves one guess as to what it is.[5]

The letter proceeds through additional events, leading up to Monday:

> In the afternoon Cecile and Mrs. H. drove out to R. G. and we all went to visit the Fultons.... But May [Fulton, the high school principal when Helen and the Halley Sisters were at Rio Grande] is beginning to look old. She is just as nice and pleasant as ever, interested to hear all about everybody—you Jean, John P. Sometime during the conversation while we were there Mrs. H. let forth with the statement that Beryl was 44 years old when her baby was born. Even Cecile looked embarrassed and I thought how furious Beryl would have been if she could have heard it. That may be one reason she doesn't want Mrs. H. over there. Cecile told me once that Chet doesn't know Beryl's age and their mother would be sure to let it slip.[6]

Apparently, sisters could keep secrets, but mothers and others of Beryl's contemporaries in Gallia County knew things about her age that one might as well maintain a discreet silence about in New York.

The ideal picture that Sobel painted of the Falkenhainer family in early 1946 apparently dissolved during the course of that year. In early

Beryl Halley

Officers
Walter Vincent,
President
Harry G. Sommers,
1st Vice-President
Katharine Cornell,
2nd Vice-President
Vinton Freedley,
Treasurer
Robert Campbell,
Secretary

•

Executive Committee
Charles Dow Clark,
Chairman
Harry G. Sommers
J. Herbert Mack
James O'Neill
Robert Campbell
George Christie

•

Finance Committee
Harry G. Sommers,
Chairman
Vinton Freedley
A. O. Brown
J. Herbert Mack
Marcus Heiman
Jacob I. Goodstein

•

Board of Trustees
Lee Shubert
Frank E. Henderson
Chas. Dow Clark
A. O. Brown
George Christie
J. Herbert Mack
Chrystal Herne
Warren P. Munsell
Sam Forrest
Raymond W. Peck
James O'Neill
Marcus Heiman
Antoinette Perry
Jacob I. Goodstein
Gilbert Miller
Jules E. Brulatour
Reed A. Albee
Alfred Lunt

1619 BROADWAY   NEW YORK

Telephones:
COlumbus 5-6440-6441

New York,
September 17th, 1943.

Mrs. Beryl Halley Falkenhainer,
10 Eton Crest,
Manhasset, L.I.

Dear Mrs. Falkenhainer:

                The Executive Committee of the Actors' Fund of America was very happy to elect you a Life Member of the Fund, yesterday.

                We are enclosing herein a Life Membership card, but an engrossed certificate will be sent you during the course of the next few weeks. These certificates are signed by Mr. Walter Vincent, President of the Actors' Fund, and the Secretary.

                The Actors' Fund appreciates your great interest in this charitable work.

                Sincerely yours,

                (Robert Campbell)
                Secretary

RC:FL

Encl.1

Address all communications to: ROBERT CAMPBELL, Secretary

By the 1940s, Beryl Halley Falkenhainer faded from the public eye. In 1943, she was recognized as a Life Member of the Actor's Fund of America.

11. New York to Texas, 1941–1953

February 1947, Beryl filed a divorce application in Broward County, Florida, against Chester. She gave her address in Broward County where the couple wintered, but gave her husband's address as Nassau County, New York.[7]

Whether or not her divorce had been granted in April cannot yet be determined, but in April she had been in Montreal, because on the 15th, she landed at LaGuardia Airport, listing herself as single, aged thirty-seven [she was actually forty-seven], and gave her place of residence as Fort Lauderdale, Florida. If not already a fact, it must have been by June 4, because the feuding couple received a new license in New York City. However, the ceremony probably was not performed under the thirty-day limit on a New York license. As related, somewhat tongue-in cheek in the *Daily News*:

> As a John Street insurance broker, Chester O. Falkenhainer knows how to figure all the angles. But there was one neatly curved question yesterday on which no underwriter could shed light. Will Chester's blonde ex-wife, Beryl Halley, former Ziegfeld and Earl Carroll dancer, remarry him?
> Late Wednesday the News learned Chester and Beryl visited the Municipal Building and took out a marriage license, and their application revealed that the prospective second-time bride had just divorced her bridegroom-to-be on March 21 in Fort Lauderdale, Fla. Grounds, cruelty.
> But when a reporter called Beryl at her home, 10 Eton Crest, Manhasset, L. I., he found her enigmatic as the Sphinx as to whether the darned paper would be used or dropped into the waste basket.
> "I came back from Florida a little over two weeks ago and Chester asked me if I wouldn't [sic] change my mind," she explained. "He's been after me and yesterday I yielded to the extent of getting a license. You'll notice though, that we didn't say when or where we would be married.
> "In fact, I have decided to put him through a cooling-off [probational] period. The license is sort of like an insurance policy; it says I have 30 days in which to take up the option. Right now I can't say when, where or whether we will be married."
> Their first marriage was solemnized Oct. 16 [other sources gave the date as September 30], 1933, about six years after Beryl's devotion to historical accuracy landed her in West Side Court because she wore only a gilded fig leaf as Eve in a Garden of Eden scene at the Broadhurst. Fortunately for Beryl, the late Magistrate Harry Gordon was a man of inquiring mind. He saw the show and dismissed her holding that her costume was a work of art, no more dangerous than revelations in paint, marble or bronze.
> Beryl appeared in the same or a similar costume seven years ago when the Ziegfeld Follies alumnae (theme song "A Pretty Girl Is Like a Melody") held their fifth annual reunion. She still looked like a work of art.[8]
> In addition Beryl took a short vacation to Bermuda in late August, returning

to LaGuardia Airport on September 2, although the thirty days expired without remarrying yet.[9]

Of his early childhood, Chester Falkenhainer, Jr., says, "I don't remember a lot about the relationship between Mom and Dad because I was only six when they got divorced." He does remember a trip or two to the Polo Grounds to watch the Giants play. He also remembers his father taking him to a Columbia vs. Army football game in the fall of 1947. Of that contest he recalls it "as really special" as "Army under Red Blaik was the national powerhouse" while "Columbia had a zilch rating," but the Lions "pulled off a 21–20 upset, to everyone's amazement." He says, "As far as I recall, it [i.e., home life] seemed to be pretty normal until in 1947."[10]

To further complicate matters, Beryl and Chester applied for another marriage certificate in Broward County on December 30, 1947. This time, they went through another marriage ceremony on January 3, 1948, performed by County Judge Boyd Anderson, who had also issued the license. For the next four or five months, nothing more appeared in print or document. However, the reconciliation failed, and in May, Mrs. Beryl Falkenhainer, accompanied by the nearly six-year-old Chester Junior, traveled westward to Reno, Nevada, already famous as the "divorce capital of the world," to seek another legal split. The estranged husband, meanwhile, filed suit in a New York Court, asking for full custody of the couple's only child.[11]

There followed a cat-and-mouse game, which continued for the next five years. A few months later, the next chapter in the drama unfolded in a courtroom in Vancouver, British Columbia. Several newspapers across the country, under an Associated Press release, carried the following:

> Justice A. M. Manson has ordered the arrest of Mrs. Beryl Falkenhainer, former Ziegfeld Follies and Earl Carroll star, on a contempt of court charge.
> The move yesterday wrote another international chapter in a child custody case.
> Her husband, Chester Otto Falkenhainer, a New York insurance executive, instituted habeas corpus proceedings to secure their 7-year-old son, Chester, Jr. The boy was with Mrs. Falkenhainer when she visited Vancouver recently. The contempt charge was preferred when she failed to appear.
> The ex–Follies star, however, returned to the United States. That left a question as to whether the court order will have any effect, since it is valid only in Canada.[12]

At least two papers opted for a bit more sensationalism. For instance, the *Miami News* referred to Beryl as "a statuesque blonde who appeared

11. New York to Texas, 1941–1953

in several editions of the 'Follies' and other Broadway revues." They added: "She was featured as a nude and several times encountered troubles with the police [once, actually] because of scenes in which she appeared in only a trifle of chiffon or less." The *Des Moines Tribune* had similar comments, adding a reminder of *The Bunk of 1926*. Although not reported at the time, Beryl apparently remarried during her Vancouver junket.[13]

Chet picks up the story from here. "I found out I had a new dad, no sign of the old one and the stability of my life vanished for awhile." The "new dad" was Jim McCormick, and he hailed from Montreal, Quebec, in Canada. To date, not much additional information about McCormick has been learned beyond what Chet remembers. He credits the vanishing stability "because we were always on the move, as I remember living in three different places with her and Jim: Three Rivers, Quebec, San Miguel de Allende, Mexico, and California, until we settled in Houston in 1950." Two reasons account for this frequent relocation. One: McCormick worked in the maritime business as a freight forwarder for various firms; two: "Dad had detectives on her trail after she took off with me."[14]

About his stepfather, Chet recalls: "Jim was twenty years younger than Mom, a small man sizewise (about 5'8", 150–160 pounds), and a fairly nice-looking guy. I never learned any details about how they started the affair and never asked as that was her business. I just figured that it was a younger man/older woman deal and let it go. Jim had a very nice personality and was always a good stepfather to me. I liked him, but never respected him like I did my dad. Lots of times Jim took me down to the port of Houston on business calls on various ships and I got to meet the captain and officers of each ship—kind of a thrill for a young kid!"[15]

Meanwhile, back in Gallia County, ninety-year-old Melissa Porter Halley died. On February 8, 1949, it was reported that "Miss Cecile Vivian Halley, Youngstown school teacher, was en route to Gallipolis today to be at the Holzer Hospital bedside of her mother, Mrs. Melissa Porter Halley, 90, oldest resident of Chambersburg." Elaborating, the *Tribune* continued, "Mrs. Halley was reported to be in poor condition after becoming ill at her home Thursday night" but that "at noon today she seemed to be in good spirits" and "that her son, Paul Halley, is with her." After mentioning Porter kinfolk by name, the report concluded, "Another daughter, Mrs. Beryl McCormick, resides in Nevada."[16]

Mrs. Halley's funeral, held at the Bethel Church near Bladen, was officiated by Rev. Charles Lusher, a well-known local minister, with singing by the Swan Creek Grange Quartet, followed by burial in the hilltop cemetery behind the church. Her will revealed that she owned but little, and "all my personal effects [are] to go to Cecile Vivian Halley. She is to give to my son, Paul Kreuger Halley, any part of personal effects that she doesn't wish for her own use." Beryl, who was not present for either the funeral or settlement of the estate, was mentioned as a resident of 467 Bonaventure Street, Three Rivers, Quebec. Regardless of who owned the house in Eureka, Paul continued to live there until shortly before his own death, in 1971.[17]

After moving to Houston in 1950, Beryl Halley McCormick would live the rest of her life there. Chet Falkenhainer became a fan of the Houston Buffaloes and recalls that his stepfather sometimes took him to see the hometown Texas League team in action. He specifically remembers being taken to a game in the Dixie Series between the Houston nine and the Atlanta Crackers. Still, for his mother, there was probably some realization that Chester Otto Falkenhainer would learn of their location and the custody case would be reopened and that, sooner or later, a permanent resolution would come. In the meantime, although Beryl and Jim McCormick had married in Canada on September 3, 1948, they repeated their nuptials in Houston on January 20, 1951.[18]

Chet Falkenhainer, a child at the time, had no knowledge of what was transpiring behind the scenes. He recalls that during the McCormick residence in Three Rivers, Quebec, Jim took him down to see the ice breaking up on the St. Lawrence. All he knew was that they seemed to be moving frequently and sometimes on relatively short notice. After settling in Houston in 1950, he attended private schools and generally enjoyed his childhood. In retrospect, he believes that the detectives were looking for him and his mother through Jim McCormick's employment, as Beryl was not working at the time. Only when those his father had on the trail caught up with him did he really learn what had been transpiring.[19]

Surprisingly, the showdown did not happen for more than two years. On November 10, 1953, the case was apparently settled—superficially, at least—to the satisfaction of both contending parties. According to the Associated Press report, datelined Houston:

> For five years a New York father hunted for his son. He spent $30,000 in his search.

11. New York to Texas, 1941–1953

In district court here, New York insurance broker C. O. Falkenhainer's effort prevailed. He had found his son, Chester, 12, and will have the boy for several months each year.

Mrs. Falkenhainer, a Ziegfeld Follies beauty of the 1920s, left New York for Reno in 1948 to obtain a divorce, taking Chester. She married Jim McCormick. The McCormicks and Chester lived in Canada, California, and Mexico. They came to Houston in 1950.

Falkenhainer won full custody of his son that year from a New York court. But he still had to find the boy.

His attorneys obtained a writ demanding that the McCormicks produce Chester in court, which they did.

"It's a wonderful day," Falkenhainer said after an agreement was reached that Chester will spend the Christmas holidays and spring and summer vacations with him.

Mrs. McCormick also appeared relieved. "I'm glad to have it settled so that everyone can get some happiness out of it," she said.[20]

The media seems to portray the settlement as a victory for Chester. In a sense, this is true. However, the original court decree in New York had given the father full custody. Yet the Texas court still gave Beryl control of her son for about thirty-two to thirty-three weeks of the year.

12

Texas, 1953–1988

Once the child custody settlement involving Beryl Halley McCormick and her former husband, Chester Otto Falkenhainer, ended, the former Ziegfeld Girl's life entered a relatively calm period. Young Chet spent the school year under his mother's care in Texas, but spent the summer with his dad, initially in New York, but with the passage of time, more of it in Broward County, Florida, after his father retired from the insurance industry. Beryl, now fifty-six (although she claimed fewer years), had fashioned a new career as a legal secretary. She worked for the firm of Butler, Binion, Rice, Cook, and Knapp. This firm, although not one of Houston's "big three" legal entities, still ranked among the larger ones, having a staff of eighty-five attorneys in 1973. According to an article in *Texas Monthly*, "Butler & Binion" as it was known, had "been described as 'a small firm that happens to have a lot of people in it.'" It was formed in the 1940s and did not go "for representation of large corporate clients," although they handled legal work for the Bank of Texas, among other companies. (The company folded in 1999). Her secretary work lasted much longer than her career on the stage and in nightclub floor shows.[1]

According to Chet, his mother worked full-time for one of the senior partners until she was in her late seventies, typed nearly ninety words a minute without error, and could make that IBM Selectric typewriter sound "like a machine gun." She always dressed as "a class act, all the way." She bought her clothes at Nieman-Marcus, owned several pairs of high-end shoes, with Ferragamo being her favorite brand. He says that whenever she went to work or was taken out to dinner, she was "always dressed like she was stepping out onto Fifth Ave. in NYC." She retained fond memories

12. Texas, 1953–1988

of her time on Broadway and spoke often of her experiences, especially with the *Follies* and the acquaintances she made there.[2]

One such trip down memory lane took place in mid–December 1955, when Lillian Roth came to Houston for an engagement at the Shamrock Houston, beginning on her birthday, the 13th. After Beryl and Lillian had performed together in the 1928 edition of *Earl Carroll's Vanities*, Miss Roth's star continued to rise and she made several films for Paramount in Astoria, New York, most notably in the classic musical-comedy *Animal Crackers* (1930), with Chico, Groucho, Harpo, and Zeppo Marx. Then she lapsed into a chronic battle with alcoholism, which for a time destroyed her career, and nearly cost her her life. Finally, after some years in obscurity, she managed to get sober with the help of her then husband, wrote the bestselling autobiography *I'll Cry Tomorrow* (1954), and successfully

Singer Lillian Roth is seated between Beryl and her second husband, Jim McCormick, in 1955.

resumed her career as a nightclub singer. At the time, Roth's comeback had been augmented by an appearance on the popular TV show *This Is Your Life* and an award-winning biopic, which earned Susan Hayward an Oscar nomination for her portrayal of Roth. Lillian, who had always credited Beryl as her mentor, enjoyed their reunion.

The photograph taken at the hotel where Roth appeared is one of those worth the proverbial thousand words. While Beryl and Lillian have only tea or coffee cups in front of them, Jim McCormick has a large bottle of Scotch in front of him and looks to be making the most of the situation. It is also suggestive of the personal crisis that over the next couple of years would engulf his personal life as well as his career in the Texas shipping business.[3]

According to Chet Falkenhainer, "Jim's curse was alcohol." He also commented that he was never physically abusive to either him or his mother. Chet explained, somewhat in his stepfather's defense, that the shipping business was "pretty high pressure and he used to drink himself … insensible on a regular basis." In 1956, "he was hospitalized with cirrhosis of the liver and barely survived." After some time in recovery "he got back on his feet and started drinking again and lost his job." His employer, Biehl Freight Forwarding, had given him more than one chance to reform, but he ultimately failed. Jim and Chet went to the Dixie Series in the fall of 1957, when the Texas League Champ Houston Buffaloes played the Southern Association leading team, the Atlanta Crackers. But not long after, their stepfather-stepson relation deteriorated. Chet, then sixteen, recalled that "after seeing him sitting around the house drinking scotch that my mom was paying for" as well as "all the house and school expenses, I got fed up and told him to either go out and get a job or get gone," giving him thirty days to do so. As a result, "about ten days later [January 15, 1958], he disappeared."[4]

Chet further related, "My mom didn't know where he had taken off to." In April 1959, she filed for divorce, which apparently was uncontested, citing Jim's "excesses, cruel treatment, outrages." Chet continues: "In 1962, she was notified by a hospital in Montreal that Jim had died of liver disease." In retrospect, Chet believes that "Jim was basically a nice man, but a weak one" who "just didn't have the strength of character to deal with the problem that was killing him." As an afterthought, Chet said, "Mom wore the pants in our house, for sure!"[5]

12. Texas, 1953–1988

The only negative event he recalls happened when he was fourteen years old. He was hit by a flying rubber band, landing him in the emergency room. The accident eventually kept him out of the service, for which he was rejected when he tried to enlist in 1961.[6]

Chet attended the private secondary St. John's Episcopal Academy, which, he says, really prepared him for college. Although St. John's dated back only to 1946, it established and maintains a reputation as one of the top prep schools in the country. It counts among its alumni such notables as William Farrish III, who served as ambassador to the U.K. in the first George W. Bush administration, and the late Molly Ivins (d. 2007), a well-known syndicated columnist. Around the same time as Chester, Peter Roussel served in the Reagan administration as a press aide.[7]

Beryl's "old maid" school teacher sister Cecile shed her longtime single status at the age of sixty-two when she married a gentleman named Harold Fitch in 1956; after her retirement, she and Harold relocated from Youngstown to Jamestown, New York. The apartment house in Youngstown where Cecile resided was owned by a family named Fitch, which probably explains how the aging couple met. She maintained close friendships with the older set of Rio Grande friends, including Helen Martin Eaton and the elderly couple Frank and Miriam Allen, who kept a boarding house near the campus. The Allen son, Donovan, was RGC's main financial supporter until the time of his death in 1959. Cecile is known to have visited the campus for a Preparatory School Reunion in 1964, as did her pal Helen, and also an RGC alumni gathering in Florida in 1966. Of course, by that time the campus looked quite different than she would have remembered it. Only Community Hall—built on the site of the old Boarding Hall—and Anniversary Hall, built in 1926, remained from earlier days. The home of Helen Martin and her parents had been demolished and replaced by a new gymnasium. Back in Jamestown, she was an active member of the League of Women Voters, and served as president of the local chapter for a term. As the legal guardian of younger brother Paul, she bought him an automobile (according to Richard James), but that did not work out. She had better luck with a television set, which he watched almost constantly until his death in 1971. At some point in the late-1950s, Cecile also visited Beryl and Chet in Houston. Harold Fitch died in 1981, but Cecile remained in Jamestown until her own death in 1987, subsequently leaving Chet a small inheritance and a larger one to Beryl.[8]

Chet also recalls the summers and holidays he spent with his biological father. He said that he "was always tough but fair with me and I both loved and respected him." The youth also had seasonal work: "I never just sat on my butt and did nothing." One summer, in Manhasset, he had to re-tar the deck over the garage. But other jobs were less strenuous, such as landscape work, which consisted of "mowing lawns and moving dirt." Chester Falkenhainer had remarried in June 1950 to a lady named Claire Breakiron, whom he described as "very nice and kind." At times, he said, his father would drink a bit too much and start complaining excessively about all the money he had spent on detectives to track him and Beryl down, which embarrassed both Chet and his stepmother. When Chet was sixteen, "I finally had enough of that and faced him down about it." After the confrontation, he became more moderate, and the two got along much better.[9]

In the late fifties, Chester and Clair settled in Florida, where they lived their remaining years in Fort Lauderdale. Chester died in June 1962, the same year of Jim McCormick's demise. By that time, Chet had finished his academy education and entered the University of Houston, where he majored in accounting, graduating in June 1964. Two years later he married a nineteen-year-old girl named Stella Amaya, who worked in a veterinarian's office. The couple had a son in 1969, but the marriage ended in 1972. Chet says it turned out be a blessing to have a mother who worked in a major law firm, because some of the lawyers at Butler & Binion assisted him "pro bono." In 1974, he married a Korean woman—nearer to his own age—named Pun Hui, who had become a U. S. Citizen in 1970. Only nine when the Korean War ended, she and her family had suffered tough times in the conflict, but at least survived.[10]

Beryl experienced another memory from her past when, in July 1958, she received a letter from Vincent Lopez. He explained that he was writing an autobiography, tentatively titled, "How I Changed My Life." He wished "to know if you want me to mention your name and the incidents which we were a part of at the time." She apparently consented as a year and a half later he wrote again, giving the new title as "Lopez Speaking" and asking for approval of the passages regarding her. Beryl gave said approval, adding: "This consent is irrevocable." Other than addressing each other by their first names, the exchanges had a businesslike tone, although Lopez did include a color postcard-sized photo of himself, signed on the reverse side.[11]

12. Texas, 1953–1988

Chet spent his working life as an accountant and marketing director, moving from Houston to Austin in July 1992. He has also been a part-time coin dealer. Pun Hui had a college degree from Seoul National University, and took more courses after coming to America. She had a career of her own as a commercial artist with an oil tool company. She later had exhibits and sold several of her works. He says that at some point in the 1970s, the couple decided to live on half of their income and thus have a comfortable and enjoyable retirement, which has worked out well for them. In 2017, the couple took an automobile trip to Chicago, visiting several historic sites associated with Abraham Lincoln. After getting back home, Chet felt exhausted from all the travel and henceforth decided to limit his travel to shorter trips out of the Austin area.[12]

Chester has also been a lifelong fan of the Houston Astros (originally the Colt .45s). He also studies Civil War and Texas history. While familiar with his mother's stage career—especially the Ziegfeld era—initially he knew almost nothing about her early life in Gallia County beyond her sister Cecile's visit in the late 1950s. As far as he knew, her life really began when she became a Ziegfeld Girl. In retrospect, he believes that the main thing he learned from his mother was to make up his own mind and go his own way. Chet also says that he never knew his mother's real age during her lifetime.[13]

Chester Otto Falkenhainer, Jr., lives in Austin, Texas. The apple of his mother's eye, Chet made this book possible with his cooperation, support, and donation of the Beryl Halley Collection to the University of Rio Grande Archives.

As she aged and eventually retired, Beryl lived out her life quietly and peacefully. She kept the electric typewriter she had used at Butler & Binion and continued using it for whatever correspondence she maintained. While she read a great deal, and undoubtedly watched a great deal of television, she didn't participate much in club activities as she had done with the Ziegfeld Girls Club. Chet says that his mother's early life was dominated by the Ziegfeld years and her later life centered on him. Reflecting back, his main criticism of his mother came as a result of her beliefs that Chet should pick a higher quality of friends while he, being somewhat more egalitarian, tried to accept people based on their character, more than their social and economic background.[14]

A son, Chester Otto "Rooster" Falkenhainer III, born on May 25, 1969, served in the Gulf War as a combat photographer. Having retired as a colonel on disability, he resides in Houston. His recollections of his grandmother tend to be positive but somewhat limited as his parents divorced when he was only three. However, he added with a bit of modern terminology, "My Grandmother is the REAL Rock Star, and I adored her."[15]

As for Beryl, she remained in good health and of sound mind until the last few months of her life. Chester recalls that well into her eighties, she usually did an hour of stretch exercises daily. She moved two or three times to different apartments, and had her driver's license renewed at age eighty-nine. However, her last move proved to be her undoing. Settling in her new residence, she fell over a box of still-unpacked possessions and suffered a broken hip. Not realizing that she sustained a fracture, Beryl drove herself to the emergency room. A hip-replacement surgery did not go particularly well. After that she went downhill fast and spent her last weeks in a nursing home at Fort Bend, in Williamson County, just outside Harris County and Houston. She died at ninety on January 2, 1988, and her remains were cremated, according to her written instructions. Sometime later, Chet and his wife "took half of her ashes ... and buried them at the base of a large tree in Central Park so that she could be near the place she loved most forever."[16]

Looking back at Beryl Halley's life, one must conclude that while her show business career was limited to her years on the stage, in nightclubs, and in a trio of relatively insignificant silent pictures, it remained atypical in many respects. She was not groomed for a life in entertainment. Over the years, a number of those who became screen and/or stage legends—

12. Texas, 1953–1988

Beryl Halley—Rio Grande College student, teacher in a one-room school, United States Navy veteran, stenographer, mother—is pictured here in this live theatrical picture by Richard Tucker in her favorite space—center stage, in full costume, ready to dazzle the audience.

from Gypsy Rose Lee and Lillian Roth to Shirley Temple, Natalie Wood, and Lindsey Lohan—had been prepared for such work from early childhood.

Girls looking for a life outside of hearth and home in rural southeastern Ohio could become school teachers, a career which usually ended when they got married. Perhaps they could—as did Melissa Porter Halley—return to the classroom when their own children reached school age, if circumstances so warranted. In rural areas such as Gallia County, until the late 1920s much teaching took place in the one-room district schools. During the summer months, they probably took additional course work in colleges like Rio Grande or in the so-called "Teacher's Institutes," usually under the sponsorship of county boards of education. Teachers who sought better opportunities could find employment in the growing industrial centers—as did Cecile Halley—and make a lifetime occupation of education, especially after the creation of state retirement systems. Those who obtained higher degrees, such as Rio Grande instructors Ruth Brockett, Chestora Carr, and May Fulton, might become college instructors.

Beryl Halley, however, looked elsewhere for a career. Whether she gained inspiration from stage events at Rio Grande or was aware of the work in New York City of such major figures as Frank Crumit, or minor figures as Marie Hall, cannot be determined; neither can they be immediately discounted. Beryl left no written record explaining her thoughts either before she joined the navy or when she went to New York. Maybe she had a stage career on her mind when she went to New York in 1921, and maybe it just happened as events transpired. With the possible exception of a brief return when her father's estate was settled, she left Gallia County behind, her only connection being her older sister. Richard James remembers that her brother, Paul, had a picture of Beryl hanging on his wall, and told friends that she was in New York (or Texas, in later years). If they communicated directly, it is unknown.

Chet Falkenhainer believes that his mother probably felt too "confined" concerning her life in Ohio. Being something of a "free spirit" by 1918, she joined the navy and later went to New York. She wanted a life beyond the narrow horizons of the Ohio Valley or the Story's Run School. She found it on the Broadway stage and in such nightclubs as the Silver Slipper. While she did not find lasting fame in the manner of a Barbara Stanwyck, Beryl experienced a stage career that endured for the better part of a decade and may well have endured longer had not the Great Depression come along. What fame she acquired came as a dancer, chorus girl, and in tableaux. Those who sustained more long-lasting fame tended also to be singers and those who exhibited dramatic skills. Beryl's talents in those areas were apparently limited, although based on critics' comments at the time, maybe the greatest actresses in the world could not have made *Half a Widow* or *The Broadway Boob* hits.

Within her realm in tableaux and dancing, Beryl gained more attention than the average Ziegfeld Girl. As one newspaper stated, she was "responsible for a good part of the Broadway traffic congestion." While this comment may have been a not-so-thinly-veiled reference to her looks (which can take you only so far in show business), she had a degree of charisma that made her a standout at the time. Beryl lasted longer than

12. Texas, 1953–1988

most showgirls—three seasons with Ziegfeld (plus part of another if you count *Palm Beach Nights* and her eventual return to *Rio Rita*) and another season with Earl Carroll. Her greatest short-term fame, or perhaps notoriety, came from her brief role as "Eve" in *The Bunk of 1926*. This enhanced her career as a nightclub dancer, but probably did less for her work on the stage. For better or worse, it seems to have been the incident that remained longest in Broadway memory, enduring for at least twenty-one years after the production terminated.

In addition to whatever looks and charisma helped to give Beryl a degree of Broadway fame, excellent health contributed to sustaining it. The average Ziegfeld Girl was still in her late teens, but Beryl was twenty-four when she joined the cast of *Tangerine*, and two years older when she first appeared in the *Follies*. While honesty may have characterized most of her life, that did not include the subject of age. On various forms after she went to New York, her 1897 birth year varied from 1900 to 1914 (she claimed an age of thirty-seven on her Texas marriage license in 1951), which, if true, would have meant that she graduated from high school at the age of two! Birth records, the 1900, 1910, and 1920 census, as well as U.S. Navy enlistment data tell a more truthful story, but for a casual observer to have unquestionably accepted her later birth dates as given, she must have had a remarkably youthful appearance.

While Beryl Halley may have left her background in the Appalachian foothills far behind and rejected some tenets of her strict upbringing, she still retained characteristics associated with country folk. One was her resilience, a trait she carried for the entirety of her ninety years. According to Chet, she always maintained a positive attitude and, with it, a large capacity to readjust to changing circumstances. When her show business livelihood faded during the Great Depression, she did not end her career on skid row or in the gutter like some of her cohorts. Instead, she almost effortlessly turned to office work and the skills she had developed in the navy. When her first marriage failed, she again went back to the office and supported her son and weak-willed second husband until he departed and continued working in the law office until she was nearly eighty years old. (Perhaps, given her claims of being much younger, her employers may also have been unaware of her real age). Asking her son if she ever expressed any regrets about her life, Chet thinks that Beryl wished she had handled the final breakup with Chester more smoothly.

Beryl Halley

Beryl Halley was certainly not the only person to come from a strict rural upbringing and modest means to make it in the entertainment world. The Nashville scene is full of such figures, with Johnny Cash, Loretta Lynn, and Dolly Parton the most notable examples. Oklahoma-born Will Rogers made it much bigger than Beryl on Broadway and in Hollywood, while hardly altering his down-home persona at all. Florenz Ziegfeld himself noted that many of his girls came from small-towns. Beryl, however, seems to be the only one who hailed from the Gallia-Jackson-Meigs-Vinton area of the Ohio hill country. In that sense, she achieved a degree of uniqueness.

Appendix:
Beryl's Buddies

The years of the "Roaring Twenties" that Beryl Halley spent on Broadway brought her into close contact with numerous figures from the entertainment world, some of whom are now legends. Others were less famous and have since been consigned to obscurity. The following sketches offer a brief view of those who had some connection with Gallia County's Ziegfeld Girl. Some became close friends or "buddies," but some may have been little more than work colleagues.

Ackerman, Bernice (1898–1995)

Bernice Ackerman was a Ziegfeld Girl and close friend of Beryl Halley; she even served as matron of honor when Beryl married Chester Falkenhainer. In addition to the *Follies* in 1923 and 1924, she also performed in *No Foolin'* in 1926 and a half-dozen other Broadway productions between 1921 and 1929. Her last came in the stage version of the Marx Brothers' classic *Animal Crackers*, which closed April 6, 1929. She is sometimes confused with another Ziegfeld Girl, Jean Ackerman.[1]

Barton, James (1890–1962)

James Barton was an actor and comedian who worked in *Palm Beach Nights* with Beryl Halley. He also appeared in its Broadway successor *No Foolin'* and a number of other productions. His most noted stage performances came after Ziegfeld's death, when he had a five-year run as

Appendix

Jeeter Lester in *Tobacco Road* and, later, as Theodore Hickman in the acclaimed 1946 production of *The Iceman Cometh*. Barton also appeared in supporting roles in such films as *Shepherd of the Hills* (1941), *Golden Girl* (1951), and *The Misfits* (1961).[2]

Basquette, Lina (1907–1994)

A California girl, born Lena Baskette, she first appeared in films at the age of six, as the original Suzie Snowflake in a silent short of the same name. At sixteen, she made her Broadway debut as Lina Basquette. Producer Charles Dillingham is alleged to have said "Lena is a cook, but Lina is an artiste." After two seasons (1923–1924) in the *Follies* and the Ziegfeld production of *Louie the XIV*, she met and married Sam Warner, the eldest member of the film-producing Warner Brothers. They became a happy, loving couple and had a daughter, Lita, but Sam Warner died in 1927 of a sinus infection that had spread to his brain. A widow at twenty, Lina was turned away by the surviving brothers, who denied her any share in the firm and much of what might have been an inheritance. This included virtually being forced to give up her daughter in exchange for a guarantee of Lita's financial security. Lina starred in a major Cecil B. DeMille silent, *The Godless Girl*, but it failed to attract much attention because moviegoers increasingly preferred sound pictures. However, Adolph Hitler, in his pre–Fuhrer days, contended that she was his favorite movie star. She even traveled to Germany in the mid-thirties, as Hitler wanted to meet her. According to legend, the Nazi leader made a move on her, and she not only rebuffed him, she kicked him in the groin and told him truthfully that she was part Jewish. Meanwhile, her own life was tumultuous as she had several broken marriages, failed suicide attempts, and a son by husband number four.

After 1943, Basquette left Hollywood, moved to a farm in Pennsylvania, and gained a new form of stardom in the canine world as a breeder and trainer of Great Danes. She wrote several guidebooks on the subject and served as a judge at American Kennel Club shows. After being able to see her daughter only twice in the thirties, Lina and Lita finally reconnected in 1977. She lived her last years in Wheeling, West Virginia, where she wrote a lengthy autobiography, *DeMille's Godless Girl*. She also appeared in one final film, *Paradise Park* (1991), in which she played an elderly lady living in an Appalachian trailer park. Basquette died at eighty-seven, and was survived by several direct descendants and a twelve-year-younger half-sister, dancer/choreographer/actress Marge Champion.[3]

Benda, Marion (1903–1986); (1904–1951)

There were two *Follies* girls who used the stage name Marion Benda. The older of the two, born Marion Bimberg, was a *Follies* Girl in 1923 who also had roles in two other later Ziegfeld hits, *Rio Rita* and *Rosalie*, the latter of which starred Marilyn Miller. In 1927, she was in the ensemble of the Marx Brothers musical play *The Cocoanuts*, when she met and married the youngest brother, Herbert "Zeppo" Marx; they divorced in 1954. Slightly younger and born Marion Wilson, the other was romantically linked with Rudolph Valentino at the time of his death in 1926. As a result, confusion has reigned, even among show business historians. Mallory Curley managed to differentiate the two, but does not identify which was the close friend and associate of Beryl Halley.[4]

Berlin, Irving (1888–1989)

Israel Baline, born in Russia to poor Jewish parents, became one the most acclaimed composers of American vernacular music in the 20th century under his Anglicized name of Irving Berlin. Coming to New York with his parents at age five, he had only two years of formal education. A list of his compositions could fill a book, but three of his most enduring are "God Bless America," "White Christmas," and "Easter Parade," the last two of which are secular songs for Christian holidays. A few other standards include "Alexander's Ragtime Band," "Blue Skies," and the World War I classic "Oh! How I Hate to Get Up in the Morning." Beryl Halley's connection with Berlin was limited to those productions where she danced to his music.[5]

Brice, Fania (Fannie, or later, Fanny) (1891–1951)

Fannie Brice achieved fame as a comedienne and singer. She first worked for Ziegfeld in *The Follies of 1910*, and intermittently thereafter for seven seasons, through 1923. Brice was especially known for her Yiddish dialect comedy, although she was equally skilled in other accents. As a vocal-

Appendix

ist, her signature songs were "My Man" and "Second Hand Rose," which were top-selling phonograph records as well as stage hits. According to one account, in early August 1923, Brice had scheduled a "facial sculpture," more commonly known as a nose job, to make her more marketable for serious drama. But because of President Harding's death and funeral, she postponed the operation, so she could get maximum publicity for her operation. Somewhat of an eccentric, she claimed that she slept while wearing her pearl necklace, because she argued that pearls were meant to be worn constantly. At one time, she was married to producer Billy Rose.

In later years, Brice earned much of her fame and fortune on radio, where she created the character "Baby Snooks" which she performed for about fourteen years, including on her own network program that ran from 1944 until her 1948 retirement. Eddie Cantor reported that when she was hospitalized a few days before her death she was on the phone placing bets on horses at racetracks all over the country. Many years after death, she was the subject of the 1964 stage play and its motion picture adaptation *Funny Girl* (1968) starring Barbra Streisand; a sequel, *Funny Lady*, was released in 1975. Beryl's only work with Brice took place in the 1923 *Follies*, which was Fannie's last and Halley's first.[6]

Brooks, Louise (1906–1985)

Mary Louise Brooks has become a cult figure. Of Kansas birth, she worked in *George White's Scandals*, and *Earl Carroll's Vanities*, in addition to a season in the *Follies* and Ziegfeld's *Louie the XIV*. The 1925 *Follies* and the 1928 *Vanities* were concurrent with Beryl Halley's work in those productions, as well as the short-lived Broadway play *Half a Widow*. Brooks also appeared in films, both before and after her Broadway career, and became famous for popularizing the bobbed hairstyle of the twenties. She starred in several motion pictures, some acclaimed and others not so. Her best films were made in Germany under the direction of G. W. Pabst: *Pandora's Box* and *Diary of a Lost Girl*. Known for her numerous affairs, the most prominent was probably with Laundromat tycoon and future Washington Redskins owner George Preston Marshall. As Richard and Paulette Ziegfeld wrote, "She saved nothing and was often broke," sometimes supporting herself by working as a department store sales clerk. But in the 1950s, renewed interest in her movies led to a renaissance, which truly gained momentum with the 1979 publication of Kenneth Tynan's *New Yorker* profile, "The Girl in the Black Helmet." In 1982, by which time she was bedridden from the effects of emphysema and osteoarthritis, a book of her essays, *Lulu in Hollywood*, was published by Knopf to wide acclaim. As Ephraim Katz noted in *The Film Encyclopedia*, "She died of a heart attack, poor, [and] alone, but not forgotten."[7]

Buck, Gene (1885–1957)

Gene Buck worked for Ziegfeld off and one for several years between 1913 and 1931, including all three seasons that Beryl was in the *Follies*. He wrote songs and was a co-founder of the American Society of Composers, Arrangers, and Publishers (ASCAP) and served as its president for several years. As a right-hand man for Ziegfeld, he brought set designer Joseph Urban to the *Follies*, a move which enhanced the productions.[8]

Burke, Katherine (Dates Unknown)

Katherine Burke worked in the 1925 *Follies*, *Palm Beach Nights*, *No Foolin'*, and replaced Beryl Halley in *Rio Rita* shortly before it opened on Broadway on February 2, 1927. Burke played the role of Montezuma's Daughter, which initially had been Beryl's part. The Halley anger was mostly directed at Ziegfeld and prompted a threatened lawsuit, which apparently came to nothing. Burke also appeared in *Rosalie*, *Whoopee!*, and the short-lived *Smiles*. Ironically, when Beryl had been the "Goddess of Feathers," Burke had been the "Goddess of the White Cobra Bird." Her Broadway career apparently ended after the 1931 *Follies* closed on November 21, 1931.[9]

Cambridge, Cynthia (d. 1929)

Cynthia Cambridge was a Ziegfeld Girl during the same three seasons as Beryl Halley. Earlier in 1923, she had been in the ensemble of *Jack and Jill*. This appears to be her sole work on Broadway.[10]

Cantor, Eddie (1892–1964)

Eddie Cantor, born Isadore Itzkowitz, to a family of poor Russian Jewish immigrants on New York's lower East Side, went on to achieve major success on stage, in motion pictures, on phonograph records, network radio, and television. Although in several editions of the *Follies*, the only one in which Beryl Halley also appeared was that of 1923. He had the advantage of being both an acclaimed comedian as well as a credible vocalist, known for his song, "Ida, Sweet as Apple Cider," named for his wife. Like a number of Ziegfeld associates, Cantor was a Masonic Lodge member—as were Will Rogers, Leon Errol, Bert Lahr, Irving Berlin, Sigmund Romberg, Rudolf Friml, Ed Wynn, Bert Williams, and even, for a time, W. C. Fields—and quite active in both Jewish and Christian charity work.

In his prime, Cantor often earned as much as five thousand dollars weekly. Although he lost much of it in the stock market crash, he regained prosperity thanks to network radio. When Flo Ziegfeld died, Eddie, along with Will Rogers, helped Billie Burke arrange his funeral. From 1954, his health declined and his career wound down, more rapidly after his wife's death. But his stature remained.[11]

Carroll, Earl (1893–1948)

Earl Carroll, along with George White, ranked as the foremost rivals to Florenz Ziegfeld as a producer of variety revues on Broadway. Carroll inaugurated his *Vanities* in 1923; they ran for eleven seasons. Ziegfeld did not care much for either rival and considered their shows to be relatively trashy, although theatregoers often failed to see much difference between them. Carroll, a Pittsburgh native, had been a pilot in World War I, and in 1926 became involved in a scandal as a result of a private party he threw, which featured a bathtub containing illegal liquor and a naked girl. For violating the Prohibition laws, he served six months in the federal prison in Atlanta.

Beryl Halley, Louise Brooks, and Lillian Roth, all served in the cast of the 1928 *Vanities*. Roth described Carroll as "a tall thin, baldish man with long whispy hair, a worn gray artist's smock over his frail body" who adamantly refused to put her name on the marquee. She also noted that Carroll had an exercise machine installed backstage to help the girls control their weight. Carroll subsequently fell for Dorothy Knapp, a former Ziegfeld Girl and Halley friend, and starred her in a play that subsequently became one of the biggest flops in Broadway history up to that time. He later went to Hollywood, where he was involved in several productions.

Beryl's Buddies

According to Bernard Sobel, by 1948, he planned "a Hollywood adaptation of Radio City, with theatre, restaurant, cabaret, executive office building and aeroplane stations and landing." But it ended later that year when he perished in a plane crash at the age of fifty-four. Sobel concluded, "Incompletion furnished the tag line for his life."[12]

Crumit, Frank (1889–1943)

Frank Poore Crumit hailed from Jackson County, Ohio, adjacent to Beryl Halley's home county of Gallia. Crumit's family had some degree of prominence in Jackson, where young Frank and Ben Ames Williams (the latter of whom became a popular novelist in the 1930s and 1940s) were childhood friends. After attending a military academy for a time, Crumit went first to Ohio University and then to Ohio State, where he earned an engineering degree. His real interest, however, was in show business. He displayed his aptitude for songwriting by penning songs for both schools: "High in the Middle and Round on the Ends" for the former, and "The Buckeye Battle Cry" for the latter (it remains quite popular even now). He worked the vaudeville circuits for a time, and in some Broadway productions, but his real hit was *Tangerine*, the show that also launched Beryl's Broadway career. While there is no evidence that the two had known each other before coming to New York, there is a strong possibility that they had mutual acquaintances, since many Jacksonians had Rio Grande connections. Crumit also had a noted recording career complete with some major hits, beginning with Columbia in 1919, and Victor from 1924. His most popular numbers included "Frankie and Johnnie," "The Gay Caballero," "I Learned About Women from Her," "Abdul Abulbul Amir," and "The Prune Song." His repertoire also included older songs, typified by "Grandfather's Clock," "The Preacher and the Bear," and "Granny's Old Arm Chair." He also recorded pseudo-folk songs of collegiate humor, such as "The Pig Got Up and Slowly Walked Away." In the thirties, he re-cut many of his earlier numbers for Decca and they remained in print in the United Kingdom well into the long-play album era. From 1929, he and his wife, Julia Sanderson (the leading lady in *Tangerine*), concentrated on network radio. By 1943, they had a daily program and a weekly prime-time program, *The Battle of the Sexes*. They retained their popularity until Frank's death in September 1943. Julia started her own program that

Appendix

December but retired soon afterward, living quietly in her Massachusetts home.[13]

Dempsey, William Harrison "Jack" (1895–1982)

Jack Dempsey, whose background was in a Colorado mining camp, was the heavyweight boxing champion from 1919 until 1926. According to Vincent Lopez, he, Dempsey, Beryl Halley, and Estelle Taylor had double dates with himself as Taylor's date and Dempsey as Beryl's escort. As the evening progressed, the guys switched girls. Dempsey and Taylor married in 1925, but it ended in failure; Lopez and Halley became serious but never married, although she apparently wanted him to propose at one point. In later years, he contacted her to gain her approval to discuss their relationship in his autobiography, *Lopez Speaking*. As for Dempsey, in addition to his boxing career, he too appeared on the screen and onstage, but was more of a show business celebrity than anything else. According to his most notable biographer, the audience "if not captivated by his acting talent, were awed by his magnetic presence."[14]

Dooley, Rachel "Ray" (1896–1984)

Rachel Dooley was born in Scotland, but grew up in Philadelphia and was on Broadway by 1917. Physically small, she often played young brats and babies in musical comedies. She worked in the *Follies* from 1919 to 1921, and again, in 1925 and 1926. She later joined *Earl Carroll's Vanities* in 1928, thus working in two seasons with Beryl Halley (1925 and 1928). She retired from performing around 1935.[15]

Drange, Alma (Dates Unknown)

Alma Drange appeared as a chorus girl in two seasons (1924 and 1925) of the *Follies* concurrent with Beryl Halley, as well as in 1922, the summer edition of 1923, and that of 1927. She was also in *No Foolin'* and five other Broadway productions between 1917 and 1929. Other than that, little is known of her.[16]

Durante, James Francis "Jimmy" (1893–1980)

Jimmy Durante was a household name entertainer on stage, screen, radio, and television for most of his adult life. According to Chet Falkenhainer, Beryl and Durante became close friends as a result of working many of the same nightclubs at the same time, although they never appeared in any productions at the same time. Durante's closing tag line in closing his radio and TV programs was always, "Goodnight, Mrs. Calabash, wherever you are."[17]

Edwards, Cliff (1895–1971)

Cliff Edwards, better known as "Ukelele Ike," came from the Mark Twain locale of Hannibal, Missouri. During the twenties, he performed in vaudeville and had a number of hit records, first for Pathé, and then Columbia, most notably "Singin' in the Rain," which was later revived as the title song for one of the all-time great musical films of the early 1950s. Even more than Frank Crumit, he made the ukulele a popular instrument in the Roaring Twenties.

His only work with Beryl Halley came in the January-to-March production of *Palm Beach Nights*. He first appeared in motion pictures in 1929, but his most notable role was as the voice of Jiminy Cricket in the Disney animated production of *Pinocchio* in 1940. The song he performed, "When You Wish upon a Star," also garnered an Oscar. The next year, he became a Western movie sidekick for Columbia's cowboy hero Charles Starrett in eight programmers, beginning with *Thunder Over the Prairie*. In the summer of 1942, he moved to better-paying RKO and their Tim Holt series for six pictures, ending with *Red River Robin Hood*. Edwards bounced around from different radio programs and early TV shows, until failing health forced him into retirement. It was said that he survived in genteel poverty on a small pension from the Disney studio.[18]

Fender, Harry (1897–1995)

Harry Fender appeared in five Broadway productions from 1918 until 1923 when he joined the cast of Ziegfeld's *Kid Boots* in 1923 and *Louie the XIV* in 1925. He also appeared in the Florida production of *Palm Beach Nights* between January 12 and March 24, 1926. His specialty songs included "Old-Fashioned Waltz" and "Florida, the Moon and You." After this, he seems to have faded from the scene.[19]

Appendix

Fields, W. C. (1880–1946)

Born in Philadelphia to "poor but dishonest" English parents, William Claude Dukenfield initiated his stage career as a juggler, but went on to become a comedy legend. He gained renown for his sarcastic wit, and creating such characters for himself as Otis Cribblecoblis, Egbert Souse, and Larson E. Whipsnade. Although notorious for his heavy consumption of alcohol, Fields could also point out correctly that he never missed a performance, neither did he ever show up late. Over the years he appeared in several seasons of the *Follies* but only in 1925 and in the 1928 season of Earl Carroll's *Vanities* did he and Beryl Halley work together to any degree.

Flo Ziegfeld did not especially care for Fields because of his heavy drinking, but had to concede that he was not only popular but could enliven a show. From his early beginnings on the stage, he conquered Broadway, Hollywood, and even network radio (his verbal duels with ventriloquist Edgar Bergen's dummy Charlie McCarthy are classics). However, as far as can be determined, he never called Beryl Halley, "My Little Chickadee."[20]

Fisher, Irving (1886–1959)

Irving Fisher's Broadway career stretched over a thirty-year period (1916–1946), with one long dry spell of eighteen years. His first *Follies* appearance was in 1917; the next two came in 1924 and 1925. He was also in the cast of *Sally* (1920–1922), in which he marries the eponymous character, played by Marilyn Miller in a star-making role. He was also in *No Foolin'* as well as some non–Ziegfeld productions. His last performance was in *Christopher Blake*, which closed in March 1947.[21]

Goddard, Paulette (1910–1990)

Paulette Goddard rose from the Ziegfeld chorus to become a screen star in the thirties and forties. She was possibly a Ziegfeld Girl in 1925, appeared in his Florida production *Palm Beach Nights*, and its Broadway successor *No Foolin'*, in which she played "Peaches." After a number of bit parts, and larger light-comedy roles opposite Bob Hope, she reached major stardom as a result of the Charlie Chaplin Hitler-spoofing classic *The Great Dictator*. She later became a member of the Hollywood Chapter of the Ziegfeld Girls Club.

Goddard remained a top star throughout the 1940s in such films as *Diary of a Chambermaid*; *Kitty*; *Suddenly, It's Spring*; and *So Proudly We Hail*, the latter of which earned her an Oscar nomination. Her star faded somewhat in the early fifties and she virtually retired. In her prime, one film historian defined her persona as "saucy sparkle." She had three famous husbands: Charlie Chaplin, Burgess Meredith, and European novelist Erich Maria Remarque. She spent her later years in Switzerland. Her main work with Beryl took place in *Palm Beach Nights*.[22]

Guinan, Mary Louise Cecilia "Texas" (1884–1933)

Texas Guinan was one of those persons whose legendary status surpasses her historical significance. During the Prohibition era, she became known in New York as a speakeasy hostess, "Queen of the Nightclubs," and for her trademark greeting, "Hello, *Sucker*." Born in Waco to Irish Immigrants, Texas entered vaudeville and, from 1917, in silent films. In 1922, she left Hollywood for New York. Her brassy style found favor with club patrons, whom she convinced to spend, spend, spend. As one might suspect, her actions led to frequent trouble with authorities, but she was never convicted of any crime, as she apparently did not own any of the clubs where she worked.

With the advent of the Great Depression, profits dwindled in the clubs, leading her to organize a show. When she took it to Europe, she was refused entry, but managed to tour some places in the U.S. and Canada. In Vancouver, in November 1933, she died from an attack caused by amoebic dysentery. Beryl Halley's friendship with Guinan, like that with characters ranging from entertainers such as Jimmy Durante and mobster Owney Madden, resulted from her work in New York nightclubs.[23]

Guy, Edmonde, and Van Duren, Ernest (d. 1930)

Edmonde Guy and Ernest VanDuren were a dance team—reportedly brother and sister—that Flo Ziegfeld imported from France as a special feature for *Palm Beach Nights*. Edmonde also sang, with her specialty

Appendix

being "I Will If You Will." Both apparently made a positive impression on Beryl Halley, as well as the Florida audience, although it may have been less than her publicity buildup had anticipated. Ernest was also a quality artist who made a pastel portrait for, and of, Beryl that she treasured for the rest of her life. Sadly, the duo's career came to a sudden end four years later when Ernest unexpectedly took his own life, leaving Edmonde devastated.[24]

Hazzard, John (1881–1935)

John Hazzard was a Broadway veteran whose career dated back to 1904. His principal connection to Beryl Halley came in *Tangerine*, her stage debut. Hazzard played the comedy role of King Home Brew, who ruled the remote tropical island where much of the play took place. His last appearance came in 1934, only a few months before his death.[25]

Healy, Dan (1888–1969)

Dan Healy was an actor and dancer who appeared in several Broadway productions. He later worked with Beryl Halley as a dancer in nightclub acts. In fact, when he and Beryl had a ballroom dancing engagement at the Silver Slipper in December 1926, it could have been a contributing reason that Ziegfeld dropped her from the cast of *Rio Rita*, as she may have skipped out on an appearance in Boston.[26]

Hickman, Art (c. 1887–1930)

Art Hickman was an orchestra leader in a manner not unlike Paul Whiteman or Vincent Lopez, but different in that his orchestra was based on the West Coast. However, he did take his group to Florida in 1926, where they supplied the music for *Palm Beach Nights*. His big hits on Columbia Records were "Hold Me" and "Love Nest." He died at the untimely age of forty-three.[27]

Johns, Brooke (1893–1987)

William Brooke Johns worked in vaudeville, had roles in six Broadway shows (including the *Follies* in 1922 and 1923), as well as in *Tangerine*. On stage, he was billed as "Six-foot-three and Oh! So Different." He apparently made records for Victor, but seems not to have scored any hits. His one motion picture was *That Old Gang of Mine*, a 1925 silent in which he played a musician (he was known to be a banjo player). Johns retired from show business in 1930 to a farm near Washington, D.C., which he turned into the Brooke Manor Country Club. Later, he owned a restaurant in Georgetown, entered politics, and served as a Republican County Commissioner in Montgomery County at a time when the area was becoming a part of suburbia. As such, he opposed "tacky postwar development," but favored more orderly growth. At times he also served on the state racing commission, hosted a children's TV show, and entertained at benefits. A colorful man to the very end, he told a local reporter, "I'm down in history now," and "I'm so egotistical I don't want the public to ever forget me."[28]

Kennedy, Flo (Dates Unknown)

Beryl's friend Flo Kennedy appeared in the *Follies* of both 1923 and 1925. She also appeared in the Broadway version of *No Foolin'* in 1926. Nothing more is known of her at this time.[29]

Knapp, Dorothy (b. 1900)

Dorothy Knapp was a Ziegfeld Girl who subsequently moved to *Earl Carroll's Vanities*. She initially came to prominence via the beauty contest route as runner-up in what later became the Miss America contest in Atlantic City. She appeared in *Earl Carroll's Vanities* in 1923, and the *Follies* in 1924. Knapp then entered the Miss America contest in 1925. Chosen "Miss Manhattan," she had to withdraw because of her past stage work, after which she went back to work for Ziegfeld, and then to the *Vanities* again.

Earl Carroll, who proclaimed her "the most beautiful girl in the world," starred her in the 1929 musical *Fioretta*, which became the biggest flop in Broadway history up that time due to her inadequate singing. She also had roles in three motion pictures. At some point she announced that she would enter a "cloistered convent"; if she did so, her stay was short, as she had a role in *Smiles* in 1931. Dorothy and Beryl worked together in the *Follies* in 1924 and 1925, as well as in the 1928 *Vanities*. After 1934,

Appendix

she faded from the Broadway scene. In 1947, she worked in Magnin's Jewelry Store in Beverly Hills, where Earl Carroll's latest girlfriend bought a watch for Earl from Knapp, who actually suggested an engraved inscription.[30]

Lane, Lupino (1892–1959)

Lupino Lane was an English-born actor and director whose real name was Henry Lupino. The family's stage ancestors career dated back to the 17th century. Henry's better-known brother was Stanley Lupino (1893–1938) and his niece the film noir star and director Ida Lupino (1914–1995). Known for his versatility, especially in comedy, it was said that he actually played twenty-five different characters in a British silent film. His film career extended from 1915 to 1920 in England, and in the States in 1920. He was back in the UK from 1930 to 1939; he also did three Broadway shows, including the 1924 season of the *Follies* and a short-lived 1925 revival of Gilbert and Sullivan's *The Mikado*.[31]

Leedom, Edna (1896–1937)

Edna Leedom was in five Broadway productions between 1923 and 1928, all but one of which were Ziegfeld-related, including the three seasons of the *Follies* featuring Beryl Halley. Over her lifetime, she survived four marriages, only to die at the age of forty.[32]

Lockhart, Gene (1891–1957)

Canada-born Gene Lockhart had a noted acting career on both stage and screen, chalking up numerous credits in both. He was also a writer and lyricist. His main connection with Beryl Halley was in *The Bunk of 1926*, where she came in as an added cast member when the production switched theatres. This prompted her arrest in the fig-leaf incident. Shortly after the play ended its run, Lockhart went on to an active career in Hollywood. In addition to his own efforts, his wife Kathleen also appeared in several films. Daughter June Lockhart (b. 1925) was a regular on several TV series, including *Lassie* (1958–1964), *Lost in Space* (1965–1968), and *Petticoat Junction* (1969–1970). Granddaughter Anne Lockhart has also been in various television shows, including *Battlestar Galactica*.[33]

Luce, Claire (1903–1989)

Claire Luce was a Rochester, New York, native whose career advanced from cigarette girl to Broadway star. She also achieved significant accomplishments in both motion pictures and on the London stage. Making her Broadway debut in 1923, she appeared in three successful plays, including Ziegfeld's *Palm Beach Nights* as "The Broadway Indian," in January 1926. She remained in the Broadway version, re-titled *No Foolin'*, from which she was dropped to the stage inside a giant sphere. In the 1927 *Follies*, Luce created a major sensation when she came onstage riding a live ostrich. She then went to London, where she starred in the play *Burlesque* before going to Hollywood where she worked as leading lady in an early Spencer Tracy film. Luce then replaced Adele Astaire as her brother Fred's dancing partner, performing with him on both the Broadway and London stages. During World War II, she took on the lead role of Katherine in Shakespeare's *Taming of the Shrew*, and later became the first American actress to play lead roles at the Shakespeare Memorial Theatre in Stratford-on-Avon, before returning to the States in 1947. A true renaissance lady, she did a one-woman show, had showings of her paintings in various art galleries, and recorded albums of poetry. She died of cancer at the age of eighty-six.

Beryl Halley and Claire had become friends during the *Palm Beach Nights* production in Florida. Luce appeared as "the Broadway Indian," while Beryl danced as the "Goddess of Feathers." Their friendship continued for some years afterward, as evidenced by postcards in the Halley collection.[34]

Madden, Owen Vincent "Owney" (1891–1965)

During Prohibition, Owney Madden was a New York gangster whom Beryl Halley called a friend, according to her son. Born in England of Irish parents, Madden came to New York City as a child with his widowed mother, settling in the Hell's Kitchen area of Manhattan, where Owney began his career of crime while his mother labored as a scrubwoman. In prison for manslaughter between 1915 and 1923, he soon became a big-time mobster. Like Frank Costello and Lucky Luciano, Owney's crime activities covered the worlds of boxing, bootlegging, gambling, and entertainment. Exactly what his involvement with Beryl Halley was has not been documented, although she probably worked in some nightclubs under his control after her work on Broadway ended. He is said to have much impact on the careers of George Raft and Mae West, who later called him "Sweet ... but oh so mean." In 1932, Madden was sent again to prison, this time for violating parole. Released the following year, he moved to Hot Springs, Arkansas, where his usual activities continued as part of what has been called the "Dixie Mafia." In 1964, the state government closed the illegal operations there. Madden died there the following year and was buried locally.[35]

Marston, William Moulton (1893–1947)

William Marston is often credited with either inventing, or at the very least popularizing, the lie detector. In one of his widely publicized demonstrations, he administered the test on some Ziegfeld Beauties, including Beryl Halley, although whether she passed or failed is unknown. His principal contribution to American culture in later years was his creation, under the pen name "Charles Moulton," of the first female comic book superhero "Wonder Woman," whose fictional exploits initially helped defeat the Axis Powers in World War II.[36]

Martin, Kathleen, a.k.a. Kathlene Martyn (b. 1903)

English-born Kathleen Martin was a *Midnight Frolics* cast member in the years 1920–1921; she also appeared in *Palm Beach Nights*, where she performed the solo song "Green Hat." Before coming to America, she had been selected as mascot for British Royal Flying Corps in 1919. Known as "the Butterfly Girl," she was an ad model for Coca-Cola and posed for other magazine ads in the early 1920s.[37]

"Mary Jane" a.k.a. Jane Catherine Young Martin Pulitzer (b. 1910)

Mary Jane Young was a Ziegfeld Girl who endured one of the most miserable marriages to a dissolute millionaire in entertainment history. She made her stage debut at the age of ten in *Jimmie*, followed by two productions in 1925. She then joined the cast of *Palm Beach Nights*, dancing the "Charleston" with Claire Luce. During the production's two-month run in Palm Beach, she found the time to win a speedboat race, for which she received a trophy. Back on Broadway, she remained in the cast for *No Foolin'* and *The Merry Malones* before joining the cast of another Ziegfeld hit, *Whoopee!*, in December 1928. During this time she met and subsequently married Samuel Klump Martin III, a millionaire playboy. They married in July 1929, and the troubled union faced its first conflict during their Paris honeymoon. It seems the young bridegroom got into a barroom brawl, which landed him in jail. Back in the States, he bought a two-hundred-acre tract in Montgomery County, Maryland. He then built a lavish, thirty-three-room home called Marwood, into which the newlyweds and their newborn son moved late in 1931. The *Washington Post* termed it "one of the show spots of the suburban area." For the next few months, they wined and dined the rich and famous. By early 1934, however, their storybook life had unraveled. They lived in Florida for a time and rented Marwood to the family of Joseph Kennedy, the new head of the Securities and Exchange Commission. Although the Martins separated, they remained married. In March 1935, Samuel died in a Savannah hotel. His lawyer blamed Jane for refusing to reconcile and blamed her for the "unbridgeable chasm" she had created for the man who died loving her with his last breath. Jane was awarded the home under the laws of Maryland. In 1937, she married Seward W. Pulitzer, grandson of newspaper tycoon Joseph Pulitzer. In 1939, she sold Marwood to H. Grady Gore, a wealthy relative of future vice president Al Gore.[38]

Nesbitt, Evelyn (1884–1967)

Evelyn Nesbitt, one of the Florodora Girls, worked briefly as a singer and was reputedly the model for the Gibson Girl. She also had an affair with noted architect Stanford White, but subsequently married the eccentric Pittsburgh millionaire Harry K. Thaw. Learning of her past and possible continuing relationship, Thaw fatally wounded White in 1906. The subsequent trials followed what was termed "the crime of the century." Thaw was found innocent by reason of temporary insanity. Nesbit subsequently appeared in some silent motion pictures until 1922 and later either owned or operated some nightclubs where Beryl Halley worked as part of a dance act in the early 1930s. Later, she worked as an art and sculpting instructor in California. In the mid–1950s, she became the subject of a major motion

Appendix

picture, *The Girl in the Red Velvet Swing*, starring Joan Collins. She then returned to relative obscurity until her death at age eighty-two.[39]

Pennington, Ann (1893–1971)

Ann Pennington may hold the record for being a Ziegfeld Girl in more seasons than any other—a total of eight. Born in Wilmington, Delaware, but reared in Camden, New Jersey, the petite Ann, who would gain fame for her dimpled knees, first danced as an amateur in Philadelphia, and moved on to Broadway at seventeen in *The Red Widow*. Pennington's career with the *Follies* extended from 1913 to the spring of 1925. Concurrently and afterward, she also spent five seasons in *George White's Scandals*. Although best known as the dancer who first popularized the African American–originated "Black Bottom," in the 1926 *Scandals*, she was also a singer. By 1920, her salary had climbed from fifty dollars weekly to one thousand. She also worked in the Ziegfeld-produced *Miss 1917* and in some of his *Midnight Frolics* shows. Her feature films included the silent *Pretty Ladies* and three early talkies: *Night Parade*, *Gold Diggers of Broadway*, and *Tanned Legs*, all in 1929; she also appeared in some short subjects, including one in which she portrayed the original "Susie Snowflake." In between Broadway and Hollywood engagements she also danced in vaudeville, thrilling audiences with her quality steps in her one-and-a-half-size shoes.Beryl Halley's three seasons in the *Follies* took place at the same time as Ann's last three. Apparently, living a frugal lifestyle—except for a disastrous gambling habit—the demure dancer roomed with Fanny Brice when in Hollywood and resided in a one-room apartment in New York City. Although engaged four times, she never married. She seemingly outlived all of her relatives and, with her memory failing, she entered a nursing home at age seventy-seven. About four weeks before her death she was moved to Beekman Downtown Hospital. Beryl Halley treasured her friendship with Pennington and kept a large, personally autographed photo of her for the rest of her life.[40]

Richman, Harry (1895–1972)

Cincinnati-born Harry Richman entertained in nightclubs, vaudeville, on the Broadway stage, recordings, and in films over a long career. Today he is probably best known for his 1929 romance with the legendary "It Girl" Clara Bow, and his 1930 motion picture *Puttin' on the Ritz*, featuring the up-and-coming superstar Joan Bennett. The latter also served as the title of his hit Brunswick record. Although impoverished in his later years, Richman authored a colorful autobiography in 1965.[41]

Rogers, Will (1879–1935)

Beyond doubt, the best-known entertainment figure born in Indian Territory, Will Rogers earned considerable fame both on the stage and in Hollywood. However, he is perhaps best remembered as a "homespun philosopher." At fourteen he became a cowboy on his father's ranch and became an expert with the lariat, not only lassoing animals but in all kinds of rope tricks. He joined Wild West shows and displayed his talents in such faraway locales as Argentina, Australia, and South Africa, before landing in New York. His comic monologues, covering topical jokes about politicians, made him a star in vaudeville and he spent six seasons in the *Ziegfeld Follies* (1916–1918, 1922, and 1924–1925, the last two concurrent with Beryl Halley). There seems to be little doubt that Rogers was Ziegfeld's favorite comedian; the two were also close friends. According to one theory, Ziegfeld considered the *Follies* comedians' main purpose was to provide time for the girls to change costumes between skits, musical and dance numbers, and tableaux. However, his appreciation for the clean-living Rogers was genuine. Eddie Cantor recalled in 1934 that the three great Ziegfeld comics were Rogers, Fields, and himself.

Rogers also appeared in motion pictures from 1918, but they were generally unexceptional until the advent of sound. He used his natural rural accent to advantage in such Fox films as *State Fair* (1932), and *David Harum* (1933). When Florenz Ziegfeld died, in 1932, Rogers and Cantor helped Billie Burke in planning his funeral. A lover of aviation, he accompanied noted pilot Wiley Post in efforts to circle the earth in the air, but the flight ended tragically for both men near Point Barrow, Alaska.[42]

Roth, Lillian (1910–1980)

Lillian Roth may have gained more fame for her best-selling autobiography as a recovered alcoholic, *I'll Cry Tomorrow*, than for her genuine achievements as a singer and actress. She entered show business as part of a child act known as the Roth Kids. She and Beryl Halley worked together in the 1928 version of *Earl Carroll's Vanities*, where Halley was called "The Form Divine." Lillian also acted and sang in sound films, including an early version of *The Vagabond King*, Cecil B. DeMille's *Madam Satan, The Love Parade*, and the Marx Brothers comedy *Animal Crackers*. Alcoholism brought her low, resulting in multiple marriages, trips to mental institutions, and, ultimately, show business obscurity. Lillian and Beryl had a reunion in Houston, Texas, on December 17, 1955.[43]

Sanderson, Julia (1884 or 1887–1975)

Julia Sanderson (born Julia Scubett) hailed from Springfield, Massachusetts, and her Broadway career commenced in 1907. She appeared in eleven major productions prior to being cast as the lead in *Tangerine*, where she first met and subsequently married Frank Crumit. Prior to *Tangerine*, her biggest successes were *The Sunshine Girl* (1913), *The Girl from Utah* (1914–1915), and *Sybil* (1916). Her 1927 marriage to Crumit—the second for both—led them to work as a team thereafter, mostly on network radio. While Crumit recorded extensively, Julia made only a few solo discs and a couple of duets with Frank. After her husband's unexpected death in 1943, she landed a show of her own, *Let's Be Charming*, although this proved to be short-lived. She retired to Springfield, where she lived her remaining thirty-two years.[44]

Segal, Vivienne (1897–1992)

Vivienne Segal was a Broadway veteran who made her debut in 1914 and first worked for Ziegfeld in *Miss 1917*. She was in the *Follies* in with Beryl in 1924 and 1925 and later appeared in several motion pictures. Following her retirement, she became one of the most active members of the Ziegfeld Girls Club.[45]

Sobel, Bernard (1887–1964)

Bernard Sobel worked tirelessly as Ziegfeld's press agent until 1931, when the economic downturn prevented Flo from being able to pay him for his services. He also worked as a drama critic, writing several books and articles on theatre history. As late as 1946, he discussed "the exquisite Beryl Halley," in an article which contained a recent photo of her and her five-year-old son.[46]

Sterling, Dolly (Dates Unknown)

Dolly Sterling played the female lead, opposite Gene Lockhart, in *The Bunk of 1926*. Like Beryl, Sterling seems to have joined the cast only with the change of venues. An El Paso native, she claimed to find the Broadway scene a bit too racy for her tastes. Apparently, she was primarily an eccentric dancer, not unlike Fanny Brice and Charlotte Greenwood. She later appeared in nightclubs in the Miami area.[47]

Taylor, Estelle (1894–1958)

Estelle Taylor was a Broadway actress who became the wife of boxing champion Jack Dempsey; the marriage ended in divorce in 1930. According to Dempsey biographer Randy Roberts, he was not particularly kind to Taylor, calling her "an ambitious, second-rate actress," He further described her as "frustrated" and "trapped in a career that was going nowhere." On a honeymoon trip to Europe, Dempsey bought her a large blue boarhound named Castor. The dog's rambunctious personality cost the couple some $10,000 in damages to the hotel room.

Although Lopez termed her a Ziegfeld Girl, the Internet Broadway Database (IBDb) does not list any credits for her, although she may have toured in Ziegfeld productions. She actually worked more in films than on the stage. In her later days, Taylor displayed considerable interest in animal welfare, initially displayed by her enthusiasm for Castor. Among other activities, she served as founder and first president of the Pet Protective League.[48]

The Tiller Girls

The Tiller Girls were a British girls precision-dance group, first organized by John Tiller in Manchester, England, in 1889. The act played in the States on numerous occasions, including in the *Follies* of 1922 and 1923.

Appendix

Some of characteristics of Ziegfeld's Chorus Girls, such as efforts to get his girls of similar size, height, and weight in certain routines had been borrowed from Tiller. From 1925, many of these characteristics, including dance numbers in geometric shapes, were also adapted from the Tiller Girls. The act, in its various incarnations, exists even now.[49]

Udell, Peggy (1905–1984)

Peggy Udell was another of Beryl's acquaintances. The girls befriended each other during the tryouts for *Rio Rita* in Philadelphia and subsequent rehearsals on Broadway. Beryl and Peggy were included among the six girls who participated in the William Marston experiment in the blonde-brunette comparison. She later appeared in three other Broadway productions: *Cross My Heart, A Wonderful Night,* and *A Night in Venice,* of which only the latter ran for more than two months. In Hollywood, her principal role came in a silent Western starring Bob Custer and Bill Cody. Although made earlier, the film's 1929 release forced it to compete with sound pictures, which were then all the rage. Custer and Cody moved on to low-budget talking pictures, but, apparently, Peggy did not.[50]

Urban, Josef (1872–1933)

Joe Urban worked as a set designer and artist on numerous Ziegfeld productions from 1915 until 1931, including many featuring Beryl. Born in Vienna, Austria, he came to the States in 1914. In addition to his contribution to Broadway, he illustrated children's books and worked as artistic director for the Metropolitan Opera. Described as "fat [and] jolly," it has been claimed that he refused to work for what he termed "girlie shows," but Flo convinced him that his productions were "art" (the promise of a hefty salary also swayed him) and the two became close friends. In later years, Urban designed the Florida estate fifty-eight-bedroom home Mar-a-Lago, for cereal heiress Marjorie Merriweather Post Hutton. When she died in 1972, the Post family donated the house to the government for use as a Winter White House, but it was returned to the family in 1981. Donald Trump purchased the property as a Florida home, which he continues to use on weekends.[51]

Varell, Charles (1891–1945)

Charles Varell worked as Beryl's ballroom dance partner during their February and March 1929 stay at the Nixon Restaurant in Pittsburgh.[52]

Vargas, Alberto (1896–1982)

Vargas, a native of Peru, became famous for his portraits of Ziegfeld Girls, including one he painted of Beryl Halley in 1924. After Ziegfeld's death, he went to Hollywood and painted many portraits of Hollywood stars, and did studio work on movies posters for both Fox and Warners, until he was blacklisted for participating in a strike in 1939. Returning to New York, he signed a contract with *Esquire Magazine*, for whom he created some 180 illustrations of "Esquire Girls," some of which he modeled after his wife, former showgirl Anna Mae Clift. From 1959 on, he did some 152 illustrations for *Playboy*.[53]

Walker, Heather "Polly" (1904–1983)

"Polly" Walker, a Chicago native, made her show business debut in *Palm Beach Nights* in January 1926. She sang two songs in the show, one of which "No Foolin,'" which became the title of the production when it moved to Broadway in June; the other was "Tent for Two." An attractive blonde, Polly played a five-stringed instrument resembling a lute. She later appeared in three other New York stage productions: *The Merry Malones*; *Billie*; and *Hello, Paris*. In Hollywood, she starred in *Hit the Deck* (1929) and *Sleepless Nights* (1933). On the London stage she was in the 1932 production *Out of the Bottle*.[54]

Wayburn, Ned (1874–1942)

On his letterhead, Ned Wayburn advertised himself as head of a "Dancing, Singing and Dramatic School, Inc." He also listed more than thirty well-known entertainment figures he had helped put "In the Spotlight," from Fred Astaire to Marilyn Miller. As the man who staged many of the *Follies* and other Broadway productions, he could hardly have been exaggerating. Among his other achievements, he is credited with having

Appendix

developed the "Ziegfeld Walk." Some of the girls considered him a hard taskmaster because of his perfectionist demands. He was also instrumental in signing Ben Ali Haggin (1882–1951) to the *Follies*; Haggin would go on to develop the popular tableaux, several of which featured Beryl. Chet Falkenhaner recalled that Wayburn also hired Beryl for the 1923 *Follies*—ironically, his last—and he remained her friend and admirer for many years, telling her that "you made a beautiful picture that is never to be forgotten, and your mighty fine character radiated from within."[55]

Weeks, Ada Mae (1896–1978)

Ada Mae Weeks was a native of Theodore Roosevelt's hometown of Oyster Bay, New York. She appeared in nine Broadway productions between 1915 and 1933. Beryl apparently first became a friend of hers when Weeks danced in Ned Wayburn's Dance Studio. Their friendship continued in Ziegfeld's *Rio Rita* in Philadelphia, and for rehearsals on Broadway.[56]

Wheeler, Albert "Bert" (1895–1968)

Bert Wheeler was best known as half of the Wheeler and Woolsey comedy team, although he had earlier been teamed in a dance act with his wife, Betty. The latter twosome appeared together in the 1923 *Follies*, which was Beryl's first year in the show. In partnership with Robert Woolsey, he also spent 1927 in Ziegfeld's *Rio Rita*, after he and Betty had split. As a team, Wheeler and Woolsey made over twenty comedy films, including the screen version of *Rio Rita*, prior to Woolsey's passing in 1938. After that, Bert's career declined; his last role was as "Smoky Joe" in the CBS-TV Western *Brave Eagle*, from 1955 to 1956.[57]

Whiteman, Paul (1890–1967)

Paul Whiteman was an orchestra leader who supplied music for the 1923 season of the *Follies*. Known as the "King of Jazz," his musical tastes were actually quite broad. Hard-core jazz fans complained that his jazz-influenced orchestral music distracted from what they considered the real thing. But there seems no doubt that his material helped to popularize that genre.[58]

Wilson, Imogene "Bubbles" (c. 1905–1948)

Imogene Wilson grew up as Mary Imogene Robertson in a Kentucky orphanage. At seventeen, she became a sensation in the 1922 productions of *Daffy Dill* and *Lady Butterfly* and was hired by Ziegfeld for the *Follies* of 1923. However, her widely publicized affair with Broadway comedian Frank Tinney (1878–1940) led to her dismissal, after which her celebrity status declined; by 1936, she was "penniless." She later wrote her memoirs but died before they were published. Aged forty-two, she suffered from malnutrition and weighed but ninety pounds. It was a sad ending for someone of whom it had been said in 1922 that she was the only person other than the president who could bring every reporter in NYC to the docks to see her off on a trans-Atlantic trip.[59]

Wooten, Stella "Cricket" (Dates Unknown)

"Cricket" Wooten had roles in five Broadway shows between 1922 and 1932, including the *Follies* with Beryl Halley in 1924 and 1925. To date, nothing else concerning her career has surfaced.[60]

Worthing, Helen Lee (1905–1948)

Helen Lee Worthing appeared in six Broadway shows between 1920 and 1924, all but two produced by Ziegfeld. The last was the *Follies* of 1923, during which she and Beryl became friends. Worthing then went to California and acted in several films. However, her 1927 wedding to an African American physician, Eugene Nelson, brought an end to her motion picture career; the marriage itself would fail by the autumn of 1930. Nearly eighteen years later, on August 25, 1948, she committed suicide.[61]

Young, Halfred (1897–1978)

Halfred Young had the leading role as the World War I officer in the short-lived *Half a Widow* in 1927. Gertrude Lang played his French bride, Babette. Young played in a total of five Broadway productions in his acting career, the biggest success of which was the Ziegfeld-produced Marilyn Miller vehicle *Rosalie* in 1928. The lead role of that show went to Jack Donohue.[62]

Chapter Notes

Introduction

1. *Gallipolis Daily Tribune*, October 19, 1933, p. 1.
2. "Beauty Secretly Weds," *New York Daily Mirror*, October 16, 1933 p. 3 (Date is uncertain although the entire page is in the Beryl Halley Collection in the Jean Lloyd Cooper Archives at the University of Rio Grande).
3. *Gallipolis Daily Tribune*, October 19, 1933, p. 1.
4. Quoted in Ivan M. Tribe, "The Hillbilly Versus the City: Urban Images in Country Music, *J E M F Quarterly* X: 2 (Summer 1974), pp. 41–51. This article discusses a number of songs that touch on views of urban life. In fact, the songs mentioned in the article are just a few examples of such that warn of the evils young girls faced in moving to the big cities. Popular literature also contained much material of this nature. Among young males, the focus tended to warn of the evils of alcohol, and less often of being seduced by loose women. As late as 1936, parents were reluctant to let their daughters go to the city to appear on radio barn dance programs (e.g., Lily May Ledford at WLS Chicago) for fear of them being sold in "white slavery," a once popular euphemism for prostitution. In addition to Henry Burr, later recordings were by Emry Arthur in 1929, and Johnny Barfield in 1940, both in the country field.

Chapter 1

1. Benjamin F. Halley, Ancestry.com; *Official Roster of the Soldiers of the State of Ohio in the War of the Rebellion, 1861–1866* (Akron: Werner Ptg..., 1887), V, p. 250. For Halley forebears, see *Gallia County, Ohio: People in History to 1980* (Paoli, PA: Taylor Pub. Co, 1980), pp. 156–157. In recent decades the Gallia County population has stabilized at about 30,000, although the African American numbers have dropped by at least half.
2. *Official Roster of Ohio Soldiers in the War with Spain* (Columbus: State of Ohio, 1916), pp. 500–515, 517.
3. For the Porter forebears, see Gallia County, Ohio: People in History, pp. 273–274. The claim of Melissa Porter Halley as possibly the first certified female teacher in West Virginia appeared in the *Gallipolis Daily Tribune*, April 7, 1949, at the time her estate was being settled. The contention may have originated with her nephew, who worked on the staff at the time.
4. Most of our knowledge on Bladen and Eureka comes from the communities' unofficial historian Richard James and is based on interviews from November 25, 2017 (taped) and February 6, 2018 (not taped); Charles Otis Gill and Gifford Pinchot, *Six Thousand Country Churches* (New York: Macmillan, 1919), p. 173.
5. James P. Averill, *History of Gallia County* (Chicago: H. H. Hardesty & Co., 1882), p. xix.
6. Richard James, telephone interview, February 6, 2018.
8. Averill, *History of Gallia County*, p. xx. Gill and Pinchot, *Six Thousand Country Churches*, p. 173; *Gallipolis Daily Tribune*, August 27, 1906, December 20, 1906, p. 4; April 16, 1907, p. 3; *Masonic Calendar*, Gallia County, Ohio, 1916 Gallipolis: The *Gallipolis Daily Tribune* Print, 1916), pp. 12–13. Halley

Notes. Chapter 2

apparently did not belong to other Masonic groups, such as the Eastern Star, York Rite, Scottish Rite, or Shrine, all of which are listed in the *Calendar*.

9. James interview, February 6, 2018; Gill & Pinchot, *Six Thousand Country Churches*, p. 173.

10. Samuel Halley, Ancestry.com, 1900 Census Enumeration for Ohio Township.

11. Ivan M. Tribe, *Gallia County, Ohio: A Brief History, in Gallia County, Ohio: People in History*, pp. 8, 12; For Edward Bouchet, see Frank Lincoln Mather, *Who's Who of the Colored Race* (Chicago: Memento Editions, 1915), p. 31.

12. For the origin and early years of Rio Grande College, see Abby Gail Goodnite and Ivan M. Tribe, *Rio Grande: From Baptists and Bevo to the Bell Tower, 1876–2001* (Ashland, KY: Jesse Stuart Foundation, 2002), pp. 1–70; See also Jacob L. Bapst and Ivan M. Tribe, *University of Rio Grande and Rio Grande Community College* (Arcadia: Charleston, SC, 2016), pp. 8–31.

13. Goodnite and Tribe, *Rio Grande*, pp. 402–403; *Gallipolis Daily Tribune*, August 27, 1909, p. 1.

14. Bapst and Tribe, *University of Rio Grande*, pp. 17, 20–21, 23.

15. Samuel Halley, Ancestry.com; Rio Grande College Board of Trustees, Minutes, June 15, 2010, p. 242.

16. Samuel Halley, Ancestry.com; "Annual Elocutionary Recital, June 10, 1910" (Program in Rio Grande College Archives).

17. *Rio Grande College Bulletin*, August 1911, pp. 27, 31, 32, 36; The girls basketball team photos for 1911 and 1916 are in the Rio Grande College Archives.

18. Undated news clipping (in Rio Grande College Archives); Rio Grande College Board of Trustees, Minutes, August 22, 1911; February 28, 1912; *Rio Grande College Bulletin*, August, 1912, p. 48.

19. Program, "Rhetorical," October 31, [1912] (Typescript in the Rio Grande College Archives).

Chapter 2

1. "Court Report," *Gallipolis Journal*, February 27, 1914; "Court News," *Gallipolis Journal*, January 29, 1915.

2. Gallia County, Ohio. Court of Common Pleas, June 15, 1915, pp. 93–94; *Gallipolis Journal*, April 23, 1915; June 18, 1915.

3. "Mr. Halley, 70, Claimed Here," *Gallipolis Daily Tribune*, August 2, 1971, p. 1.

4. See Tom Diemer, Lee Leonard, and Richard G. Zimmerman, James A. Rhodes: *Ohio Colossus* (Kent: Kent State University Press, 2014), p. 8, for an atypical example. One might add that, like Beryl Halley, James Rhodes became a college dropout, although she did complete one full year of college.

5. Helen C. Martin, 1910 Census, Ancestry.com. Helen Martin subsequently married three times: to Cornelius K. "Kate" Berridge, a prominent Rio student (A. B. 1916) who served as a captain in World War I; architect Harry Wanger; and Jasper Frank Eaton, another RGC alumnus (A. B. 1916) who became an attorney and judge in Huntington, West Virginia. Ironically, despite her lifelong close connections with the college, Helen seems not to have graduated from anything beyond the Preparatory Department, although she did receive a 1916 diploma in the Music Program and, as she had demonstrated, considerable piano skills. By the time she divorced Berridge in 1933, Helen was a law student and later became an attorney. She died in 1968.

6. "Obituary, Joseph F. Martin," Typescript in Helen Martin Collection (Jeanne Lloyd Cooper Archives, University of Rio Grande, Rio Grande, Ohio); *Gallipolis Daily Tribune*, May 31, 1929, p. 1.

7. J. F. Martin Obituary; *Gallipolis Daily Tribune*, May 31, 1929, p. 1. The Martin House in Rio Grande later became the site of the Lyne Center Gymnasium.

8. *Rio Grande College Bulletin*, July 1915, p. 67; October 1915, p. 16; July 1916, p. 52, October 1916, pp. 21–22; July 1917, pp. 62, 64–65, 82; *The Grandion 1913* (n.p.: n.p., 1913), p. 12.

9. Rio Grande College, *The Grandion*, 1916 (Columbus: Champlin Press, 1916), p. 59.

10. Program, "Public Rhetoricals," March 23, 1916; Program "The 15th of January," May 9, 1916 (both in Jean Lloyd Cooper Archives, University of Rio Grande).

11. Stanley Crawford Neal, Ancestry.com; Draft Registration Card for Stanley Crawford Neal; Stanley Crawford Neal in Ohio Military, Ancestry.com; *The Grandion*, 1916, pp. 51–53, 66–67.

12. Rio Grande College, *The Grandion*, 1916 (Columbus: Champlin Press, 1916), p. 29.

13. Rio Grande College, *The Grandion*, 1917 (Columbus: Champlin Press, 1917).

Notes. Chapter 3

14. *The Grandion*, 1917, pp. 42, 51, 57.

15. *Ibid.*, pp. 21, 59.

16. Grade report of Lola M. King, December 21, 1916 (copy in Archives, reprinted in Jacob L. Bapst and Ivan M. Tribe, *University of Rio Grande and Rio Grande Community College* (Charleston, SC: Arcadia Publishing, 2017), p. 32; Rio Grande College Transcript, Beryl Halley, October 28, 1966 (copy in Archives). For examples of Beryl Halley and her friends' trips to Gallipolis for shopping and socializing, see the *Gallipolis Daily Tribune*, September 11, 1915, p. 3; January 15, 1916, p. 4; April 1, 1916, p. 4; June 23, 1916, p. 4; August 23, 1916, pp. 2, 3; October 9, 1916, p. 1; October 27, 1916, p. 1; and December 23, 1916, p. 4. Sometimes her address is given as Angola or Crown City, rather than Rio Grande or Bladen. These were also small hamlets down river from Gallipolis, where her mother may have resided at the time. Ziegfeld girls were expected to get their names in the newspapers as often as possible. However, the Halley sisters seem to have attained expertise in this area even before leaving Gallia County. In fact, two trips to the dentist for Beryl even made the *Gallipolis Daily Tribune* on February 27, 1917, p. 4, and April 2, 1917, p. 4.

17. Estivaun Matthews, Charles A. Murray and Pauline Rife, *Gallia County One-Room Schools: The Cradle Years* (Gallipolis, OH: Gallia County Historical Society, 1993), p. 126; Cecile Virran [sic] Halley, 1920 Census, Ancestry.com.

18. Matthews, et al., *Gallia County One-Room Schools*, pp. 115, 308, 313.

19. "23 Years Ago Today," *Gallipolis Daily Tribune*, July 20, 1940, p. 2; Matthews, et al., *Gallia County One-Room Schools*, p. 71. Among Beryl's possessions shipped to the University of Rio Grande Archives was a small pictures of the Civil War Soldier's Monument in Vinton County. Since this seems to have been the only time she was ever in McArthur, the photo must date from her July 1917 visit. Efforts by the authors to pinpoint the exact location of Story's Run School did not yield results, although one more familiar with the area might know.

20. Paul Porter Halley, Ancestry.com. Some of the information is under the name Paul R. Holley, but given the fact that birth, death, and name of mother is the same, there can be no doubt of the identity *Gallipolis Daily Tribune*, August 2, 1971, p. 1; *Cemeteries of Ohio Township* (Gallipolis: Gallia County Historical Society, 1980), p. 8; additional information is from Paul's military discharge, read via telephone by Gallia County Recorder, Roger Walker to Jacob Bapst on March 13, 2018. Although he has a Veteran's Administration tombstone, Paul's name is incorrectly spelled as "Holley" on the stone, but corrected in the above publication.

21. *Gallipolis Daily Tribune*, February 22, 1916, p. 3; February 28, 1916, p. 3; May 4, 1916, p. 3; "Marie Hall," Internet Movie Database, Internet Broadway Database. She also had film credits under the names Maybelle Halsey and Miss Halsey. The IBDb makes no mention of a Ziegfeld connection.

22. *Gallipolis Daily Tribune*, September 25, 1918. Nina Beryl Halley, Ohio Military Men [sic], Ancestry.com. For women's service in World War I, see Nathaniel Patch, "The Story of the Female Yeomen during the First World War," Prologue 38:6 (Fall 2006), on line in http://www.archives.gov/publications/prologue/2006/fall/yeomen-f.html. A more comprehensive treatment is by Jean Ebbert and Marie-Beth Hall, *The First, the Few, the Forgotten: Navy and Marine Corps Women in World War I* (Annapolis, MD: U.S. Naval Institute Press, 2002).

23. Patch, "The Story of the Female Yeoman." These lyrics first appeared *in Newport Recruit 1918*, and have been altered slightly hear to fit the Norfolk naval base.

24. Patch, "The Story of the Female Yeomen"; Nina Beryl Halley, Ohio Military Men [sic], Ancestry.com; The Official Roster of Ohio Soldiers, Sailors and Marines in the World War 1917–18 Vol. XX (Columbus: The F. J. Heer Printing Co., 1928), p. 792.

Chapter 3

1. Norfolk City Directory, 1920, p. 469; *Chicago Tribune*, March 23, 1924, p. 102.

2. Samuel L. Leiter, ed., *Encyclopedia of the New York Stage, 1920–1930* (Westport, CT: Greenwood Press, 1985), p. 894.

3. Robert Edgar Ervin, *Jackson County, Ohio: Its History and Its People, 1900–1950* (Jackson, OH: Sheridan Books, 2008), pp. 164–166; "Tangerine" Internet Broadway Database (hereafter referred to as IBDb); "Frank Crumit"; Joel Whitburn, *Pop Memories, 1890–1954* (Menominee Falls, WI: Record Research, 1986), pp. 115–116. Frank Crumit's biggest hit record, "The Gay Caballero," a spoof on Latin American romantic types, came in 1928.

Notes. Chapter 3

4. Ervin, *Jackson County*, pp. 164–166.

5. "Tangerine," IBDb. For Oscar Eagle and possible connections, see "Gallipolis People on Broadway," *Gallipolis Daily Tribune*, October 24, 1925, p. 1; "Oscar Eagle," IBDb. Several members of the Eagle Family also had close ties to Rio Grande College, although Oscar's name is not among them.

6. *Hartford Courant*, June 14, 1922; "Florence Moore" IBDb; "Cheating the Thermometer," *Pittsburgh Post-Gazette*, June 18, 1922, p. 14. Kellerman may not have quite swum the Channel but she was still widely acclaimed and later became the subject of a biopic, *Million Dollar Mermaid*, starring Esther Williams. Gertrude Ederle became the first woman to successfully swim the English Channel, in the 1920s.

7. *Brooklyn Life*, September 23, 1922, p. 12; "Hazel Dawn," IBDb; "Glenn Anders"; IBDb; *Philadelphia Inquirer*, October 8, 1922, p. 80; P. M. A.-A. E. A. [Producing Managers' Association-Actors' Equity Association], Minimum Contract, August 26, 1922 (Beryl Halley Collection, Rio Grande Archives); Leiter, ed., *Encyclopedia of the New York Stage*, p. 200.

8. Undated clipping from *San-Francisco Chronicle* (Beryl Halley Collection); *Washington Star*, December 17, 1922 (Image 89); *Longreach Leader*, February 23, 1923, p. 1; "California Beauty," *Chicago Tribune*, December 27, 1922, p. 4.

9. *Philadelphia Inquirer*, January 16, 1923, p. 8. See IBDb for Allen, Ballou, and Ruggles. For a deeper discussion of the latter's film career, see Ephraim Katz, revised by Fred Klein and Ronald Dean Nolen, *The Film Encyclopedia, Fourth Edition* (New York: Harper Resource, 2001), p. 1191. Ruggles had a major supporting role in the Howard Hawks classic *Bringing Up Baby* (1938).

10. *Harper's Bazaar*, April 1923, page number unknown (found in Beryl Halley Collection, University of Rio Grande).

11. This condensed history of Florenz Ziegfeld and his production is derived from a compendium of the following secondary sources: Randolph Carter, *The World of Flo Ziegfeld* (New York: Praeger, 1974); Marjorie Farnsworth, *The Ziegfeld Follies* (New York: Bonanza Books, 1956); Ethan Mordden, *Ziegfeld: The Man Who Invented Show Business* (New York: St. Martin's Press, 2008); and Richard and Paulette Ziegfeld, *The Ziegfeld Touch: The Life and Times of Florenz Ziegfeld, Jr.* (New York: Henry Abrams, 1993). A modern feminist perspective is offered by Linda Mizejewski, *Ziegfeld Girl: Image and Icon In Culture and Cinema* (Durham, NC: Duke University Press, 1999). The most recent (and perhaps most definitive) account is by Cynthia Brideson and Sara Brideson, *Ziegfeld and His Follies: A Biography of Broadway's Greatest Producer* (Lexington: University Press of Kentucky, 2015). Lewis A. Erenberg, *Steppin' Out: New York Nightlife and the Transformation of American Culture, 1890–1930* (Chicago: University of Chicago Press, 1981), p. 207.

12. "Ziegfeld Discusses Girls," *Brooklyn Daily Eagle*, May 6, 1923, p. 74.

13. *Ibid.*

14. *New York Morning Telegraph* (1925); quoted in "What Makes a Ziegfeld Girl?" in "Musicals101.com; accessed in http://musicals 101.com/Ziegfeldspeaks.htm.

15. *Ibid.*

16. *Ibid.*

17. Brideson and Brideson, *Ziegfeld and His Follies*, pp. 94–95. For a more detailed study of Lorraine, whose relationship with Ziegfeld ended before Beryl Halley joined the Follies, see Nils Hanson, *Lillian Lorraine: The Life and Times of a Ziegfeld Diva* (Jefferson, NC: McFarland, 2009).

18. Eaton quoted in Michael Kantor and Laurence Maslon, *Broadway: The American Musical* (New York: Bulfinch, 2004), p. 21; Brideson and Brideson, *Ziegfeld and his Follies*, p. 64. Doris Eaton Travers (1904–2010) also wrote a perceptive autobiography, *The Days We Danced: The Story of My Family from Ziegfeld to Arthur Murray and Beyond* (Norman: University of Oklahoma Press, 2003). Anna Held and Ziegfeld, who, in a sense, made each other legendary, are discussed in Eve Golden, *Anna Held and the Birth of Ziegfeld's Broadway* (Lexington: University Press of Kentucky, 2000).

19. Bernard Sobel, *Broadway Heartbeat: Memoirs of a Press Agent* (New York: Hermitage House, 1953), p. 107.

20. WOR Radio Program typescript, April 30, 1937 (copy in Beryl Halley Collection).

21. Michael Lasser, "The Glorifier: Florenz Ziegfeld and the Creation of the American Showgirl," *The American Scholar* 63: 3 (Summer 1994), pp. 441–448.

22. George C. Warren, "Five Ziegfeld Beauties Pay Chronicle Visit," *San Francisco Chronicle*, September 24, 1923, p. 11. The trip to the West Coast seems likely to have been Elise Sparrow's only experience with a Zieg-

Notes. Chapter 4

feld shows, as her name graces no lists of Ziegfeld girls, nor indeed on the Internet Broadway Database.

23. *Ibid.*

24. "Ziegfeld Beauties in Film" and "Dancers See Film Selves," *San Francisco Examiner*, May 24, 1923; *The Enemies of Women*, IMDb. Ironically, none of the threesome discussed herein are credited in the IMDb; Bow, Dumont, and Worthing are, however.

25. *New York Daily News*, September 10, 1923, p. 20; October 10, 1923, p. 25; O. O. McIntyre, "New York Day by Day" Olean, *New York Times Herald*, January 19, 1924, p. 27. McIntyre was, of course, correct, but it also took the Great Depression to make it happen.

26. Ziegfeld and Ziegfeld, *The Ziegfeld Touch*, pp. 257; Brideson and Brideson, *Ziegfeld and His Follies*, pp. 274–275, 453–454.

27. New Amsterdam Theatre. pp. 5, 31, 33, 37, 39 (February 1924, Program in Beryl Halley Collection).

28. Joseph Bennett, "Brother Vincent Lopez: Anatomy of a Band Leader," accessed http://www.KnightTemplar/articles/lopez.htm//Top.

29. Vincent Lopez, *Lopez Speaking* (New York: Citadel Press, 1960), p. 177.

30. *Ibid.* pp. 177–178.

31. *Ibid.* p. 178; Bennett, "Brother Vincent Lopez."

32. For an example, see *Chicago Tribune*, March 24, 1924, p. 102.

33. False claims of birthplaces have long been common in the entertainment world. Two examples: 1920s cowboy movie star Ken Maynard claimed to be from Mission, Texas, when he was actually born in Indiana; country singer Lloyd "Cowboy" Copas, gave his birthplace as Muskogee, Oklahoma, at about the same time he was applying for a delayed birth certificate in Adams County, Ohio. In fact, the first modern star to claim a phony birthplace may have been the original Ziegfeld star, Anna Held, who, although born in Poland, claimed Paris.

34. For fan letter examples, see "Ward M. Miller to My Dear Miss Halley," February 23, 1924; "Frederick T. Howard to My Dear Miss Halley," February 14, 1924; "Marjorie Stewart to Dear Miss Halley," undated (all in Beryl Halley collection).

35. "Walter J. Kingsley, to My Wonderful Beryl," October 20, 1923; "Winfield Scott, Jr., to Dearest Beryl," February 11, 1924 (both in Beryl Halley Collection).

36. Jim Bishop, *The Mark Hellinger Story: A Biography of Broadway and Hollywood* (New York: Appleton-Century-Crofts, Inc., 1952), pp. 80–81. Mark Hellinger in 1929. Successfully married Ziegfeld Girl Gladys Glad (1907–1983), one of the six on the list.

37. "Bladen Girl Attracts Attention," *Gallipolis Daily Tribune*, May 6, 1924, p. 2. The picture from *Red Book* became known to the authors when the folded page dropped out of her friend Helen Martin's *Grandion* yearbook that had been donated to the University of Rio Grande Archives.

Chapter 4

1. Chorus Equity Association of America, Contract between Ziegfeld Follies Inc. and Miss Beryl Halley, June 17, 1924 (in Beryl Halley Collection).

2. "S. H. Nickerson to Dear Miss Halley," July 27, 1924 (in Beryl Halley Collection).

3. Incoming Passenger Lists, Southampton, 1924 (Ancestry.com); "London Wants Ziegfeld Show," *New York Daily News*, June 11, 1924; June 30, 1924, p. 64; "Ziegfeld Plans 3 Shows here, 'Boots' Overseas," July 14, 1924, p. 16.

4. Incoming Passenger Lists, New York, 1924 (Ancestry.com); Cunard Line "Saloon Passenger List, R.M.S. Berengaria, Sailing from Southampton to New York" (via Cherbourg), Saturday, August 23, 1924. (in Beryl Halley Collection).

5. *Ibid.*

6. *Ibid.*

7. For background on Richard Kyle Fox and his building of *The Police Gazette*, see Michael T. Isenberg, *John L. Sullivan and His America* (Urbana: University of Illinois Press, 1988), pp. 92–94; *The National Police Gazette*, August 23, 1924, front cover. For a more in depth look and the Gazette and its impact, see Guy Reel, *The National Police Gazette and the Making of the Modern American Man, 1879–1906* (New York: Palgrave Macmillan, 2006).

8. *All Peppered Up* (New York: Leo Feist Inc., 1924), front cover (In Beryl Halley Collection at University of Rio Grande). The only Halley portrait which can even compare to that of the Vargas effort was the one by Ernest Van Duren made during the 1926 *Palm Beach Nights* in Florida.

9. Vincent Lopez, *Lopez Speaking* (New York: Citadel Press, 1960), pp. 193.

Notes. Chapter 5

10. Joseph E. Bennett, "Brother Vincent Lopez: Anatomy of a Band Leader," www.knighttemplar.org/KnightTemplar/articles/lopez; Lopez, *Lopez Speaking*, p. 208.

11. *Ibid.*

12. *Ibid.* In addition to keeping up with Vincent Lopez's playboy image, some doubt exists as to whether or not, he was still married to his first wife, which may explains his reluctance to be serious about marriage.

13. *Harrisburg [PA] Telegraph*, August 8, 1925, p. 9.

14. *Indianapolis Star*, December 7, 1924, p. 80.

15. "The Finale at the Follies Dress Rehearsal," March 1925, Reprinted in Edmund Wilson, *The American Earthquake: A Documentary of the Twenties and Thirties* (New York: Octagon Books, 1971), p. 44.

16. *Ibid.* pp. 44–45.

17. *New York Daily News*, October 10, 1926, p 82; *Exhibitor's Trade Review*, August 29, 1925, p. 13; "First National Has Great List Planned for Next Three Months," *Moving Picture World*, October 17, 1925, p. 548. For Barthelmess, Gish, Powell, and Puglia, see Ephraim Katz, *The Film Encyclopedia, Fourth Edition* (New York: Harper Resource, 2001), pp. 95–96, 532–533, 1101, 1113.

18. *Buffalo Courier*, March 8, 1925, p. 7; another undated clipping from the *New York Times* showing silhouettes is in the Beryl Halley Collection.

19. "Wasn't My Chin, Actress Wails, Asking $75,000," *Daily News*, October 24, 1925, p. 23. With modifications, this article was repeated in other newspapers, including the *Shreveport Times*, October 25, 1925, p. 1, and another edition of the *Daily News*.

20. Alfred Albelli, "Beryl's Double Chin in Ad Nets Her $5,000 in Damages," *Daily News* (NY), November 23, 1928, p. 51.

21. For the Castles' career and impact, see Lewis A. Erenberg, *Steppin' Out: New York Nightlife and the Transformation of American Culture, 1890–1930* (Chicago: University of Chicago Press, 1981), pp. 158–171; see also Irene Castle, et al., *Castles in the Air* (Garden City, NY: Doubleday & Co, 1958).

22. "The Frivolity," *Variety*, November 25, 1925, p. 52; December 9, 1925, p. 40.

Chapter 5

1. "Bound for South," *New York Daily News*, January 10, 1926, p. 106; "Show Headed South," *Tampa Tribune*, January 9, 1926, p. 18.

2. Patricia Ziegfeld, *The Ziegfelds' Girl: Confessions of an Abnormally Happy Childhood* (New York: Little, Brown, 1964), p. 120; Billie Burke, *With a Feather on My Nose* (New York: Appleton Century Crofts, 1949), p. 184. For a broad discussion on the ideas behind the production, see Cynthia Brideson and Sara Brideson, *Ziegfeld and His Follies: A Biography of Broadway's Greatest Producer* (Lexington: University Press of Kentucky, 2015), pp. 306–314. For Edmonde Guy, see "Almost the Bride of Her Own Brother," *Galveston Daily News*, October 25, 1925, p. 11.

3. Richard and Paulette Ziegfeld, *The Ziegfeld Touch: The Life and Times of Florenz Ziegfeld, Jr.* (New York: Harry N. Abrams, Inc., 1993), p. 129; Program, *Ziegfeld's Palm Beach Nights* (West Palm Beach: Tropical Sun Press, 1926), p. 1. How much the wives had to do with persuading their husbands cannot be confirmed, but the *New York Daily News*, January 17, 1926, p. 84, stated that Singer and Biddle "are reported as the angels for 'Ziegfeld's Palm Beach Nights.'"

4. For more detail on the Singers, see Ruth Brandon, *Singer and the Sewing Machine: A Romance* (New York: Kadisha International, 1977); see also "Anthony J. Drexel Biddle Dead; Ambassador to Spain was 64, Envoy and Officer in World War II—Tributes Paid by Kennedy and Eisenhower," Obituary, *New York Times*, November 14, 1961.

5. Program, *Ziegfeld's Palm Beach Nights*, pp. 3–5, 9.

6. *Ibid.*, pp. 11–21.

7. *Ibid.*, pp. 23–27.

8. *Ibid.*, pp. 27–31.

9. *Palm Beach Post*, February 5, 1926, p. 8; "Florenz Ziegfeld Produces 'Follies,'" *Orlando Sentinel*, February 7, 1926, p. 59; "The New Eve," May 1926, p. 44; Brideson and Brideson, *Ziegfeld and His Follies*, pp. 314–315; Ziegfeld, *The Ziegfeld Touch*, pp. 129–130.

10. *New York Daily News*, January 1, 1926, p. 17; "Florida Bathers Feel Laws' Lash Must Wear Wraps Going to and from Beach," *Ogden [Utah] Standard*, February 18, 1926, p. 6; "Mary Jane receives Trophy at Montmartre," *Palm Beach Post*, March 18, 1926, p. 10.

11. "Ziegfeld Star Bemoans Lack of Equine Companionship," *Palm Beach Post*, March 15, 1926, p. 7.

12. Betsy Schuyler, "Gorgeous Apparel at

Notes. Chapter 6

Ziegfeld 'Nights.'" *Palm Beach Post*, January 27, 1926, p. 19; see also Schuyler's "Winter's Most Brilliant Event Brings Out Gorgeous Apparel," *Richmond* [Indiana] *Item*, January 24, 1926, p. 7.

13. "Glenn Hunter," IMDb; IBDb. "The Broadway Boob," IMDb. Chances are that Beryl's earlier film, *The Beautiful City*, was also made in New Jersey.

14. *Ibid*.; *Exhibitor Herald*, March 13, 1926, p. 66.

15. "The Bunk of 1926," IBDb: *New York Daily News*, May 10, 1926, p. 56; *New York Times*, May 10, 1926, p. 19; for a discussion see Thomas S. Hischak, *Off-Broadway Musicals Since 1919: From Greenwich Village Follies to The Toxic Avenger* (Lanham, MD: The Scarecrow Press, 2013), pp. 12–13.

16. Will Page, *Behind the Curtains of the Broadway Beauty Trust* (New York: Edward A. Miller, N. P., 1927), opposite p. 16.

17. "Eve Driven Out of Stage Eden," *St. Louis Post-Dispatch*, May 11, 1926, p. 1; *Elmira Star-Gazette*, May 11, 1926, p. 1; "N.Y. Actress Is Asked to Explain Her Role of Eve," *Salt Lake Telegram*, May 11, 1926, p. 1.

18. "Nude? No! Wore a Leaf! Eve Pleads in Court," *Pittsburgh Post-Gazette*, May 12, 1926, p. 11.

19. *Brooklyn Eagle*, May 12, 1926, p. 25.

20. "Turn Over New Leaf? No Need. Eve Goes Free," *New York Daily News*, May 15, 1926, p. 7.

21. Leon M. Siler, "Fig Leaf Wins," *Wilkes-Barre Times Leader*, May 24, 1926, p. 10; See also *Muncie* [Indiana] *Evening Press*, May 21, 1926, p. 1.

22. "'Bunk of 1926' Found Naughty, Closed By Jury," *New York Daily News*, June 8, 1926. p. 115.

23. "Broadway Shocked at the Attempts Made to Improve Its Morals," *Santa Cruz Evening News*, June 9, 1926, p. 1.

24. "'Bunk' Reopened Tonight Under Court's Shield," *New York Daily News*, June 9, 1926, p. 2. Ironically, one of the biggest critics of what he termed "shocking trends" was none other than Ziegfeld tableaux arranger Ben Ali Haggin, who while never mentioning *The Bunk of 1926*, his comments in the June 12 *Daily News* (p. 83) are obviously related. It tempts one to think that Haggin opposed any tableaux of near nudity that he did not create.

25. "Naughty Niceties," *The Harvard Crimson*, June 10, 1926.

26. "A Letter to a Certain Party," *New York Daily News*, June 13, 1926, p. 83; Samuel L. Leiter, ed., *The Encyclopedia of the New York Stage, 1920–1930* (Westport, CT: Greenwood Press, 1985), pp. 103–104.

27. Contract between George H. Maines, Press Representative and Beryl Halley, May 12, 1926 (in Beryl Halley Collection). Whether the contract was something that would have transpired anyway, or was based on her newfound "fame" cannot be determined.

28. "The Venus of the Twentieth Century," *Los Angeles Times*, June 10, 2016, p. 30. Silent film star Claire Windsor has been cited as another of the fifteen most beautiful women in America the artist had chosen for a portrait.

29. "Eyes Versus Legs—Which Allures Mere Male More?" Appleton, *Wisconsin Post-Crescent*, December 11, 1926, p. 1.

30. *Ibid*.

31. *New York Daily News*, August 22, p. 130; Brideson and Brideson, *Ziegfeld and His Follies*, p. 292.

32. "Beauty to Tour," *New York Daily News*, June 28, 1926, p. 79; *Daily News*, October 10, 1926, p. 82.

33. Brideson and Brideson, *Ziegfeld and His Follies*, pp. 318–321; "New Ziegfeld Show at Forrest," *Philadelphia Inquirer*, January 11, 1927, p. 14.

34. "Invitation to Cornerstone laying," December 9, 1926 (in Beryl Halley Collection); Irene Thirer, "Ziegfeld Lays Cornerstone as Beauties Glow," *New York Daily News*, December 10, 1926, p. 138.

35. *New York Daily News*, December 25, 1926; *Brooklyn Daily Eagle*, December 29, 1926, p. 1.

36. *New York Morning Telegraph*, January 2, 1927, not paginated; *Philadelphia Inquirer*, January 10, 1927, p. 10; "She Will Be 'Venus,'" *St. Louis Post Dispatch*, January 9, 1927, p. 105; "Premiere," *New York Daily News*, January 19, 1927, p. 33.

37. Grace Cutler, "Blonde Venus Hunts Ziegfeld With Writ," *New York Daily News*, January 19, 1927, p. 2.

Chapter 6

1. See Ira Rosenwaike, *Population History of New York City* (Syracuse, NY: Syracuse University Press, 1972), pp. 1–12, 58. Subsequent paragraphs are condensed from this work.

Notes. Chapter 6

2. David Wallace, *Capital of the World: A Portrait of New York City in the Roaring Twenties* (Guilford, CT: Lyons Press, 2011), p. IX.

3. Burton W. Peretti, *Nightclub City: Politics and Amusement in Manhattan* (Philadelphia: University of Pennsylvania Press, 2007), p. 4.

4. The best brief development in baseball in the 1920s are adequately covered in the chapter "The Golden Twenties" by Charles Alexander, *Our Game: An American Baseball History* (New York: Henry Holt and Co., 1991), pp. 130–155.

5. John A. Lucas and Ronald A. Smith, *Saga of American Sport* (Philadelphia: Lea & Febiger, 1978), pp. 308–311; Benjamin G. Rader, *American Sports: From the Age of Folk Games to the Age of Spectators* (Englewood Cliffs, NJ: Prentice-Hall, Inc., 1983), pp. 186–193.

6. *Ibid.*, pp. 182–186; Lucas and Smith, *Saga of American Sport*, pp. 315–317.

7. Rader, *American Sports*. For a more thorough study, see Herbert Warren Wind, *The Story of American Golf* (New York: Knopf, 1975).

8. Wallace, *Capital of the World*, pp. 138–151.

9. *Ibid.*, pp. 153–163.

10. For the "Harlem Renaissance," see Gilbert Osofsky, *Harlem: The Making of a Ghetto, Negro New York, 1890–1930* (New York: Harper Torchbooks, 1968), pp. 179–187.

11. Wallace, *Capital of the World*, pp. 165–187.

12. Russel Nye, *The Unembarrassed Muse: The Popular Arts in America* (New York: The Dial Press, 1970), pp. 250–252.

13. Wallace, *Capital of the World*, pp. 109–117. For a more thorough look at Henry Luce, see James Baughman, *Henry R. Luce and the Rise of American News Media* (Boston: Twayne, 1987) and W. A. Swanberg, *Luce and His Empire* (New York: Scribner, 1972).

14. Wallace, *Capital of the World*, pp. 77–90. For Hopper and Parsons, see Ephraim Katz, *The Film Encyclopedia*, Fourth Edition (New York: Harper Resource, 2001), pp. 445–446, 1065.

15. *Ibid.*; See also Frederick Lewis Allen, *Only Yesterday: Informal History of the Nineteen Twenties* (New York: Harper and Brothers, 1931), pp. 77–79.

16. Wallace, *Capital of the World*, pp. 113–

117. For a more comprehensive look at radio and its overall impact, see Thomas S. Lewis, *Empire of the Air: The Men Who Made Radio* (New York: Burlingame/Harper Collins, 1991).

17. Quoted in Wallace, *Capital of the World*, pp. 16, 18.

18. *Ibid.* p. 20.

19. This and succeeding paragraphs concerning the Mafia are condensed from chapters 3 and 4 in Wallace, *Capital of the World*, pp. 31–56, with some added from the in-depth study by David Critchley, *The Origins of Organized Crime in America: The New York City Mafia, 1891–1931* (New York: Routledge, 2009), and Humbert S. Nelli, *The Business of Crime* (New York: Oxford University Press, 1976).

20. Peretti, *Nightclub City*, p. 112.

21. Lewis A. Erenberg, *Steppin' Out: New York Nightlife and the Transformation of American Culture, 1890–1930* (Chicago: University of Chicago Press, 1891), pp. 238–239; Wallace, *Capital of the World*, pp. 13–14.

22. *Ibid.* 1–4; Erenberg, *Steppin' Out*, p. 255.

23. *Ibid.*, pp. 5–7; Wallace, *Capital of the World*, pp. 222–227.

24. Nils Thor Granlund, *Blondes, Brunettes, and Bullets* (New York: David McKay, Co. Inc. 1957),

25. Peretti, *Nightclub City*, p. 7. For a map of the Broadway theater district, see Ziegfeld, *The Ziegfeld Touch*, p. 320. The theaters are: Century, Cosmopolitan, Ziegfeld, Warwick, Manhattan, Thorley's House of Flowers, Globe, Palace, New York, Majestic, Dinty Moore's, Lyric, New Amsterdam, Casino, and Koster & Bial's. More theaters were added in later years. In addition, many of the better-known nightclubs, featuring entertainment by Broadway showgirls, were in the same area.

26. Cynthia Brideson and Sara Brideson, *Ziegfeld and His Follies* (Lexington: University of Kentucky Press, 2015), pp. 23–24. Samuel Nixon's name had been Anglicized from Nirdlinger. For the 1926 situation, see Will Page, *Behind the Curtains of the Broadway Beauty Trust* (New York: Edward A. Miller, pub., 1927), pp. 10–12.

27. Brideson and Brideson, *Ziegfeld and His Follies*, p. 24.

28. *Ibid.*, 59–60.

29. Granlund, *Blondes, Brunettes, and Bullets*, p. 203.

30. Linda S. Watts, Alice L. George, and

Notes. Chapter 7

Scott Beekman, *Social History of the United States: The 1920s* (Santa Barbara: ABC Clio, 2009), pp. 85–95.

31. Beretti, *Nightclub City*, pp. 142–145. For a comprehensive look at the mayor, see Thomas Kessner, *Fiorello H. LaGuardia and the Making of Modern New York* (New York: Viking, 1989).

32. For a different perspective, read Roderick Nash, *The Nervous Generation: American Thought, 1917–1930* (Chicago: Ivan R. Dee, 1970).

33. Granlund, *Blondes, Brunettes, and Bullets*, pp. 162–169.

Chapter 7

1. Dave Tabler, "She Came Rollin' Down the Mountain," Appalachian History.net, www.appalachianhistory.net/2016/04/she-came-rollin'-down-mountain.html. Although initially designed as a spoof on rural folk, the song's popularity among country music people has been widespread. It has been recorded under various titles by the Callahan Brothers, Sweet Violet Boys (a.k.a. Prairie Ramblers), Homer and Jethro, Tex Morton (in Australia), and an unreleased field effort by Billy Cox.

2. Linda S. Watts, Alice L. George, and Scott Beekman, *Social History of the United States: The 1920's* (Santa Barbara: ABC-CLIO, Inc., 2009), p. 23.

3. H. Ellis Sibley. "William Giddings Sibley and Hiram Ellis Sibley" in *Gallia County, Ohio: People in History to 1980* (Paoli, PA: Taylor, 1980.) p. 314.

4. *Gallipolis Daily Tribune*, November 6, 1920, p. 2.

5. Office of Strategic Research, Ohio Department of Development, "Decennial Census of Population by County: 1910 to 2010." www.development.ohio.gov/reports/reports_censusarchive_map.htm.

6. "Detailed Census Figures Show Loss in County," *Gallipolis Daily Tribune*, May 29, 1931, p. 1.

7. "Notes Important Changes Toward City Betterment," *Gallipolis Daily Tribune*, June 15, 1926, p. 1.

8. David M. Kennedy, *Freedom from Fear: The American People in Depression and War, 1929–1945* (New York: Oxford University Press, 1999), pp. 41–42.

9. *Gallipolis Daily Tribune*, February 16, 1931, p. 4.

10. "Farm News and Views," *Gallipolis Daily Tribune*, September 26, 1931.

11. Ivan Tribe. "Gallia County, Ohio: A Brief History" in *Gallia County, Ohio: People in History to 1980*, p. 13.

12. *Gallipolis Daily Tribune*, July 22, 1920, p. 2.

13. "Community Association Opposes Gas Rate Increase," *Gallipolis Daily Tribune*, December 10, 1920, p. 1.

14. Stephan G. Bullard, Bridget J. Gromek, Martha Fout, Ruth Fout, and the Point Pleasant River Museum, *The Silver Bridge Disaster of 1967* (Charleston, SC: Arcadia Publishing, 2012), p. 16. On December 15, 1967, the Silver Bridge collapsed into the Ohio River, plunging thirty-one vehicles into the river, causing forty-six deaths. The communities of Point Pleasant, West Virginia, and Gallipolis, Ohio, carry the scars of this tragedy to the present day.

15. "R. Grande College Made Accessible By New Highways," *Gallipolis Daily Tribune*, February 25, 1938, p. 1.

16. *Fortieth Annual Catalog of Rio Grande College* (Rio Grande, OH: Rio Grande College, 1916), p. 17.

17. "The Telephone Operators Strike At Pomeroy," *Gallipolis Daily Tribune*, November 17, 1920, p. 2.

18. "Number Telephones Here Reaches All Time Peak, 1245," *Gallipolis Daily Tribune*, February 1, 1939, p. 5.

19. "A Radio Log," *Gallipolis Daily Tribune*, November 3, 1923, p. 4.

20. *Gallipolis Daily Tribune*, November 6, 1929, p. 3.

21. "Talkie Talk Takes Place of Gossip in Conversation Thurs," *Gallipolis Daily Tribune*, January 16, 1930, p. 1.

22. "History of BREC—Buckeye Rural Electric." Buckeye Rural Electric, https://www.buckeyerec.coop/index.php/history-of-brec/, August 6, 2018.

23. "Almost Half Ohio Farms Electrified," *Gallipolis Daily Tribune*, February 6, 1931, p. 4.

24. United States Department of Agriculture. "Rural Electrification" by Robert T. Beall in *Yearbook of Agriculture, 1940*, pp. 790–809.

25. John L. Neufeld, "Rural Electrification," May, 2017. www.chicago.universitypress scholarship.com.

26. "BREC Makes County's Electrical Dream Reality," *Gallipolis Daily Tribune*, August 27, 1940, p. 7.

27. This is the family history as told by

Notes. Chapter 7

Janet Bapst, mother of the co-author. Since 1952, the house has received electricity from the Buckeye Electric Co-Operative.

28. Lowe Stokes and His North Georgians, "Prohibition Is a Failure," Brunswick 491, 1930.

29. Elizabeth Stevenson, *Babbits and Bohemians: The American 1920's* (New York: Macmillan, 1967), p. 89.

30. *Gallipolis Daily Tribune*, from 1895 to 2017, is available online through the Samuel Bossard Memorial Library of Gallia County, Ohio. Searching is done by an optical scan of terms entered.

31. "Sheriff Makes Find When Auto Hits Tree," *Gallipolis Daily Tribune*, August 27, 1920, p. 1.

32. "Gun Battle in Meigs County," *Gallipolis Daily Tribune*, September 2, 1920, p. 1.

33. "I Am No Dry Detective," *Gallipolis Daily Tribune*, August 15, 1921, p. 4.

34. The collection of houses along the Meigs–Gallia County Line is still called "Pity Me." The name derives from the Epitome Coal Company, which had a mine in that area at the turn of the 20th century.

35. "No Offense Intended to a Big Meigs County Industry," *Gallipolis Daily Tribune*, April 11, 1923, p. 1.

36. "Jackson County Constable Sentenced To Pen," *Gallipolis Daily Tribune*, January 1, 1925, p. 1.

37. "Bootleg Gangs Obtain Revenge at Gallipolis," *Dayton Herald*, July 29, 1925, p. 1.

38. "Blame Bootleggers," *Dayton Herald*, August 13, 1925, p. 10.

39. "Local Flapper Gets Soaked in Pomeroy Justice Court," *Gallipolis Daily Tribune*, June 21, 1926, p. 1.

40. *Gallipolis Daily Tribune*, January 15, 1929, p. 1.

41. Lowe Stoke, "Prohibition Is a Failure," Brunswick 491, 1930.

42. "Whipping Post as Deterrent to Petty Crimes is Discussed by Veteran Commentator," *Gallipolis Daily Tribune*, September 2, 1932, p. 1.

43. "Suggests Birth Control," *Gallipolis Daily Tribune*, February 8, 1933, p. 1.

44. *Gallipolis Daily Tribune*, March 10, 1934, p. 2.

45. From "Ain't No Bugs on Me," by Fiddlin' John Carson, OKeh 45259, 1928.

46. Rory McVeigh, *The Rise of the Ku Klux Klan: Right-wing Movements and National Politics* (Minneapolis: University of Minnesota Press, 2009) p. 143.

47. *Gallipolis Daily Tribune*, November 18, 1925, p. 4.

48. *Gallipolis Daily Tribune*, February 6, 1926, p. 4.

49. *Gallipolis Daily Tribune*, August 19, 1926, p. 4.

50. "Ku Klux Klan Organizes," *Gallipolis Daily Tribune*, April 28, 1923, p. 1.

51. "No Ku Klux At Court House," *Gallipolis Daily Tribune*, May 14, 1923, p. 1.

52. "Large Crowd Saw Klan Demonstration at Fair Grounds," *Gallipolis Daily Tribune*, September 21, 1923, p. 1.

53. "Klan to Burn Cross on River Front," *Gallipolis Daily Tribune*, July 31, 1925, p. 4.

54. "Ku-Klux-Klan Outing," *Gallipolis Daily Tribune*, June 26, 1928, p. 1.

55. "All I Got's Gone" by Ernest and Eddie Stoneman, Vocalion 02901, 1934.

56. *Gallipolis Daily Tribune*, October 30, 1929, p. 1.

57. "Letters From Tribune Readers," *Gallipolis Daily Tribune*, April 6, 1934, p. 4.

58. "Women's Flesh and Ruling Power," *Gallipolis Daily Tribune*, May 29, 1929, p. 4.

59. *Gallipolis Daily Tribune*, May 7, 1923, p. 4.

60. "New York Notes," *Gallipolis Daily Tribune*, August 6, 1926, p. 4.

61. *Gallipolis Daily Tribune*, October 14, 1926, p. 3.

62. Internet Broadway Database, *The Broadway League*, https://www.ibdb.com/shows. November 3, 2018.

63. "Demand for Tickets Precedes Advertising," *Gallipolis Daily Tribune*, February 27, 1927, p. 1.

64. *Gallipolis Daily Tribune*, February 28, 1927, p. 4.

65. *Gallipolis Daily Tribune*, March 3, 1927, p. 3.

66. *Gallipolis Daily Tribune*, March 7, 1927, p. 1.

67. Jacob L. Bapst and Ivan M. Tribe, *University of Rio Grande and Rio Grande Community College* (Charleston, SC: Arcadia, 2017), p. 31.

68. Abbie Gail Goodnite and Ivan M. Tribe, *Rio Grande: From Baptists and Bevo to the Bell Tower, 1876–2001* (Ashland, KY: The Jesse Stuart Foundation, 2002), pp. 97–98.

69. Bapst and Tribe, p. 23.

70. This information comes from the original program for "The Historical Pageant Rio Grande College Fifty Golden Years, 1876–1926." This rare twelve-page document

is kept at the Jean Lloyd Cooper Archives at the University of Rio Grande.

71. "Thousands See Pageant Celebrating Fiftieth Year," *Gallipolis Daily Tribune*, June 12, 1926, p. 1.

72. Bapst and Tribe, p. 43.

73. Goodnite and Tribe, *Rio Grande From Baptists and Bevo to the Bell Tower, 1876–2001*, pp. 113–149.

74. Proceedings of the Executive Committee of Rio Grande College, June 11, 1928–May 22, 1936 (Jean Lloyd Cooper Archives at the University of Rio Grande).

75. Bapst and Tribe, p. 50.

76. "Rio Grande Trustees Open Way for Dancing by Students," *Gallipolis Daily Tribune*, January 2, 1930, p. 1.

77. Larue Habercom Duffy to Dr. Marcella Barton, professor of history at Rio Grande College, on October 21, 1986 (Jean Lloyd Cooper Archives at the University of Rio Grande).

Chapter 8

1. Grace Cutler, "Blonde Venus Hunts Ziegfeld With Writ," *New York Daily News*, January 19, 1927. p. 2.

2. *Ibid.*; "Demands $100,000," *Poughkeepsie Evening News*, January 22, 1927, p. 7; "Beauty Seeks 100,000 from Ziggie," *Pittsburgh Press*, January 23, 1927, p. 4; "Demands $100,000," *Chillicothe Gazette*, January 21, 1927, p. 8; *Philadelphia Inquirer*, January 13, 1927, p. 14; *Baltimore Sun*, January 17, 1927, p. 4. In a related piece, Kathryn Burke tried to avoid taking sides, saying only that "I think controversy is beneath the dignity of a Ziegfeld showgirl." See "Chorine Filling Beryl's Role Kicks in with Dignified Line," *New York Daily News*, January 20, 1927, p. 10.

3. *New York Daily News*, March 20, 1927, p. 84; "Rufus LaMaire," IBDb. Samuel L. Leiter, ed., *The Encyclopedia of the New York Stage, 1920–1930* (Westport, CT: Greenwood Press, 1985), p. 782.

4. *Ibid.*; *New York Daily News*, May 22, 1927, p. 27.

5. "Profit in Being Dumb Beauties," *Canandaigua* [New York] *Daily Messenger*, March 18, 1927, p. 4.

6. *Ibid.*

7. Leiter, Ed., *The Encyclopedia of the New York Stage*, p. 363; *Brooklyn Life*, August 6, 1927, p. 16.

8. Quoted in *New York Daily News*, September 15, 1927, p. 367; "War and Music," *Brooklyn Daily Eagle*, September 13, 1927, p. 38.

9. Burns Mantle, "A History," *New York Daily News*, September 17, 1927; *Allentown* [PA] *Morning Call*, September 4, 1927, p. 14; Leiter and Hill, eds., *Encyclopedia of the New York Stage*, p. 363.

10. *Brooklyn Daily Eagle*, September 27, 1927, p. 3; *New York Daily News*, September 28, 1927, p. 340.

11. *New York Daily News*, December 5, 1927, p. 295; "Changes Name," *New York Daily News*, February 4, 1928, p. 80; undated clipping in Beryl Halley Collection (University of Rio Grande).

12. For the "Arden Stuart" connection, see "The Single Standard," *Wilmington* [DE] *Morning News*, June 9, 1928, p. 17.

13. "Girls to Undergo Heart Throb Test," *New York Daily News*, January 27, 1928, p. 320; "Blondes Lose Out in Film Love Test," *New York Times*, January 31, 1928, p. 25.

14. *Ibid.*

15. *Ibid.* The experiment received wide press coverage, including "Brunettes Are More Stirred by Sentiment than Blondes," *St. Louis Post-Dispatch*, February 6, 1928, p. 33. Perhaps the most interesting comment came from Illinois in the *Decatur Evening Herald*, February 1, 1928, p. 8, which asked the question "If Blondes and Brunettes Act This Way, What Would Redheads Do?" Marston, who is perhaps better known today as the creator of the comic book super-heroine "Wonder Woman" during World War II, was an unusual character in his own right. A more recent study from a feminist viewpoint is by Jill Lepore, "The Last Amazon: Wonder Woman Returns," *New Yorker*, September 22, 2014, https://newyorker.com/magazine/2014/09/22/last-amazon.

16. *Brooklyn Daily Eagle*, March 15, 1928, p. 34.

17. Burton W. Peretti, *Nightclub City: Politics and Amusement in Manhattan* (Philadelphia: University of Pennsylvania Press, 2007), p. 112.

18. "City to Rain Gold Upon Infant, 1927," *New York Times*, December 31, 1926.

19. *Ibid.*

20. "Miss Morgan Big Game in Dry Attack," *New York Daily News*, October 21, 1928, p. 154.

21. Ethan Mordden, *Ziegfeld: The Man Who Invented Show Business* (New York: St.

Martin's Press, 2008), p. 190; "Earl Carroll," IBDb.

22. Ken Murray, *The Body Merchant: The Story of Earl Carroll* (Pasadena: Ward Ritchie Press, 1976), pp. viii–ix. Evidently, Murray (1903–1988) was well acquainted with and had worked for Carroll in 1935, and wrote much his book in the first-person. Murray had also been a performer in vaudeville, on Broadway, and in film. Much of his work was with Marie Wilson (1915–1972), famous for her portrayals of the typical "dumb blonde," especially *My Friend Irma*.

23. Murray, *The Body Merchant*, pp. 8–33.

24. Actors' Equity Association Contract, Vanities Producing Corp. and Beryl Halley, June 22, 1928 (In Beryl Halley Collection). "Saint Earl of the 7th Avenue," *New York Daily News*, August 5, 1928, p. 51.

25. Burns Mantle, "Stalking B'dway Show Girls," *New York Daily News*, June 24, 1928, p. 111.

26. "Earl Carroll's Vanities of 1928," IBDb.

27. *New York Daily News*, August 8, 1928, p. 245; "Newly Discovered," *Brooklyn Daily Eagle*, October 21, 1928, p. 63.

28. Lillian Roth (with Gerold Frank, Mike Connelly), *I'll Cry Tomorrow* (New York: Frederick Fell, Inc., 1954), p. 52.

29. *Ibid.*, 52–53.

30. *Ibid.*, 53. Halley and Roth had a pleasant reunion in Houston on December 17, 1955. Ironically, Roth had been initially angered at Earl Carroll because her name had not been in lights on the marquee on opening night. She claims she would have quit if she had not been threatened by a lawsuit from both Carroll and Actor's Equity. He later complimented her on her weight loss, but the initial argument with him remained a sore spot. Nonetheless, according to Ken Murray, she attended his funeral.

31. Leiter, ed., *Encyclopedia of the New York Stage*, p. 232. Leiter points that his work covers only productions in Manhattan. Off-Broadway is included on Manhattan Island (New York County), but omits other cities, including Brooklyn, which apparently had numerous theaters.

32. *Pittsburgh Press*, February 24, 1929, p. 66; March 3, 1929, p. 86; "Dancers at Nixon," *Pittsburgh Press*, March 17, 1929, p. 93.

33. "1,000 at Stockton for Opening Dance," *Asbury Park Press*, July 27, 1929, p. 2; "Vet Operators Meet," *Brooklyn Daily Eagle*, August 18, 1929, p. 58.

34. "WOR—Newark," Bridgewater, New Jersey, *Courier-News*, August 31, 1929, p. 7.

35. "To Wed Artist," *New York Daily News*, December 9, 128, p. 81.

36. Lewis A. Erenberg, *Steppin' Out: New York Nightlife and the Transformation of American Culture* (Chicago: University of Chicago Press, 181), pp. 223–224.

37. Walter Winchell, "On Broadway," *Scranton Republican*, October 8, 1928, p. 19.

Chapter 9

1. Paul Johnson, *A History of the American People* (New York: Harper Perennial, 1997), p. 735. Amity Shales, *The Forgotten Man: A New History of the Great Depression* (New York: Harper Collins, 2007), and Martin L. Fausold, *The Presidency of Herbert Hoover* (Lawrence: University Press of Kansas, 1985).

2. Johnson, *History of the American People*, pp. 741, 744–745; Joel Whitburn, *Pop Memories, 1890–1954* (Menomonee Falls, WI: Record Research, Inc., 1988), pp. 480, 506.

3. Richard Masseck, "About New York," *Gettysburg Times*, January 16, 1930, p. 10. While Beryl and Dorothy Knapp were closely associated, Joyce Hawley was unconnected with the former. Although she had been in the Greenwich Village Follies in 1925–1926, her only other claim to fame resulted from a party thrown by Earl Carroll on February 22, 1926, in which she posed nude in a champagne-filled bathtub. Carroll was later arrested for his involvement in the stunt.

4. Alec MacKenzie, "The Rhythm Glide," *The Dance Magazine*, November 1929, pp. 28–29. Whether the new dance caught on or became a casualty of the depression cannot be determined.

5. Rian James, "Reverting in Type," *Brooklyn Daily Eagle*, April 21, 1930, p. 19.

6. "Death Takes S. T. Halley," *Gallipolis Daily Tribune*, February 26, 1930, p. 1; Estate Record of Samuel T. Halley (Property of Gallia County Probate Court, but housed in the Gallia County Historical and Genealogical Society, Gallipolis, Ohio).

7. For typical coverage of Ernst Van Duren's demise, see "Intimate Truths about the Romantic Tragedy of Europe's Handsomest Man and Loveliest Girl," *Shreveport Times*, p. 40.

8. Mark Barron, "A New Yorker at Large,"

Notes. Chapter 10

Wilkes-Barre Record, August 9, 1930, p. 19; also printed in *Galveston* [TX] *Daily News*, August 10, 1930, p. 13.

9. "Walter Winchell's Day by Day Biography of the Main Stem," *The Dance Magazine*, November 1930, p. 14; December 1930, p. 16.

10. The account of Florenz Ziegfeld's last years was adapted from Cynthia Brideson and Sara Brideson, *Ziegfeld and His Follies: A Biography of Broadway's Greatest Producer* (Lexington: University of Kentucky Press, 2015), pp. 360–396, 439–460; and Richard and Paulette Ziegfeld, *The Ziegfeld Touch: The Life and Times of Florenz Ziegfeld, Jr.* (New York: Henry Abrams, 1993), pp. 152–169.

11. Samuel L. Leiter, ed., *The Encyclopedia of the New York Stage, 1920–1930* (Westport CT: Greenwood Press, 1985), pp. 272–273. Ken Murray, *The Body Merchant: The Story of Earl Carroll* (Pasadena: Ward Ritchie Press, 1976), pp. 150–157.

12. *Ibid.* pp. 162–181.

13. Mark Barron, "Broadway Is Own Censor," *Detroit Free Press*, January 24, 1932, p. 30.

14. *New York Daily News*, December 1, 1931, p. 40. For Granlund and his restaurant, see *Blondes, Brunettes, and Bullets*, pp. 203 ff. Although the Hollywood did not serve alcoholic drinks, some customers brought flasks, resulting in a raid. The restaurant owners took out a paid advertisement, titled, "We Apologize to Our Patrons," *New York Daily News*, April 29, 1930.

15. Clark Kinnaird, "Professor Picks Most Beautiful Legs Among 2,000 Which Acted in Follies," *San Bernardino Daily Sun*, July 16, 1933.

16. Mark Barron, "Tears with Orchids in the 'Follies,'" *Florence* [SC] *Morning News*, July 30, 1932.

17. *Dayton Daily News* (undated clipping in Beryl Halley Collection); *New York Daily News*, November 14, 1932, p. 26.

18. "Gallia Co. Girl Among Typical Ziegfeld Girls," *Gallipolis Daily Tribune*, July 25, 1932, p. 1.

19. "Bladen Girl Called Most Perfect Figure of Ziegeld's [sic] Glorified 'Follies' Girls," *Gallipolis Daily Tribune*, August 2, 1932, p. 1.

20. O. O. McIntyre, *San Bernardino County Sun*, February 12, 1933, p. 20.

Chapter 10

1. "Beauty Secretly Weds," *New York Daily Mirror*, October 16, 1933, p. 3; *Gallipolis Daily Tribune*, October 19, 1933, p. 1.

2. *Ibid.*

3. *Ibid.*

4. U.S. Census, 1930, Chester Falkenhainer; Chet Falkenhainer to Jake Bapst, March 27, 2017; March 20, 2018 (copies in Beryl Halley Collection, University of Rio Grande); *Columbia University Alumni Directory*, p. 266; For Falkenhainer at Columbia, see "Alumni to Argue Business Needs," *Columbia Daily Spectator*, April 19, 1933, p. 4; "Job Openings Are Larger, Wells Declares," *Columbia Daily Spectator*, March 11, 1936, p. 1; "250 Take Part in Second Day of Conference," *Columbia Daily Spectator*, April 8, 1937, p. 4. For A. H. Bull & Co., see *New York Tribune*, December 30, 1920, p. 19.

5. Ship Passenger Lists, 1935; George Tucker, "'Round About New York," *Harrisburg Telegraph*, November 21, 1935, p. 10.

6. Richard and Paulette Ziegfeld, *The Ziegfeld Touch: The Life and Times of Florenz Ziegfeld, Jr.* (New York: Harry N. Abrams, Inc., 1993), pp. 171–174.

7. Clarksville, TN, *Leaf-Chronicle*, April 2, 1936, p. 3. See also "So the Glorified Follies Girls formed the 'Ziegfeld Alumnae,'" *Battle Creek* [MI] *Enquirer*, June 14, 1936, p. 23.

8. "Dance to Help Broke 'Follies' Girls June 28," *New York Daily News*, June 14, 1936, p. 60.

9. *Detroit Free Press*, August 12, 1936, p. 20.

10. "Opening Today," *Pittsburgh Post-Gazette*, August 28, 1936, p. 28.

11. "Glorified Follies Top Next RKO-Boston Show," *Boston Globe*, September 22, 1936, p. 29; "RKO-Boston," *Boston Globe*, September 25, 1936, p. 28. On September 28 a brief article, "Faithful Till Yesterday," appeared in the *Globe* (p. 6) that featured tap dancer Judy Stewart, who (according to the *Globe*) was not a former Ziegfeld star, but was identified as having been in the cast of *Hot Cha*, although part of the show since the Detroit opening had been missing from her performance on the 27th.

12. "Footlights," *Akron Beacon Journal*, October 21, 1936, p. 26; *Akron Beacon Journal*, October 23, 1936, p. 32.

13. "Girls," *Akron Beacon Journal*, October 24, 1936, p. 12.

14. "'Glorified Follies of 1936' Is Stage

Attraction Opening Today at Lyric," *Indianapolis Star*, October 30, 1936, p. 20; "Bewitched," *Cincinnati Enquirer*, November 1, 1936, p. 2; "Ziegfeld Beauties Strut Stuff in 'Glorified Follies of 1936,'" *Cincinnati Enquirer*, November 8, 1936, p. 21.

15. Betty Kern, "Reviews," *Dayton Herald*, November 14, 1936, p. 5; "Colonial," *Dayton Daily News*, November 17, 1936, p. 8.

16. *Chicago Tribune*, November 26, 1936, p. 31; "At Loew's," *Montreal Gazette*, December 19, 1936, p. 10.

17. *New York Daily News*, September 14, 1936, p. 36; "Glorified Lunch," *New York Daily News*, November 17, 1936, p. 44; Phil M. Daly, "Along the Rialto," *The Film Daily*, January 22, 1937, p. 4.

18. Alice Logan, "Ex-'Follies' Girl Finds Happiness as Mother," *Brooklyn Daily Eagle*, November 29, 1936, p. 11.

19. "Follies Girls Hold Reunion," *Rochester Democrat and Chronicle*, April 13, 1937, p. 7.

20. WOR Radio Program type script, April 23, 1937 (Copy in Beryl Halley Collection).

21. "Stage Door Prowlers Can't Remember," *Atlanta Constitution*, July 11, 1937, p. 48.

22. *Ibid*.

23. "The Social Register Still Frowns Snobbishly on the Theater, But—Stage Beauties Make Successful Society Wives," *New York Sunday Mirror*, Magazine Section, May 23, 1937, pp. 3, 19.

24. *Gallipolis Daily Tribune*, August 25, 1937, p. 3.

25. *Bradford* [PA] *Evening Star*, November 26, 1937, p. 9; *Daily Reporter* [Greenfield, IN], December 8, 1937; Louis Sobol, "The Voice of Broadway," *Miami News*, December 20, 1937, p. 14.

26. *Variety*, November 2, 1938; "Ziegfeld Chorus Girls Back Ruth," *Dispatch* [Moline, IL], October 20, 1938, p. 5; "Ziegfeld Girls Hope Everything Will Work Out for Ruth Etting," *Lincoln Star*, October 31, 1938, p. 13.

27. "Former Ziegfeld Follies Beauties Hold Reunion," *St. Louis Star and Times*, December 16, 1938, p. 32; Ned Wayburn to Beryl Halley Falkenhainer, April 24, 1939 (copy in University of Rio Grande Archives).

28. Alice Hughes, "A Woman's New York," *Dayton Daily News*, May 3, 1940, p. 22; Julia McCarthy, "Ziegfeld Alumnae," *New York Daily News*, April 28, 1940, p. 268.

29. Beryl Falkenhainer, U.S. Federal Census, 1940 (Ancestry.com); Chester O. Falkenhainer, U.S. Federal Census, 1940 (Ancestry.com); *New York Daily News*, June 6, 1947, p. 4.

30. "'Follies' Girls Club Convenes Every Year," *San Antonio Light*, April 22, 1941, p. 15; Geraldine Smith, "—And Some Have No Reunions," *Philadelphia Inquirer*, April 6, 1941, p. 125.

31. "Beryl Halley Heard," *Gallipolis Daily Tribune*, December 18, 1941, p. 6; *St. Louis Post Dispatch*, December 14, 1941, p. 6.

Chapter 11

1. Robert Campbell to Beryl Halley Falkenhainer, September 17, 1943, Actors' Fund Certificate, September 16, 1943 (both In Beryl Halley Collection at University of Rio Grande).

2. Bernard Sobel, "The Ziegfeld Girls Carry On," *Stage Pictorial* 2:3, 1946, pp. 39–41, 57. A slightly edited version of this article appeared in *Variety*, January 5, 1949, p. 254.

3. *Ibid*. p. 41.

4. *Ibid*. p. 39.

5. Helen [Martin] Wanger to Mrs. Jean Martin, undated letter, c. July 10, 1946 (in Rio Grande College Archives), p. 4. *Gallipolis Daily Tribune*, May 3, 1946, p. 5, mentions that Cecile had visited Beryl during Easter vacation. The *Tribune* (July 6, 1946, p. 5) also mentions Cecile's trip to visit Beryl as well as their joint trip to Canada, as discussed in Helen's letter. Cecile and Helen had another reunion at Rio Grande, this time in 1949, at the home of Frank and Miriam Allen, who kept a boarding house for students. The same building in 2018 houses the Greer Museum and the Jean Lloyd Cooper Archives. One might add that having a relative on the *Tribune* staff proved helpful in tracking the Halleys in the 1940s.

6. Wanger to Martin. pp. 9–10.

7. "Three Divorce Suits," *Miami News*, February 5, 1947, p. 8.

8. Steve Patterson, "Ex-Dancer Has License, Can't Decide to Renewed," *New York Daily News*, June 6, 1947, p. 4.

9. Beryl H. Falkenhainer, Marriage License Indexes, 1907–1995, June 4, 1947; Beryl Falkenhainer in *New York Passenger Lists, 1820–1957*, September 2, 1947, Ancestry.com.

10. Chet Falkenhainer to Jake Bapst, May 5, 2017; April 4, 2018 (copies in Beryl Halley Collection).

11. "Ex-'Follies' Girl Ordered Held for

Notes. Chapter 12

Contempt," *Binghamton* [NY] *Press* and *Sun-Bulletin*, September 16, 1948, p. 1; "Judge Orders Arrest of Mrs. Falkenhainer," *Lewiston* [ME] *Evening Journal*, September 16, 1948; "Former 'Follies' Star Faces Court Contempt," *Montgomery Alabama Journal*, September 16, 1948, p. 23; See also "Falkenhainer v. Falkenhainer, Nassau County, New York, March 29, 1950."

12. "Vancouver, B. C." *Miami News*, September 16, 1948, p. 8; "For Contempt in Child Case," *Des Moines Tribune*, September 16, 1948, p. 3.

13. Falkenhainer to Bapst, May 5, 2017.

14. *Ibid.*

15. *Ibid.* Problems concerning Jim McCormick will become apparent in the next chapter.

16. "Report Mrs. Halley As Seriously Ill," *Gallipolis Daily Tribune*, February 18, 1949, p. 2.

17. "Halley, Melissa," *Gallia Times*, February 26, 1949, p. 2; Estate Record of Melissa Porter Halley, March 15, 1949 (Gallia County Probate Court in Gallia County Historical and Genealogical Society). This document appears to be the only time Paul Halley's middle name is given as "Kreuger." According to one who knew him, Paul used a number of middle names at one time or another, often in jest.

18. James McCormick, Beryl Halley McCormick, Marriage Certificate, Harris County, Texas; January 20, 1951 (Copy in Beryl Halley Collection); "Beryl Halley McCormick in the Texas Select County Marriage Records, 1837–2015. Ancestry.com.

19. Recorded telephone interview between the authors and Chester O. Falkenhainer, Jr., August 15, 2018.

20. "Father's Lengthy Search Rewarded, Secures His Son," *Corsicana Daily Sun*, November 12, 1953, p. 8. Substantially the same A. P. release appeared in the *Sulphur Springs News-Telegram*, November 11, 1953, p. 2, and the *Orange Leader*, November 11, 1953, p. 1 (all papers in Texas).

Chapter 12

1. For information the law firm, see Griffin Smith, Jr. "Empires of Paper," *Texas Monthly*, November 1973. (htts://texasmonthly.com/articles/empires-of-paper/).

2. Chet Falkenhainer to Jake Bapst, March 27, 2017; May 5, 2017.

3. The autographed 8 × 10 photo of Lillian Roth flanked by Beryl and Jim McCormick dated 12/17/55 is in the Beryl Halley Collection at Rio Grande. For a contemporary account of Lillian Roth and her comeback tour, see Lucy Key Miller, "Front Views & Profiles: Tomorrow's Tears," *Chicago Tribune*, December 8, 1955, p. 58, and *Los Angeles Times*, December 3, 1955, p. 23d. The Susan Hayward film was scheduled to make its premiere ten days after Roth's Houston opening. See Pericles Alexander, "Impact of Roth Film Is Solid," *Shreveport Times*, December 14, 1955. Like Beryl and others in show business, Roth claimed to be forty when she was actually forty-five.

4. Chet Falkenhainer to Jake Bapst, May 5, 2017.

5. *Ibid.*; Houston and Harris County Daily Court Review, April 7, 1959, p. 2; May 4, 1959.

6. Taped telephone interview with Chester O. Falkenhainer, August 15, 2018.

7. St. Johns [Academy, Houston, Texas] Website, https://sjs./org.

8. Chet Falkenhainer to Jake Bapst, April 4, 2018 (in Beryl Halley Collection). Cecile Halley (Fitch); Ancestry.com.

9. *Ibid.*; Falkenhainer to Bapst, March 27, 2017; April 24, 2017; May 5, 2018 (in Beryl Halley Collection); New York Marriage License Index, 1907–1995, No. 16369.

10. "C. O. Falkenhainer," *Fort Lauderdale News*, June 6, 1962, p. 12; Falkenhainer Interview, August 15, 2018.

11. Vincent Lopez to Beryl Halley McCormack [*sic*], July 21, 1958; Vincent Lopez to Beryl H. McCormick, February 11, 1960; McCormick to Lopez, ca. February 16, 1960 (all in Beryl Halley Collection at University of Rio Grande).

12. Falkenhainer Interview, August 15, 2015.

13. Falkenhainer Interview, August 15, 2018.

14. *Ibid.*

15. Chester O. Falkenhainer III to Jake Bapst, March 30, 2017; April 5, 2018.

16. Falkenhainer to Bapst, May 5, 2017; Falkenhainer Interview, August 15, 2018. A posthumous magazine feature written by Larry Engelmann, "The Love Test: Gentlemen, it turns out prefer brunettes," appeared in the *San Francisco Examiner*, January 31, 1988, pp. 166–167. At least it wasn't one more retelling of the "fig leaf" story.

Appendix

1. "Bernice Ackerman," Internet Broadway Database (Hereafter referred to as IBDb); "Beauty Secretly Weds," *New York Daily Mirror* (undated clipping in Beryl Halley Collection at University of Rio Grande).
2. "James Barton," Internet Movie Database (Hereafter referred to as IMDb).
3. For a reliable sketch and filmography of Lina Basquette, see Buck Rainey, *Sweethearts of the Sage: Biographies and Filmographies of 258 Actresses Appearing in Western Movies* (Jefferson, NC; McFarland, 1992), pp. 256–259; see also Richard and Paulette Ziegfeld, *The Ziegfeld Touch: The Life and Times of Florenz Ziegfeld, Jr.* (New York: Harry N. Abrams, 1993), pp. 284–285.
4. "Marion Benda," IMDb; "Zeppo Marx," IMDb; see also *Mallory Curley, Zeppo Marion Benda and Valentino's Marion Benda: A Legacy of Confusion* (n.p.: Randy Press, 2016).
5. Ziegfeld, *The Ziegfeld Touch*, pp. 285–286. For more detailed studies on Berlin, see Jeffrey Magee, *Irving Berlin's Musical Theatre* (New York: Oxford University Press, 2012) and Benjamin Sears, ed., *The Irving Berlin Reader* (New York: Oxford University Press, 2012).
6. "Fannie Brice," IBDb; Ziegfeld, *The Ziegfeld Touch*, p. 287. Brice has been the subject of two extensive biographies: Herbert G. Goldman, *Fannie Brice: The Original Funny Girl* (New York: Oxford University Press, 1993) and Barbara Grossman, *Funny Woman* (Bloomington: Indiana University Press, 1992); David Wallace, *Capital of the World: A Portrait of New York City in the Roaring Twenties* (Guilford, CT: Lyons Press, 2011), pp. 92–93.
7. "Louise Brooks," IBDb; IMDb; Ziegfeld, *The Ziegfeld Touch*, p. 287; Ephraim Katz, *The Film Encyclopedia Fourth Edition* (New York Harper Research, 2001), pp. 182–183; *Quinlan's Film Stars 5th Edition* (Washington, DC: Brassey's, Inc.), p. 77.
8. Gene Buck, IBDb; Ziegfeld, *The Ziegfeld Touch*, pp. 51, 287–288.
9. "Katherine Burke," IBDb. *Rio Rita*, February 2, 1927 (Program in Beryl Halley Collection).
10. "Cynthia Cambridge," IBDb.
11. "Eddie Cantor," IBDb; IMDb. Two good studies of Cantor are Gregory Koseluk, *Eddie Cantor: A Life in Show Business* (Jefferson, NC: McFarland, 1995), and Herbert G. Goldman, *Banjo Eyes: Eddie Cantor and Birth of Modern Stardom* (New York: Oxford University Press, 1997).
12. "Earl Carroll, IBDb; IMDb; Lillian Roth (Frank and Connelly), *I'll Cry Tomorrow* (New York: Frederick Fell, Inc., 1954) p. 51; Bernard Sobel, *Broadway Heartbeat: Memoirs of a Press Agent* (New York: Hermitage House, 1953), p. 99; The only biography to date is a personal memoir by entertainer Ken Murray, *The Body Merchant: The Story of Earl Carroll* (Pasadena: Ward Ritchie Press, 1976).
13. "Frank Crumit," IBDb; Tim Gracyk, "Frank Crumit," http://www.gracyk.comfrankcrumit.html). See also Robert Edgar Ervin, *Jackson County: Its History and Its People* (n.p.: Sheridan Books, 2008), pp. 164–166. The best information on Crumit is still the four-part article in Jim Walsh's series "Favorite Pioneer Recording Artists" in *Hobbies—The Magazine for Collectors*, which was published between September and December 1953.
14. The best biography of Jack Dempsey is Randy Roberts, *Jack Dempsey: The Manassa Mauler* (Baton Rouge: Louisiana State University Press, 1979, quoted on p. 193.
15. "Ray Dooley," IBDb; Ziegfeld, *The Ziegfeld Touch*, p. 291.
16. "Alma Drange," IBDb.
17. Katz, *The Film Encyclopedia Fourth Edition*, p. 399; Tim Brooks, *The Complete Directory of Prime Time TV Stars, 1946–Present* (New York: Ballantine Books, 1987), p. 266.
18. For more on Cliff Edwards, see David Rothel, *Those Great Cowboy Sidekicks* (Waynesville, NC: WOY Publications, 1984), pp. 138–143; Joel Whitburn, *Pop Memories, 1890–1954* (Menomonee Falls, WI: Record Research, Inc., 1986), pp. 145–146; Katz, *The Film Encyclopedia Fourth Edition*, p. 412; *Palm Beach Nights*, p. 9 (Program in Beryl Halley Collection).
19. Harry Fender, IBDb; *Palm Beach Nights*, program, pp. 23, 27.
20. "W. C. Fields," IBDb; For a more thorough examination, see Wes D. Gehring, *W. C. Fields: A Bio-Bibliography* (Westport, CT: Greenwood Press, 1984).
21. "Irving Fisher," IBDb.
22. "Paulette Goddard," IBDb, IMDb; For a good sketch of Paulette Goddard, see the biographical chapter in James Robert Parish, *The Paramount Pretties* (New Rochelle, NY: Arlington House, 1972), pp. 372–407.
23. A brief sketch of Guinan can be found

Notes. Appendix

in Handbook of Texas Online, Debbie Mauldin Cottrell, "Guinan, Mary Louise Cecilia [TX], accessed April 27, 2018, http://www.fshaonline.org/handbook/online/articles/fgu21. A scholarly biography is Louise Berliner, *Texas Guinan: Queen of the Night Clubs* (Austin: University of Texas Press, 1993).

24. Edmonde Guy, IMDb; Ernst Van Duren, IMDb; *Palm Beach Nights*, program, p. 11.
25. "John Hazzard," IBDb.
26. "Dan Healy," IBDb; IMDb.
27. Whitburn, *Pop Memories, 1890–1954*, pp. 211–212.
28. "Brooke Johns," IBDb; IMDb; Eugene L. Meyer, "Brooke Johns, Vaudevillian, Ex-Md. Politician Dies at 93," *Washington Post*, December 5, 1987.
29. "Flo Kennedy," IBDb.
30. "Dorothy Knapp, IBDb; IMDb; Ziegfeld, *The Ziegfeld Touch*, pp. 120–122; Murray, *The Body Merchant*, p. 219.
31. "Lupino Lane," IBDb; IMDb; Katz, *The Film Encyclopedia, Fourth Edition*, p. 786.
32. "Edna Leedom," IBDb.
33. Gene Lockhart, IBDb; IMDb; Katz, *The Film Encyclopedia*, p. 837.
34. "Claire Luce," IBDb; IMDb; "Claire Luce, 1920s Star of 'Follies.'" *New York Times*, September 4, 1989; Ziegfeld, *The Ziegfeld Touch*, pp. 225, 227, 303–304.
35. See Shirley Tomkievicz, "Owen Vincent Madden," *The Encyclopedia of Arkansas History and Culture*, http://www.encyclopediaofarkansas.net/encyclopedia/entry-detail.aspx?entryID=1702.
36. Marston is profiled in Roy Thomas, *Wonder Woman: The War Years, 1941–1945* (New York: Chartwell, 2015), pp. 8–10.
37. "Kathleen Martin, IBDb; see also *Palm Beach Nights* program in Beryl Halley Collection.
38. "Mary Jane," IBDb; "Mary Jane Receives Trophy at Montmartre," *Palm Beach Post*, March 18, 1926, p 10; "Broken Heart Killed Millionaire Playboy," *New York Daily News*, March 10, 1935, p. 43; Mark Walston, "Potomac's Marwood estate, fashioned after European palaces, hosted American royalty," Riverside Palace, March 13, 2018.
39. "Evelyn Nesbitt [*sic*]," IBDb; IMDb. See Cecilia Rasmusssen, "Girl in Red Velvet Swing Longed to Flee Her Past," *Los Angeles Times*, December 11, 2005, http://articles.latimes.com/2005/dec/11/local/me-then11.
40. "Ann Pennington," IBDb, IMDb; William M. Freeman, "Ann Pennington, Dancing Star Dies," *New York Times*, November 5, 1971, p. 46.
41. "Harry Richman," IBDb, IMDb.
42. Katz, *The Film Encyclopedia Fourth Edition*, pp. 1173–1174; Ziegfeld, *The Ziegfeld Touch*, p. 311; Brideson and Brideson, *Ziegfeld and His Follies*, pp. 161–163, 171–172. The Rogers career is covered in Ben Yagoda, *Will Rogers: A Biography* (Norman: Oklahoma University Press, 2000).
43. "Lillian Roth," IBDb; IMDb; "Halley, Roth, McCormick, December 17, 1955" (Dated photo in Beryl Halley Collection). See also Lillian Roth (with Frank and Connelly), *I'll Cry Tomorrow* (New York: Frederick Fell, Inc., 1954).
44. "Julia Sanderson," IBDb; Gracyk, "Frank Crumit." For Julia Sanderson's recordings and radio program, see Jim Walsh, "Favorite Pioneer Recording Artists: Frank Crumit, Part One," *Hobbies—The Magazine for Collectors*, September 1953, pp. 23–24; Part Four, December 1953, pp. 29–30.
45. "Vivienne Segal," IBDb; IMDb; Ziegfeld, *The Ziegfeld Touch*, pp. 311–312; WOR Radio typescript, April 30, 1937 (In Beryl Halley Collection); Katz, *The Film Encyclopedia, Fourth Edition*, p. 1231.
46. Ziegfeld, *The Ziegfeld Touch*, pp. 121–122, 159–160; Bernard Sobel, "The Ziegfeld Girls Carry On," *Stage Pictorial*, 1946, pp. 2–3.
47. Dolly Sterling, IBDb; "Dolly Shuns the Nude Under Disguise of Art," *El Paso Evening Post*, September 2, 1927, p. 8; Alexandria [LA] *The Town Talk*, April 20, 1931, p. 7.
48. "Estelle Taylor," IBDb; IMDb. For the Dempsey-Taylor relationship, see Roberts, *Jack Dempsey: The Manassa Mauler*, pp. 203–211, 265. For what it is worth, Roberts differs from Lopez as to when his first meeting with Estelle Taylor took place. Lopez places it in a time frame not long after the Dempsey-Firpo fight, on September 13, 1923. Roberts suggests early summer 1924 as a more likely time. In addition, the pair could not marry until Taylor received her divorce from a prior husband in January 1925. What is not in dispute is that Taylor and Dempsey were legally married on February 7, 1925.
49. Ziegfeld, *The Ziegfeld Touch*, pp. 258, 260; "Tiller Girls," IBDb.
50. "Peggy Udell," IBDb, IMDb. Udell also had a checkered career in matrimony including one in which she married in the evening, and the marriage ended at breakfast the following morning.

Notes. Appendix

51. Ziegfeld, *The Ziegfeld Touch*, pp. 314–315; Brideson and Brideson, *Ziegfeld and His Follies*, p. 155. For more on Mar-a-Lago, see Judge Jeanine Pirro, *Liars, Leakers, and Liberals* (New York: Center Street, 2018), p. 188.

52. Other than the Pittsburgh appearance with Beryl, and one in New Jersey, no other data has surfaced on Charles Varell.

53. Ziegfeld, *The Ziegfeld Touch*, pp. 315. A black-and-white reproduction of the Beryl Halley portrait is in Robert Varal, *Revue: A Nostalgic Reprise of the Great Broadway Period* (New York: Fleet, 1962), p. 42, and also in full color in Ziegfeld, *The Ziegfeld Touch*, p. 211.

54. "Polly Walker," IBDb; IMDb; Ziegfeld, *The Ziegfeld Touch*, pp. 128, 225; *Palm Beach Nights* program, pp. 5, 29.

55. For more information on Wayburn, see Brideson and Brideson, *Ziegfeld and His Follies*, pp. 156–157 and Ziegfeld, *The Ziegfeld Touch*, pp. 62–64, 316; for Wayburn's extensive career, see Barbara Stratymar, Ned Wayburn and the Dance Routine (New York: Society of Dance History Scholars, 1996); Ned Wayburn to Beryl Halley Falkenhainer letter, April 24, 1939 (in Beryl Halley Collection). For Haggin, see Ziegfeld, *The Ziegfeld Touch*, p. 298.

56. "Ada Mae Weeks," IBDb. (Note in Beryl Halley Collection).

57. "Bert Wheeler," IBDb; IMDb; Katz, *The Film Encyclopedia, Fourth Edition*, p. 1456; *Quinlan's Film Stars*, 5th Edition, p. 537.

58. "Paul Whiteman," IBDb; Whitburn, *Pop Memories, 1890–1954*, pp. 447–454; Ziegfeld, *The Ziegfeld Touch*, p. 317. For a complete view of Whiteman and his influence on popular music, see Don Rayno, *Paul Whiteman: Pioneer of American Music, 1890–1930* (New York: Scarecrow Press, 2003).

59. "Imogene Wilson," IBDb; Ziegfeld, *The Ziegfeld Touch*, p. 318.

60. "'Cricket' Wooten," IBDb.

61. "Helen Lee Worthing," IBDb; IMDb. See also *Pittsburgh Post-Gazette*, December 11, 1930.

62. "Halfred Young," IBDb; "Gertrude Lang," IBDb; Samuel L. Leiter, *The Encyclopedia of the New York Stage, 1920–1930* (Westport, CT: Greenwood Press, 1985), p. 363.

Bibliography

Books

Alexander, Charles. *Our Game: An American Baseball History.* New York: Henry Holt and Company, 1991.
Allen, Frederick Lewis. *Only Yesterday: An Informal History of the Nineteen Twenties.* New York: Harper and Brothers, 1931.
Allen, Robert Clyde. *Horrible Prettiness: Burlesque in American Culture.* Chapel Hill: University of North Carolina Press, 1991.
Averill, James P. *History of Gallia County.* Chicago: H. H. Hardesty & Co., 1882.
Bapst, Jacob L., and Ivan M. Tribe. *University of Rio Grande and Rio Grande Community College.* Charleston, SC: Arcadia Publishing, 2017.
Baral, Robert. *Revue: A Nostalgic Reprise of the Great Broadway Musical.* New York: Fleet Publishing Corp., 1962.
Baughman, James. *Henry R. Luce and the Rise of American News Media.* New York: Twayne, 1987.
Berliner, Louisa. *Texas Guinan: Queen of the Night Clubs.* Austin: University of Texas Press, 1993.
Bishop, Jim. *The Mark Hellinger Story: A Biography of Broadway and Hollywood.* New York: Appleton Century Crofts, Inc., 1952.
Blum, Daniel. *A Pictorial History of the American Theatre, 1900–1951.* New York: Greenberg Publisher, 1951.
Boardman, Gerald. *American Musical Theatre: A Chronicle.* New York: Oxford University Press, 2001.
Brandon, Ruth. *Singer and the Sewing Machine: A Romance.* New York: Kadisha International, 1977.
Brideson, Cynthia, and Sara Brideson. *Ziegfeld and His Follies: A Biography of Broadway's Greatest Producer.* Lexington: University Press of Kentucky, 2015.
Brooks, Tim. *A Complete Directory of Prime Time TV Stars, 1946–Present.* New York: Ballantine Books, 1987.
Bullard, Stephan G., Bridget J. Fout, Martha Ruth Fout, and the Point Pleasant River Museum. *The Silver Bridge Disaster of 1967.* Charleston, SC: Arcadia, 2012.
Burke, Billie. *With a Feather on My Nose.* New York: Appleton Century Crofts, 1949.
____. *With Powder on My Nose.* New York: Coward-McCann, 1959.
Buxton, Frank, and Bill Owens. *The Big Broadcast, 1920–1950.* New York: Flare Books, 1973.
Cantor, Eddie, and David Freedman. *Ziegfeld: The Great Glorifier.* New York: Alfred K. King, 1934.
Carter, Randolph. *The World of Flo Ziegfeld.* New York: Praeger, 1974.
Castle, Irene, with Bob and Wanda Duncan. *Castles in the Air.* Garden City, NY: Doubleday & Co., 1958.

Bibliography

Cemeteries of Ohio Township. Gallipolis: Gallia County Historical Society, 1980.
Churchill, Allen. *The Theatrical 20s*. New York: McGraw-Hill Book Company, 1975.
Clark, Norman H. *Deliver Us from Evil: An Interpretation of American Prohibition*. New York: W. W. Norton & Co., 1976.
Critchley, David. *The Origins of Organized Crime in America: The New York City Mafia, 1891–1931*. New York: Routledge, 2009.
Curley, Mallory. *Zeppo's Marion Benda and Valentino's Marion Benda: A Legacy of Confusion*. N. P.: Randy Press, 2016.
Diemer, Tom, Lee Leonard, Richard G. Zimmerman and James A. Rhodes. *Ohio Colossus*. Kent, OH: Kent State University Press, 2014.
Ebbert, Jean, and Marie-Beth Hall. *The First, The Few, The Forgotten: Navy and Marine Corps Women in World War I*. Annapolis MD: U.S. Naval Institute Press, 2002.
Erenberg, Lewis A. *Steppin' Out: New York Nightlife and the Transformation of American Culture, 1890–1930*. Chicago: University of Chicago Press, 1981.
Ervin, Robert Edgar. *Jackson County, Ohio: Its History and Its People*. Jackson, OH: Sheridan Books, 2008.
Evans, Benjamin Rees. *A History of Rio Grande College*. Jackson: Martin Printing Company, 1939.
Evans, Henrietta C., John E. Lester and Mary R. Wood. *Gallipolis, Ohio: A Pictorial History, 1790–1990*. Charleston, WV: Pictorial History Publishing Company, 1990.
Farnsworth, Marjorie. *The Ziegfeld Follies*. New York: Bonanza Books, 1956.
Fausold, Martin L. *The Presidency of Herbert C. Hoover*. Lawrence: University Press of Kansas, 1985.
Feis, Herbert. *1933: Characters in Crisis*. Boston: Little, Brown, 1966.
Gallagher, John S., and Alan H. Patera. *The Post Offices of Ohio*. Burtonsville, MD: The Depot, 1979.
Gallia County, Ohio: People in History to 1980. Paoli, PA: Taylor, 1980.
Garrett, Charles. *The LaGuardia Years: Machine and Reform Politics in New York City*. New Brunswick, NJ: Rutgers University Press, 1961.
Gehring, Wes. *W. C. Fields: A Bio-Bibliography*. Westport, CT: Greenwood Press, 1984.
Gill, Charles Otis, and Gifford Pinchot. *Six Thousand Country Churches*. New York: Macmillan, 1919.
Giordano, Ralph G. *Satan in the Dance Hall: Rev. John Roach Straton, Social Dancing, and Morality in 1920s New York City*. Lanham, MD: Scarecrow Press, 2008.
Golden, Eva. *Anna Held and the Birth of Ziegfeld's Broadway*. Lexington: University Press of Kentucky, 2000.
Goldman, Herbert G. *Fannie Brice: The Original Funny Girl*. New York: Oxford University Press, 1993.
_____. *Banjo Eyes: Eddie Cantor and the Birth of Modern Stardom*. New York: Oxford University Press, 1997
Goodnite, Abby Gail, Ivan M. Tribe. *Rio Grande: From Baptists and Bevo to the Bell Tower, 1876–2001*. Ashland, KY: Jesse Stuart Foundation, 2002.
Gordon, Lucile Duff. *Discretions and Indiscretions*. New York: Frederick Stokes, 1932.
Granlund, Nils Thor. *Blondes, Brunettes, and Bullets*. New York: David McKay Company, 1957.
Grossman, Barbara. *Funny Woman*. Bloomington: Indiana University Press, 1992.
Hanson, Nils. *Lillian Lorraine: The Life and Times of a Ziegfeld Diva*. Jefferson, NC: McFarland, 2009.
Higham, Charles. *Ziegfeld*. Chicago: Regnery, 1972.
Hischak, Thomas S. *Off-Broadway Musicals Since 1919: From Greenwich Village Follies to The Toxic Avenger*. Lanham, MD: Scarecrow Press, 2011.
Isenberg, Michael T. *John L. Sullivan and His America*. Urbana: University of Illinois Press, 1988.
Jacobs, Dick. *Who Wrote That Song?* White Hall, VA: Betterway Publications, 1988.
Johnson, Paul. *A History of the American People*. New York: Harper Perennial, 1997.
Kantor, Michael, and Laurence Maslo. *Broadway: The American Musical*. New York: Bulfinch, 2004.
Katz, Ephraim, ed. *The Film Encyclopedia: Fourth Edition*. New York: Harper Resources, 2001.

Bibliography

Kennedy, David M. *Freedom from Fear: The American People in Depression and War, 1929–1945.* New York: Oxford University Press, 1999.
Kessner, Thomas. *Fiorello H. LaGuardia and the Making of Modern New York.* New York: Viking Press, 1989.
Knapp, Raymond, Mitchell Morris, Stacy Wolfe. *The Oxford Handbook of the American Musical.* New York: Oxford University Press, 2011.
Koseluck, Gregory. *Eddie Cantor: A Life in Show Business.* Jefferson, NC: McFarland, 1995.
Leiter, Samuel L., and Holly Hill. *Encyclopedia of the New York Stage, 1920–1930.* Westport, CT: Greenwood Press, 1985.
Lewis, Thomas S. *Empire of the Air: The Men Who Made Radio.* New York: Burlingame/HarperCollins, 1991.
Lopez, Vincent. *Lopez Speaking.* New York: The Citadel Press, 1960.
Lucas, John A., and Ronald A. Smith. *Saga of American Sport.* Philadelphia: Lea & Febiger, 1978.
Mather, Frank James. *Who's Who of the Colored Race.* Chicago: Memento Editions, 1915.
Matthews, Estivaun, Charles A. Murray, and Pauline Rife. *Gallia County One-Room Schools: The Cradle Years.* Gallipolis, OH: Gallia County Historical Society, 1993.
McVeigh, Rory. *The Rise of the Ku Klux Klan: Right Wing Movements and National Politics.* Minneapolis: University of Minnesota Press, 2009.
Miller, Edward H. *The Hocking Valley Railway.* Athens: Ohio University Press, 2007.
Mizejewski, Linda. *Ziegfeld Girl: Image and Icon in Culture and Cinema.* Durham, NC: Duke University Press, 1999.
Mooney, Michael. *Evelyn Nesbit and Stanford White, Love and Death in the Gilded Age.* New York: William Morrow, 1976.
Mordann, Ethan. *Ziegfeld: The Man Who Invented Show Business.* New York: St. Martin's Press, 2008.
Murray, Ken. *The Body Merchant: The Story of Earl Carroll.* Pasadena: Ward Ritchie Press, 1976.
Nash, Roderick. *The Nervous Generation: American Thought, 1917–1930.* Chicago: Ivan R. Dee, 1970.
Nelli, Humbert S. *The Business of Crime.* New York: Oxford University Press, 1976.
Nye, Russel. *The Unembarrassed Muse: The Popular Arts in America.* New York: Dial Press, 1970.
Oliver, John William, Jr., James A. Hodges, and James H. O'Donnell. *Cradles of Conscience: Ohio's Independent Colleges and Universities.* Kent, OH: Kent State University Press, 2003.
Osofsky, Gilbert. *Harlem: The Making of a Ghetto, Negro New York, 1890–1930.* New York: Harper Torchbooks, 1968.
Pabst, Anna C. Smith. *The Haning-Atwood Vision.* Delaware, OH: N. P., 1969.
Page, Will. *Behind the Curtains of the Broadway Beauty Trust.* New York: Edward A. Miller, 1927.
Parish, James Robert. *The Paramount Pretties.* New Rochelle, NY: Arlington House, 1972.
Parker, Derek, and Julia Parker. *The Natural History of the Chorus Girl.* Indianapolis: Bobbs-Merrill, 1975.
Peretti, Burton W. *Nightclub City: Politics and Amusement in Manhattan.* Philadelphia: University of Pennsylvania Press, 2007.
Pirro, Judge Jeanine. *Liars, Leakers, and Liberals: The Case Against the Anti-Trump Conspiracy.* New York: Center Street, 2018.
Porter, James Sherman. *Lamp of the Hills: The Authorized Centennial History of Rio Grande College.* [c. 1977].
Quinlan's Film Stars. 5th Edition. New York: Brassey's Inc., 2001.
Rader, Benjamin G. *American Sports: From the Age of Folk Games to the Age of Spectators.* Englewood Cliffs, NJ: Prentice Hall, 1983.
Rainey, Buck. *Sweethearts of the Sage: Biographies and Filmographies of 258 Actresses Appearing in Western Movies.* Jefferson, NC: McFarland, 1992.
Rayno, Don. *Paul Whiteman: Pioneers of American Music.* New York: Scarecrow Press, 2003.
Reel, Guy. *The National Police Gazette and the Making of the Modern American Man, 1879–1906.* New York: Palgrave Macmillan, 2006.
Rio Grande College. *Bulletin* [aka *Catalog*], 1911–1917.

Bibliography

Rio Grande College, *Grandion* [College Yearbook], 1913, 1915, 1916, 1917.
Roberts, Randy. *Jack Dempsey: The Manassa Mauler*. Baton Rouge: Louisiana State University Press, 1979.
Rosenwaike, Ira. *Population History of New York City*. Syracuse: Syracuse University Press, 1972.
Roth, Lillian (with Gerold Frank, Mike Connelly). *I'll Cry Tomorrow*. New York: Frederick Fell, 1954.
Rothel, David. *Those Great Cowboy Sidekicks*. Waynesville, NC: World of Yesterday Publications, 1984.
Sanders, Theresa. *Approaching Eden: Adam and Eve in Popular Culture*. Lanham, MD: Rowman & Littlefield, 2009.
Shales, Amity. *The Forgotten Man: A New History of the Great Depression*. New York: HarperCollins, 2007.
Sobel, Bernard. *Broadway Heartbeat: Memoirs of a Press Agent*. New York: Hermitage House, 1953.
_____. *A Pictorial History of Burlesque*. New York: G. P. Putnam's Sons, 1956.
Stevenson, Elizabeth. *Babbitts and Bohemians: The American 1920s*. New York: Macmillan, 1967.
Stratyman, Barbara. *Ned Wayburn and the Dance Routine*. New York: Society of Dance History Scholars, 1996.
Swanberg, W. A. *Luce and His Empire*. New York: Scribner's, 1972.
Thomas, Roy. *Wonder Woman: The War Years, 1941–1945*. New York: Chartwell Books, 2015.
Travers, Doris Eaton. *The Days We Danced: The Story of My Family from Ziegfeld to Arthur Murray and Beyond*. Norman: University of Oklahoma Press, 2003.
Wallace, David. *Capital of the World: A Portrait of New York City in the Roaring Twenties*. Guilford, CT: Lyons Press, 2011.
Watts, Linda S., Alice L. George, and Scott Beekman. *Social History of the United States: The 1920s*. Santa Barbara: ABC Clio, 2009.
Whitburn Joel, comp. *Pop Memories, 1890–1954*. Menomonee Falls, WI: Record Research, Inc. 1986.
Wilson, Edmund. *The American Earthquake: A Documentary of the Twenties and Thirties*. New York: Octagon Books, 1971.
Wind, Herbert Warren. *The Story of American Golf*. New York: Knopf, 1975.
Woods, Perry Daniel. *The First Fifty Years of Rio Grande College*. Rio Grande: College Bulletin. 1926
Yagoda, Ben. *Will Rogers: A Biography*. Norman: University of Oklahoma Press, 2000.
Ziegfeld, Patricia. *The Ziegfelds' Girl: Confessions of an Abnormally Happy Childhood*. New York: Little, Brown, 1964.
Ziegfeld, Richard and Paulette. *The Ziegfeld Touch: The Life and Times of Florenz Ziegfeld, Jr.* New York: Henry Abrams, 1993.

Periodical Articles

Bapst, Jacob L., and Ivan M. Tribe. "From Bladen to Broadway: Rio Grande's Forgotten Ziegfeld Girl," *The Bulletin*: Southeast Ohio History Center 38:4, Summer 2017.
Kaye, Joseph. "Master of the Follies," *The Dance Magazine*. October–December 1929.
Lasser, Michael. "The Glorifier: Florenz Ziegfeld and the Creation of the American Showgirl," *The American Scholar* 63:3, Summer 1994.
MacKenzie, Alec. "The Rhythm Glide (Ballroom Routine)," *The Dance Magazine*. November 1929.
Patch, Nathaniel. "The Story of the Female Yeoman during the First World War," *Prologue* 38:6, Fall 2006.
Smith, Griffin, Jr. "Empires of Paper," *Texas Monthly*, November 1973.
Sobel, Bernard. "The Ziegfeld Girls Carry On," *Stage Pictorial* 2:3, 1946.
Tribe, Ivan M. "The Hillbilly Versus the City," *J E M F Quarterly* 10:2, 1974.
Walsh, Jim. "Favorite Pioneer Recording Artists: Frank Crumit," *Hobbies—The Magazine for Collectors*. September–December 1953.

Bibliography

Government Records

Gallia County, Ohio, Court of Common Pleas, 1915.
Gallia County, Ohio, Probate Courts, 1930, 1949, 1971.
Harris County, Texas, Marriage, and Divorce Records, 1951, 1966.
Nassau County, New York, *Falkenhainer v. Falkenhainer*, March 29, 1950.
New Jersey Marriage License Index, 1933.
New York Marriage License Index, 1947, 1950.
Official Roster of Ohio Soldiers in the War with Spain. Columbus: State of Ohio, 1916.
Official Roster of Ohio Soldiers, Sailors and Marines in the World War 1917–1918. 23 vols. Columbus: F. J. Heer Printing Co., 1928.
Official Roster of the Soldiers of the State of Ohio in The War of the Rebellion, 1861–1866. 49 vols. Akron: Werner Ptg., 1887.
Ohio. Office of Strategic Research, Ohio Department of Development. "Decennial Census of Population by County, 1910–2010." www.development.ohio.gov/reports/reports_census archive_map.htm.
United States, Census, 1900. Gallia County, Ohio, Ohio Township.
_____, 1910. Gallia County, Ohio, Ohio Township, Raccoon Township.
_____, 1920, Gallia County, Ohio, Clay Township.
_____, 1920, Mahoning County, Ohio, Youngstown City.
_____, 1930, New York County, New York.
_____, 1940. New York County, New York.
_____, 1940. Mahoning County, Ohio.
United States Department of Agriculture, Yearbook of Agriculture, 1940.

Newspapers

Akron Beacon Journal
Alexandria, LA, *Town Talk*
Allentown, PA, *Morning Call*
Appleton, WI, *Post Crescent*
Asbury Park News
Baltimore Sun
Battle Creek Enquirer (Michigan)
Binghamton Press and *Sun Bulletin*
Boston Globe
Bradford, PA, *Evening Star*
Brooklyn Daily Eagle
Brooklyn Life
Buffalo Courier
Canandaigua Daily Messenger
Chicago Tribune
Chillicothe Gazette
Clarksville, TN, *Leaf-Chronicle*
Columbia Daily Spectator (Columbia University)
Corsicana Daily Sun
Dayton Daily News
Dayton Herald
Des Moines Tribune
Detroit Free Press
El Paso Evening Post
Elmira Star-Gazette
Florence Morning News (South Carolina)
Gallia Times
Gallipolis Daily Tribune
Gallipolis Journal
Galveston Daily News

Bibliography

Greenfield, IN, *Daily Reporter*
Harrisburg Telegraph
Hartford Courant
Harvard Crimson (Cambridge, MA)
Houston Daily Court Review
Indianapolis Star
Lewiston, Maine *Evening Journal*
Lincoln Star (Nebraska)
Longreach Leader (Queensland, Australia)
Los Angeles Times
Miami News
Moline, IL, *Evening Star*
Montgomery Alabama Journal
Montreal Gazette
Muncie Evening Post (Indiana)
New York Daily Mirror
New York Daily News
New York Morning Telegraph
New York Times
Ogden, UT, *Standard*
Olean, NY, *Times Herald*
Orange Leader
Orlando Sentinel
Philadelphia Inquirer
Pittsburgh Post-Gazette
Pittsburgh Press
Poughkeepsie Evening News
Richmond Item (Indiana)
St. Louis Post Dispatch
St. Louis Star and Times
Salt Lake Tribune
San Antonio Light
San Bernardino County Sun (California)
San Francisco Chronicle
San Francisco Examiner
Santa Cruz Evening News
Scranton Republican
Sulphur Springs News Telegram
Tampa Tribune
Washington Post
Wilkes-Barre Record
Wilkes-Barre Times Leader
Wilmington, DE, *Morning News*

Websites

Ancestry.com All entries for Chester Otto Falkenhainer, Beryl Halley (Falkenhainer), Cecile Halley (Fitch), Melissa Halley, Paul Halley, Samuel Halley, Helen Martin, Stanley Neal.
History of BREC-Buckeye Rural Electric https://www.buckeyerec.coop/index.php/historyofbrec/.
Internet Broadway Database (IBDb)
Internet Movie Database (IMDb)
St. John's School, Houston, Texas
Tabler, Dave. "She Came Rollin' Down the Mountain." 12 April 2016. Appalachian History.net. www.appalachianhistory/2016/04she-came-rollin'-down-mountain.html.
Ziegfeld 101.

Bibliography

Archival Sources

Beryl Halley Collection
Chester O. Falkenhainer, Jr., to Jake Bapst, 2017, 2018
Helen Cherrington Martin Eaton Collection
Jean Lloyd Cooper Archive, University of Rio Grande, Rio Grande, Ohio
Other scattered archival material and photographs

Interviews

Chester O. "Chet" Falkenhainer, Jr., Taped Telephone Interview, August 15, 2018.
Richard and Mary James, Gallipolis, Ohio

Index

Numbers in **_bold italics_** indicate pages with illustrations

Ackerman, Bernice 114, 122, 153
Ackerman, Jean 153
Actor's Equity Association 67
Actor's Fund of America 133, **_136_**
Alda, Frances 68
"All I Got's Gone" (song) 95
Allen, Donovan "Don" 16, 145
Allen, Frank 145
Allen, Joseph 32
Allen, Miriam 145
Allen, Thomas 6
Amaya, Stella 146
American Scholar 38
Anders, Glenn 31
Animal Crackers (film) 143
Anniversary Hall 99, 145
Astaire, Adele 53, 117, 119, 175
Astaire, Fred 53, 117, 119, 175
Astor, John Jacob VI 48
Atwood Hall 14, 100
Atwood, Nehemiah 14, 15
Atwood, Permelia 14, 15
Auer, Florence 51

Bacon, Faith 111
Baer, Charles 6
Ballou, Marian 32
Barrymore, Lionel 39
Barthelmess, Richard 51
Bartlett, Willard 99
Barton, James 69, 71, 154–155
Basquette, Lina 5, 40, 41, 103
Battle of the Sexes (radio) 133
Bayes, Nora 34
The Beautiful City (film) 51
Benchley, Robert 64, 75

Benda, Marion (both of them) 70, 155
Berengaria (ship) 47
Berlin, Irving 33, 155, 158
Beryl Halley, a Beauty Chat (radio) 113
Beryl Halley's Beauty Tips (radio) 113
Beth Be Good (show) 29
Betsy (show) 70
Biddle, Anthony J. Drexel 58
Bing, Grayum 23
Bing, Simeon 15, 23
Bird's Christmas Carol 16
Bladen, Ohio 9, 10, 11, 12, 24, 35, 45, 54, 72, 85, 139
Blaney and Farrar 56, 61
Boarding Hall 14, 16, 17, 18, 19
Bolger, Ray 81
Botticelli 38
Bouchet, Edward 14
Bow, Clara 39
Breakiron, Claire 146
Brice, Fania "Fanny" 5, 33, 40, 125, 155–156
Brideson, Cynthia 36
Brideson, Sara 36
Broadhurst Theater 64, 66
The Broadway Boob (movie) 63, 150
Brockett, Ruth 15, 150
Brooks, Louise 5, 110, 156–157
Buck, Gene 41, 157
Buckeye Battle Cry (song) 29
The Bunk of 1926 (show) 63–68
Burke, Billie 33, 34, 57, 69, 131
Burke, Katherine 56, 60, 97, 102, 120, 157
Burr, Henry 6
Butler, Binion, Rice, Cook, and Knapp 142, 146, 148

205

Index

Cambridge, Cynthia 157
Cantor, Eddie 5, 33, 40, 157–158, 171
Capital of the World (book) 73
Carr, Chestora McDonald 15, 16, 99, 150
Carroll, Earl 34, 109–112, 158–159
Carroll, Gracie 84
Cash, Johnny 150
Castle, Irene 53, 56–57
Castle, Vernon 53, 56–57
Chambers, John 12
Chambersburg, Ohio *see* Eureka, Ohio
Chautauqua 15, 25
Chilton, H.G. 47
Clark, Clarence 15
Clift, Anna Mae 175
Coburn, Gladys 41
Coca, Imogene 81
Collins, Joan 170
Community Hall 23, 145
Corbett, Jim "Gentleman" 1, 5
Crumit, Frank 5,29, 56, 132, 159–160, 172; *see also* Sanderson, Julia
Cugat, Xavier 42

Dahm, Marie 41
Daly, Joseph 6
The Dance Magazine 117
Davenport, Marie Degollere 68
Davies, Marion 33
Davis, Gussie L. 6
Davis, John Merrill 15
Dawn, Hazel 31
Day, Colleen 60
Day, Doris 131
DeCarlton, Grace 29
Dell, Claudia 107
The Demi-Virgin (show) 31–32
DeMille, Cecil B. 154
Dempsey, William H. "Jack" "Manassas Mauler" 5, 42–43, 74, 160, 173
Dere, Demaris 56
Diamond, Jack "Legs" 84
Dobbins, Helen 47
Donahue, Jack 177
Dooley, Ray 110, 160
Dorothy Gray Preparations 51–53
Dorsey Brothers 42
Downey, Morton 56
Drange, Alma 160
Dresser, Paul 6
Duchess of Oporto 47
Duke, Mary 58
Dulzell, Paul 67
Dumont, Margaret 39
DuPont family 48
Durante, Jimmy 160–161

Eagle, Oscar 30, 88
Earl Carroll Vanities (show) 53, 143
Eaton, Doris 37
Eaton, Mary 37, 40
Eddy, Nelson 29
Edwards, Cliff "Ukulele Ike" 56, 60, 161
Empire Girls 40, 41
The Enemies of Women (film) 39
Erenberg, Lewis A. 34
Errol, Leon 33
Etting, Ruth 119, 130–131
Eureka, Ohio 12–13, 25

Falkenhainer, Chester (first husband) 123, *124*, 129, 131, 133–134, 137, 138, 142
Falkenhainer, Chester, Jr. (son) 6,7, 132, 138, 142, 144, 145, 146, *147*, 148, 150, 151
Falkenhainer, Chester III (grandson) 148
Falkenhainer, Pun Hui 146, 147, 148
fan letters 44, 45, 46
Farris, William III 145
Fender, Harry 56, 59, 60, 61, 68, 161
Fields, W.C. 5, 33, 111, 162
Firpo, Luis 43
Fisher, Clyde 23
Fisher, Irving **44**
Fitch, Harold 145
Fort Lee, New Jersey 63
Fox, Dorothy Brown 128–129, 134
Fox, Richard Kyle 48
Frances, Helen 29
Francis, Clarence "Bevo" 5
Francis, Noel 56
Frelinghuysen 48
French, Edna 38–39
Friml, Rudolph 33, 41
Frivolity (club) 54
Fulton, Stella May 15, 135, 150

Gallagher, Rose 107
Gallia County, Ohio 9, 29, 45, 122–123, 135, 139, 147, 149
Gallia Lodge No. 469 Free and Accepted Masons 12,13
Gallipolis, Ohio *see* Gallia County, Ohio
Gershwin, George 33
Gish, Dorothy 51
Gish, Lillian 51
Glad, Gladys 45, 69, 71
The Glorified Follies of 1936 (show) 126–127
Gluck, Walter 104–105
Goddard, Paulette 5, 33, 57, 59
Gordon, Arthur (judge) 65–66
Granlund, Nils Thor 80–83
Gray, William B. 6

206

Index

The Great Ziegfeld (film) 125
Greenwich Village Follies (show) 29
Grey, Yvonne 56
Guinan, Mary Louise Cecilia "Texas" 108, 163
Guy, Edmonde *56*, 59,61, 62, 63; *see also* Van Duren, Ernest

Habercom, LaRue 100–101
Haggin, Ben Ali 38, 41, 176
Half a Widow (show) 104–105, 150
Hall, Marie 25–26
Hall, Wendell 56
Halley, Benjamin Franklin 9, 10
Halley, Beryl Falkenhainer McCormick *2*, *21*, *30*, *32*, *58*, *113*, *114*, *149*; birth 9; death 148; films 39, 51, 63; nicknames 21, 31, 39, 43, 48, 54, 69, 70, 71, 108, 118, 127; radio 113, 132; at Rio Grande College 16–24; stage shows 16, 28–32, 40–45, 53–69, 102–112, 142
Halley, Cecile Vivian (sister) 7, 9, *10*, 13, 16–17, 20, 23–25, 118, 130, 134–135, 139–140, 145
Halley, John 10
Halley, Melissa Porter (mother) 9, *10*, 11, 13, 16–18, 24, 130, 134–135, 139
Halley, Paul (brother) 9, 13, 16, 19, 25, 139, 140
Halley, Samuel (father) 9, 10, *11*, 13, 117, 118, 119
Haning, Ira Z. 2, 14
Harkrider, John 57
Harper's Bazaar 53
Harris, Charles K. 6
Hawley, Joyce 117
Hayward, Susan 144
Hazzard, John 164
Healey, Dan 70
Hearst, William Randolph 69
Heckschur Theater 66
Held, Anna 33, 37
Hellinger, Mark 33, 45
Herbert, Victor 33
Hickman, Art and Orchestra 57, 60, 164
Hill, Bunny *70*
Hitler, Adolf 154
Hoffman, Harry and Orchestra 112–113
Holley (surname) *see* Halley
Hopwood, A.H. 31
Houf, Horace 98
Houf, Ruth 98
Hunter, Glenn 63
Hurley, Marion 56
Hutton, Marjorie Merriweather Post 174

I'll Cry Tomorrow (book) 143
"In the Heart of the City That Has No Heart" (song) 6–7
"Indian Love Call" (song) 29
Ivins, Molly 145

James, Richard 12, 145
Johns, Brooke 41, *54*, 164–165
Johnson, Naomi 56
Jones, Benner 29

Keeler, Ruby 81
Kellerman, Annette 6, 30
Kennedy, Flo *42*, 165
Kennedy, John F. 59
Kern, Jerome 33
Kid Boots (film) 97
Kid Boots (show) 47
Kings of Harmony 42
Kitchen, Dorothy 30
Klein, Arthur 69
Knapp, Dorothy 45, 110, 112, 120, 165–166
Knights of the Golden Eagle Il K.G.P. 12–13
Knowlton, Alice 41
Koontz, Fredrica (Freda) 17
Kramer, John F. 91–92
Ku Klux Klan 94–95

LaGuardia, Fiorell 83–84
Lake Hoptacong, New Jersey 30
Lambert, Laverge 130–131
Lane, Lupino 166
Lang, Gertrude 177
Lascelles, Alan 47, 48
Lasser, Michael 38
Lee, Gypsy Rose 149
Leedom, Edna *41*, 166
Leiter, Samuel 67
LeSuer, Lucille Fay (aka Joan Crawford) *107*
Leviathan (ship) 47, 49
Levy, Aaron 66
Levy, Harry 65
Lewis, Ted 103
Lewis, William 100
Linenkamp, Ernest 68
Lockhart, Gene 63, 64, 166
Lohan, Lindsey 149
Loos, Anita 75
Lopez, Vincent 5, 42–43, 49–50, 55, 111, 146, 160
Lopez Speaking (book) 146
Lorraine, Lillian 1, 33, 37, 132
Luce, Claire 56, 59–*61*,68,167
Lunnay, Mildred 56

207

Index

Lusher, Charles 140
Lynn, Loretta 152

MacDonald, Jeanette 29
Madden, Owen "Owney" 80, 167, 168
Mafia 78–80
Maines, George 61, 68
Marion Davies Girls 41
Marston, William Moulton 5, 106–107, 168
Martin, Helen Berridge Wanger Eaton 17, 19, 20, 134, 145
Martin, Joseph 19–20
Martin, Katherine (aka Kathlene Martyn) **59**
Marx, Chico 143
Marx, Groucho 39, 143
Marx, Harpo 143
Marx, Zeppo 143, 155
Marx Brothers 30, 114, 155
Mary Jane (aka Jane Catherine Young Martin Pulitzer) 56, **60**, 62, 168–169
McCarthy, Joseph 49
McCormick, Jim 139, 140, 141, ***143***, 144, 146
McIntyre, O.O. 40, 122
Midnight Frolics (show) 34
Miller, Glenn 42
Miller, Marilyn 33, 70, 127, 175, 177
Mineralava Face Finish 42
Monroe, Edward Thayer 2, 43, 50
Montmartre Dinner Theater 55
Moore, Florence 30
Morgan, Helen 33
Moulton, Charles *see* Marston, William Moulton
Mountbatten, Louis 47
Mulhern, Mary 45
Murray, J. Harold 69

National Police Gazette 48
Naughty Diana (show) 31–32
Neal, Stanley Crawford "Scooty" 22
Nesbitt, Evelyn 6, 118
New Amsterdam Theater 34, 40, 70
New York's Play Jury 66
Nine O'Clock Review (show) 34
No Foolin' 61, 63, 68
Nolen, Mary *see* Wilson, Imogene "Bubbles"
Norworth, Jack 34

O'Day, Patsy 107
Oh! By Jingo (song) 29
Ohio State University 29
Ohio University 29
Ortmann, Will 32

Page, Will 64
Palm Beach Nights (show) 56–68, 151; see also *No Foolin'*
Palm Beach Supper Club 57
The Parisian Model (show) 37
Parton, Dolly 152
Pearl, Jack 126
Penman, Katheryn 59, 68
Pennington, Anne 5, 33, 41, 46, **52**, 68, 170
Petrosino, Guisseppe "Joseph" 79
The Pink Lady (show) 31
Porter, Cole 33
Porter, Daniel T. 11
Porter, James Sherman 11, 135
Powell, William 51
Prince of Wales, later King Edward VIII 47
Prohibition 77–80, 91–94
"Prohibition Is a Failure" song 94
Puglia, Frank 51

Quinault, Robert 41

Raft, George 81
Ray, Kathryn 45
Rebecca of Sunnybrook Farm (book) 16
Reno, Nevada 138
Reynolds, James 40
Rhodes, James A. 19
Rice, Mary Alice 134
Richman, Harry 170–171
Rio Grande College 3, 6, 7, 14, **15**, 16–25, 29, 35, 98–101, 144, 145
Rio Rita (show) 60, 69, 70, 71, 97, 102–103, 176, 151
Roberts, Beatrice 56
Roberts, Marion "Kiki" 84
Rogers, Ginger 53
Rogers, Will 5, 33, 152, 158, 171
Romberg, Sigmond 33
Roosevelt, Franklin 91
Roth, Lillian 5, 31, 111–112, ***143***–144, 158, 171–172
Rothstein, Arnold 80
Roussel, Peter 145
Rowe, Iris 41
Rufus LeMaire's Affairs (show) 103–104, 110
Ruggles, Charles 32
Rural Electrification System 91
Ryan, Mildred 63

St. Clair, Malcolm ***111***
St. Johns, Adele Rogers 106
St. John's Episcopal Academy 145
Sally (show) 71
Salmon, Patricia **39**

Index

Sanderson, Julia 29, 132, 159–160, 172; *see also* Crumit, Frank
Sandow, Eugen 33
Schuyler, Betsy 62, 63
Segal, Vivienne 172–173
Shaw, Artie 43
"She Came Rollin'Down the Mountain" song 86
"Shine On August Moon" (song) 34
Short, Antrim 63
Sibley, William Giddings 86–87
Siler, Leon M. 66
Silver Slipper (nightclub) 69, 70–71, 79, 80, 81–84, 150
Simonetta (tableaux) 38
Singer, Isaac 58
Singer, Paris E. 58
Smallwood, Norma 45
Smith, Mrs. Alfred E. 64, 65
Smith, George (Hardboiled) 64–65
Sobel, Bernard 33, 37, 122, 125, 128, 133, 134, 135, 172, 173
Sparrow, Elise *37*, 38, 39
Stanwyck, Barbara 1, 5, 33, 150
Steger, Julie 59
Sterling, Dolly 64, 70, 173
Stevenson, Frederick Boy 65
Storey, Bobby 56
Story's Run School 25
Stryker, Muriel *36*, 38, 39, 40
Stuart, Arden *see* Halley, Beryl
Sunny (show) 71
Swan Creek Grange Quartet 140
Sweet Lady (song) 29

Tangerine (show) 28–30, 104, 159, 172
Taylor, Estelle 42, 173
Temple, Shirley 149
Terry, Ethelind 69
Thayer, Frances 38
"There Ain't No Bugs on Me" (song) 94
This Is Your Life (TV show) 144
Thomas, Olive 33
The Tiller Girls 41, 173–174
Tinney, Frank 177
Trotter, G.F. 47
Troutman, George 29
Trump, Donald 174

Udell, Peggy 107, 174
University of Rio Grande *see* Rio Grande College
Urban, Josef 58, 69, 174

Valentino, Rudolph 155
Vancouver, British Columbia 138
Vanderbilt, Gertrude 134
Van Duren, Ernst *56*, 59, 61, 118, 163–164; *see also* Guy, Edmonde
Vargas, Alberto 32, 49, 175
Varrel, Charles (or Richard) 112–113, 175
Vitak, Albertina 56

Walker, Heather "Polly" 57, 59, 61, 175
Walker, James J. "Jimmy" 83
Wallace, David 73
Wallace, Ramsey 65, 66
Ware, Dick 112–113
Warner, Lita 154
Warner, Sam 103, 154
Warner Brothers 154
Warren, George C. 38
Warrington, Betty 41
Waxman, Percy 63
Wayburn, Ned 38, 58, 131, 175–176
Weed, Charles 23
Weeks, Ada Mae 69, 70, *71*
West, Mae 168
Wheeler, Alberta "Bert" 69, 176
White, George 34
White Throne School 24–25
Whiteman, Paul 42, 57, 59, 176
Wiggin, Kate Douglas 16
Wilson, Edmund 50
Wilson, Imogene "Bubbles (aka Nolen, Mary) 41, 122, 129, 177
Winchell, Walter 115, 118
Wood, Cyrus 32
Wood, Natalie 149
Woods, A.H. 31
Woolsey, Robert 176
Wooten, Stella "Cricket" 177
Worthing, Helen Lee 40, 41, *51*, 177
Wynn, Ed 33

Young, Halfred 104, 177

Ziegfeld, Florenz 32–38
Ziegfeld, Patricia 57, 69–70, 131
Ziegfeld Girls Club 125, *126*–132
Ziegfeld Midnight Follies (show) 30
Ziegfeld Theater 69
Zits Theatrical Chronicler 50